HAMPTON-BROWN
HIGH POINT

SUCCESS IN LANGUAGE • LITERATURE • CONTENT

ALFREDO SCHIFINI
DEBORAH SHORT
JOSEFINA VILLAMIL TINAJERO

HAMPTON-BROWN

Curriculum Reviewers

Tedi Armet
ESL Coordinator
Fort Bend Independent School District
Sugar Land, Texas

Maggie Brookshire
ELD Teacher, Grade 6
Emerald Middle School
Cajon Valley Unified School District
El Cajon, California

Lily Dam
Administrator
Dallas Independent School District
Dallas, Texas

Judy Doss
ELD Teacher and Coordinator
Burbank High School
Burbank Unified School District
Burbank, California

Rossana Font-Carrasco
ESOL Teacher
Paul W. Bell Middle School
Miami-Dade County School District 5
Miami, Florida

Jillian Friedman
ESOL Teacher
Howard Middle School
Orange County Public Schools
Orlando, Florida

Vivian Kahn
ESL Teacher/Site Coordinator
Halsey Intermediate School 296
Community School District 32
New York, New York

Suzanne Lee
Principal
Josiah Quincy School
Boston, Massachusetts

Carolyn McGavock
ESL Teacher
Rafael Cordero Bilingual Academy
Junior High School 45
Community School District 4
New York, New York

Juan Carlos Méndez
ESL/Bilingual Staff Developer
Community School District 9
Bronx, New York

Cynthia Nelson-Mosca
Language Minority Services Director
Cicero School District 99
Cicero, Illinois

Kim-Anh Nguyen
Title 7 Coordinator
Franklin McKinley School District
San Jose, California

Ellie Paiewonsky
Director of Bilingual/ESL
Technical Assistance Center of Nassau
Board of Cooperative Educational Services
Massapequa Park, New York

Jeanne Perrin
ESL Specialist
Boston Public Schools
Boston, Massachusetts

Rebecca Peurifoy
Instructional Specialist
Rockwall Independent School District
Rockwall, Texas

Marjorie Rosenberg
ESOL/Bilingual Instructional Specialist
Montgomery County Public Schools
Rockville, Maryland

Harriet Rudnit
Language Arts Reading Teacher
Grades 6–8
Lincoln Hall Middle School
Lincolnwood, Illinois

Olga Ryzhikov
ESOL Teacher
Forest Oak Middle School
Montgomery County, Maryland

Dr. Wageh Saad, Ed.D.
*Coordinator of Bilingual and
Compensatory Education*
Dearborn Public Schools
Dearborn, Michigan

Gilbert Socas
ESOL Teacher
West Miami Middle School
Miami-Dade County Public Schools
Miami, Florida

Acknowledgments

Every effort has been made to secure permission, but if any omissions have been made, please let us know. We gratefully acknowledge the following permissions:
Children's Book Press: "George Littlechild" and "Nancy Hom" from *Just Like Me*. Pages 9–10 copyright © 1997 by Nancy Hom; pages 11–12 copyright © 1997 by George Littlechild. Overall book project copyright © 1997 by Harriet Rohmer. **Acknowledgements continue on page 463.**

Hampton-Brown
P.O. Box 223220
Carmel, California 93922
1–800–333–3510

Printed in the United States of America
ISBN 0-7362-0901-8

03 04 05 06 07 08 09 10 9 8 7 6

UNIT 1

A VERY
Unique You

UNIT 2 UNITED, WE STAND

Making
Connections

UNIT 4

Communities Count

UNIT 5 STORIES TO TELL

Curiosity: The Food of the Heart, David Díaz, digital illustration, Copyright © 1999.

A VERY Unique You

In this picture, the artist shows parts of his identity: his favorite colors, his favorite food, a word that describes him, and something that is important to him. Make a four-part picture for yourself. Compare pictures with your classmates. Is your picture exactly like any other? What did you learn about people being unique?

Discover Yourself

- What words describe the way you look?
  What words describe the way you are?

- What do you want to find out about yourself?
  How can you learn more about yourself?

- What kind of person do you want to become?
  How can knowing about yourself help you now
  and later?

THEME-RELATED BOOKS

Grandfather's Journey
by Allen Say

In this Caldecott Medal-winner, Say looks at his grandfather's life in two countries. This helps him understand his own identity.

People
by Peter Spier

An award-winning author/ illustrator looks at similarities and differences among people all over the world.

Weslandia
by Paul Fleischman

An award-winning author tells the story of a boy who finds happiness when he creates his own unique identity.

Build Language and Vocabulary

DESCRIBE PEOPLE

Listen to the poem. Then say it as a group.

Outside and In

Sometimes people tell me,

"You are graceful on the stage!"

"Your voice is smooth and silky."

"You are clever for your age!"

But I have a secret—

There is something they don't know.

I'm more than what I do,

How I act, and what I show.

Those things are on the outside.

They're what everyone can see.

But there is even more to love

Deep down inside of me!

—Daphne Liu

MAKE A WORD CHART

Make a chart like this one. Write words about the girl from the poem in the chart.

What the Girl Does	What She Is Like
dances	graceful

BUILD YOUR VOCABULARY

People Words Work with a group to think of more words about people. Write the words in your chart. Keep adding new words to this chart. You will find many words about people in this unit.

USE LANGUAGE STRUCTURES ▶ PRESENT TENSE VERBS; ADJECTIVES

Speaking: Describe an Interesting Person Work with the class to make up a new poem about an interesting person or a character in a story.

- Think of words that tell what the person is like on the outside: how he or she looks and acts, and what he or she does.
- Then think of words that tell what the person is like on the inside.
- Follow this pattern to make up a new poem.

Example:

Outside and In

On the outside,
he is a cowboy,
he rides a pig,
and he swats flies.

On the inside,
he is funny,
he likes to dream,
he's a surprise!

Discovery

poem
by John Y. Wang

THINK ABOUT WHAT YOU KNOW

Make a Circle Graph What words describe you?
Show what you are like on a circle graph.

funny
happy
tired
angry
good student
friendly

character Your **character** is what you are really like.

discover When you **discover** something, you learn about it for the first time.

intelligent You are **intelligent** if you are smart.

irresponsible People who are **irresponsible** do not do what they say they will do.

irritable You are **irritable** when you get upset easily.

lazy A **lazy** person does not want to work or do anything.

merits Someone's good points are called **merits**.

optimistic You are **optimistic** when you are cheerful and hopeful.

positive You are **positive** when you are sure that things will work out well.

shortcomings Someone's bad points are called **shortcomings**.

LEARN KEY VOCABULARY

Relate Words Study the new words. Work with a group to make a chart. Write the new vocabulary words where they belong.

Discover Your Character

Merits	Shortcomings
intelligent	lazy

LEARN TO CLASSIFY IDEAS

When you **classify** things, you put them in a group. Classifying ideas helps you remember what you read.

READING STRATEGY

How to Classify Ideas

1. Look for ideas that are about the same thing. Put them in the same group.
2. Give the group a name that tells how the ideas are alike.

sad
happy

FEELINGS

Now read "Discovery." Stop after each page to classify the ideas.

Discovery

by John Y. Wang

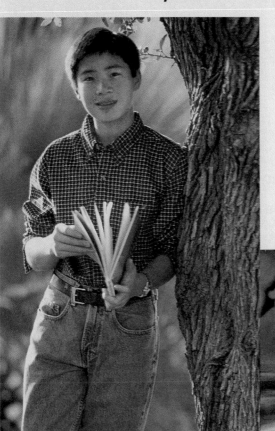

MANY TEENAGERS WANT TO FIND OUT THINGS ABOUT THEMSELVES AND THEIR WORLD. HERE IS WHAT ONE TEENAGER WANTS TO DISCOVER.

I like to **discover.**

I love to discover.

I want to discover.

I want to discover everything.

I want to discover the cure for AIDS.

I want to discover the

whole world.

Above all, I want to discover myself.

I want to discover what kind of man I am:

My **character,**

my personality,

my hobbies.

---

cure for AIDS way to stop a sickness that often kills people

my personality the things I do or say that make me different from everyone else

hobbies favorite things to do

I discover more about myself every day.
Up to now, I have discovered
I am this kind of person:
I am **intelligent.**
I am **optimistic.**
I am **positive.**

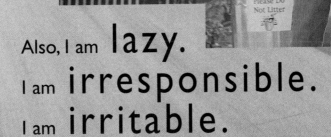

Also, I am **lazy.**
I am **irresponsible.**
I am **irritable.**

BEFORE YOU MOVE ON...

1. **Vocabulary** Make a list of words about John. Now make a list of words about yourself.

2. **Personal Experience** What are you like? Finish this sentence: *I am ___ .*

Discovery **17**

These discoveries are very helpful to me.

I know what my **merits** are.

I will keep them going.

I know what my

shortcomings are..

I can plan how to correct them.

I will keep on discovering.

I will discover more about myself.

I like to discover.

I love to **discover.**

BEFORE YOU MOVE ON...

1. **Prediction** What job do you think John will have? Why?

2. **Judgments** Is it a good idea to "keep on discovering?" Why or why not?

to correct them to change them in a way that is better

keep on go on

ABOUT THE AUTHOR

John Y. Wang went to Charlestown High School in Boston, Massachusetts. His poem was published in 1993 in a book of poems written by students on the topic of "discovery."

Respond to the Poem

Check Your Understanding

SUM IT UP

Classify Ideas How does John describe himself? Copy this chart. Add ideas from the poem.

Things John Knows About Himself	Things John Wants to Discover
He is intelligent.	He wants to discover what kind of man he is.

Write Sentences Tell what John is like. Tell what he wants to discover.

Example:
John is intelligent.
He wants to discover the cure for AIDS.

THINK IT OVER

Discuss Talk about these questions with a partner.

1. **Comparisons** How are you like John? How are you different?

2. **Opinion** Would John be a good friend? Why or why not?

3. **Personal Experience** How did the poem make you feel?

4. **Prediction** What do you think John will do in the future?

EXPRESS YOURSELF ▶ DESCRIBE PEOPLE

Tell a partner about yourself. Listen to your partner. Then tell the class what you learned about each other.

Example:
Veronica is smart.
Her favorite class is science.
She likes computers.

Respond to the Poem, continued

Language Arts and Literature

GRAMMAR IN CONTEXT
VOCABULARY

USE VERBS AND CHARACTER TRAITS

Learn About Verbs *Am*, *is*, and *are* are verbs.

- Use **am** with the word *I*.

  I **am** intelligent.

- Use **is** with the words *he* or *she*.

  He **is** optimistic. She **is** lazy.

- Use **are** with the words *we*, *you*, or *they*.

  We **are** irritable. You **are** positive.

  They **are** irresponsible.

Compare Character Traits Words that describe people are **character traits**. Work with a partner. Compare your character traits.

Venn Diagram

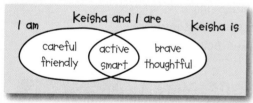

Practice Write sentences. Use the verbs *am*, *is*, and *are*. Add character traits that describe you and your partner.

Example:

I **am** careful. Keisha **is** brave. We both **are** active.

LITERARY ANALYSIS
WRITING/SPEAKING

WRITE A FREE-VERSE POEM

"Discovery" is a free-verse poem. A **free-verse poem** does not rhyme or have a regular rhythm.

1 Create a Discovery Poem Copy the poetry frame. Then add words that tell about you.

Poetry Frame

> I love to _____ .
> I want to discover a _____.
> Up to now, I have discovered I am this kind of person:
> I am _____.
> I am _____.
> I love to discover.

2 Share Your Poem Read your poem to a group. Listen to the other poems. Tell each other what you like about the poems.

Content Area Connections

SCIENCE

TECHNOLOGY/MEDIA

RESEARCH A SCIENTIST

Scientists make discoveries in areas like medicine, electronics, and farming. Study a scientist like:

- George Washington Carver
- Marie Curie
- Galileo Galilei
- Robert Goddard

1 Find Information Look for a book about the scientist, ask a science teacher, or search the Internet. Take notes.

Use the scientist's name as a key word for your search. These on-line encyclopedias may be helpful, but remember that new sites appear every day!

INTERNET

INFORMATION ON-LINE

Web Sites:
➤ **On-line Encyclopedias**
- www.encarta.msn.com
- www.britannica.com

2 Create Your Poster Write about the scientist. Then add art that shows the scientist or something about his or her discovery.

3 Share Your Poster Tell why the discovery is important. Explain how you found the information.

George Washington Carver

George Washington Carver was a famous botanist. He lived from 1864 to 1943. He made many discoveries about the peanut.

Learn how to do **research**.
See Handbook pages 366–370.
Learn to use the **Internet** on pages 364–365.

Build Language and Vocabulary

ASK AND ANSWER QUESTIONS

Look at this photograph. Read the interviewer's question.

PREDICT AND LISTEN

How do you think Anna will answer the question on page 22? Look at Anna's room for clues. Explain your answer.

 Now listen to the interview and find out what Anna said.

BUILD YOUR VOCABULARY

Question Words This picture shows six question words you can use to ask a question. Here are examples of questions for Anna:

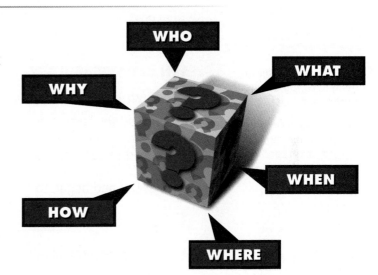

Who is your favorite singer?
What do you do after school?
When do you practice?
Where do you go to school?
How did you learn to play the trumpet?
Why did you choose the trumpet?

Now, make a list of questions you want to ask Anna.

USE LANGUAGE STRUCTURES ▶QUESTIONS

Speaking: Conduct an Interview Work with a partner. Use your list of questions for Anna. Think about Anna's answers. Then:

- Practice your interview. One of you will be the interviewer and ask the questions. The other will be Anna.

- Present your interview to the class.

  Example:
  Interviewer: When did you begin to play the trumpet?
  Anna: I began in 5th grade.

Could I Ask You a Question?

interview
by Gilbert Socas

Prepare to Read

THINK ABOUT WHAT YOU KNOW

Make a Word Web What happens during an interview? Show your ideas in a web.

asks questions

interviewer — subject

Interview

---

adapt When you **adapt** to something new, you change to get used to it.

culture People's **culture** includes their art, customs, beliefs, food, music, and clothing.

enjoy When you **enjoy** something, you like it.

felt When we **feel**, we can be happy, sad, scared, and so on. **Felt** is the past tense of *feel*.

island An **island** is land that has water on all sides.

miss When you **miss** something, you feel sad because it is not there.

situation A **situation** is something that happens.

strange Something is **strange** when it is different from what people are used to.

LEARN KEY VOCABULARY

Use New Words in Context Study the new words. Then write each sentence. Add the correct word.

1. I moved to here from the ___(island / situation)___ of Taiwan.

2. I was sad and began to ___(miss / enjoy)___ my friends in Taiwan.

3. Then I started to ___(felt / adapt)___ to my new life.

4. Now I know more about the ___(culture / strange)___ of the U.S.

LEARN TO MAKE COMPARISONS

You make **comparisons** to see how things are the same and how they are different.

READING STRATEGY
How to Make Comparisons

1. When you read about a person, think about what the person says or does.

2. Ask yourself: Does the person act or think the same way I do? How is the person different from me?

3. Ask yourself: How would I feel or act in the same situation?

Now read "Could I Ask You a Question?" Take notes about how you and Téssely are the same and different.

Could I Ask You a Question?

by Gilbert Socas

Téssely Estévez was born in Puerto Rico and moved to Florida one year ago. In this interview, she talks with her ESL teacher about herself and her new life in Miami.

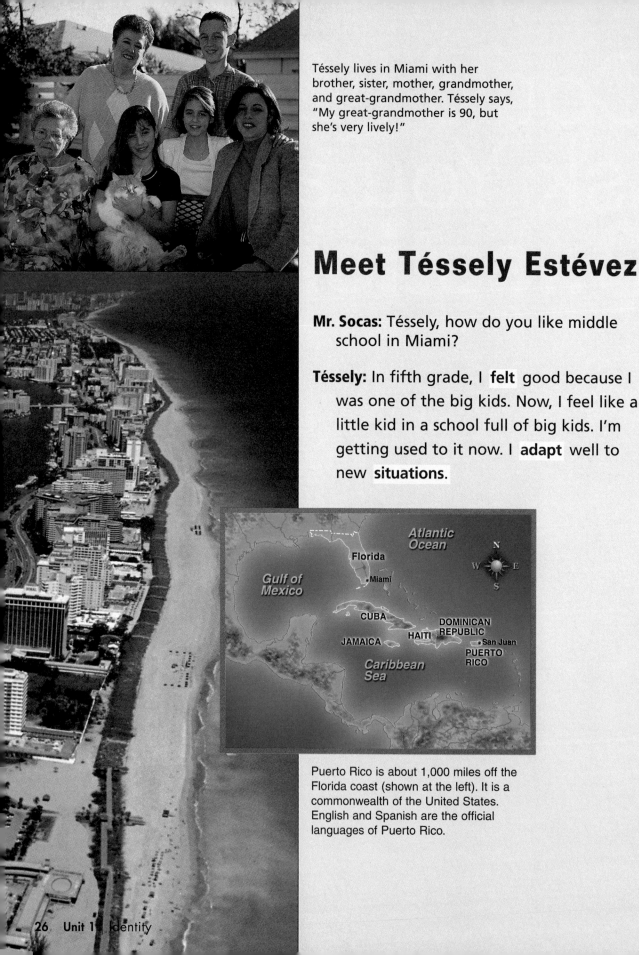

Téssely lives in Miami with her brother, sister, mother, grandmother, and great-grandmother. Téssely says, "My great-grandmother is 90, but she's very lively!"

Meet Téssely Estévez

Mr. Socas: Téssely, how do you like middle school in Miami?

Téssely: In fifth grade, I **felt** good because I was one of the big kids. Now, I feel like a little kid in a school full of big kids. I'm getting used to it now. I **adapt** well to new **situations**.

Puerto Rico is about 1,000 miles off the Florida coast (shown at the left). It is a commonwealth of the United States. English and Spanish are the official languages of Puerto Rico.

The *coquí* is a tiny frog from Puerto Rico. It lives in forests like Toro Negro, shown here with its beautiful waterfall.

Mr. Socas: So, was it easy to adapt to life in the United States?

Téssely: I feel **strange** sometimes. Some things are **the same** here, because Puerto Rico is part of the United States, but the **culture** is different.

Mr. Socas: What do you **miss** about Puerto Rico?

Téssely: I remember the beautiful mountains and **waterfalls**. The sky at night was so full of stars. I really miss that.

BEFORE YOU MOVE ON...

1. **Details** What are some of the things from Puerto Rico that Téssely misses?
2. **Personal Experience** Do you adapt well to new situations? Think of some examples.

---

the same the way they were in Puerto Rico

waterfalls places where rivers go over the edge of a hill or mountain

Téssely works on a computer at the West Miami Middle School computer lab in Miami, Florida.

Mr. Socas: What do you **enjoy** about life in Miami?

Téssely: I like the fact that we speak English. I love languages. In school, I like my French class **best.** That language is kind of **weird**, and I guess I like strange things.

Mr. Socas: If you could have anything you want, what would it be?

Téssely: I would love to have a computer of my own so that I could **chat on-line** with my **Boricua** friends from the **island**!

BEFORE YOU MOVE ON...

1. **Opinion** Do you think new languages are strange or weird? Why?
2. **Details** What would Téssely do if she had her own computer?
3. **Personal Experience** Which class do you like best? Why?

....

best the most; better than all the other classes
weird strange, different, unusual
chat on-line send and receive messages on a computer using the Internet
Boricua Puerto Rican

ABOUT THE INTERVIEWER

Gilbert Socas has been a teacher for 20 years. He loves teaching ESL classes because the students remind him of himself when he came to the United States. Mr. Socas was born in Cuba. He has lived in the United States for 34 years. He has published two books of poetry in Spanish and is now writing a children's book about young immigrants.

Respond to the Interview
Check Your Understanding

SUM IT UP

Compare Experiences Copy the chart. Add information about Téssely and yourself.

All About Téssely	All About _____
Téssely was born in Puerto Rico.	

Draw Conclusions Work with a partner. Ask and answer questions like these:

Question: How are you and Téssely the same?
Answer: We both adapt well to new things.

Question: How are you and Téssely different?
Answer: Téssely likes to learn French, but I like to learn Spanish.

THINK IT OVER

Discuss Talk about these questions with a partner.

1. **Character's Point of View** How does Téssely feel about the changes in her life?

2. **Opinion** What are some of Téssely's merits?

3. **Personal Experience** What change did you make this year?

EXPRESS YOURSELF
▶ ASK AND ANSWER QUESTIONS

Role-play an interview with a partner. One person asks questions. The other person answers as the character. Choose one of these ideas:

- Mr. Socas interviews Téssely again.

- Téssely interviews Mr. Socas.

- Mr. Socas interviews John Wang, the author of "Discovery."

- Mr. Socas interviews Téssely in five years.

Respond to the Interview, continued
Language Arts and Literature

GRAMMAR IN CONTEXT

ASK QUESTIONS

Learn About Statements and Questions
Make a **statement** to tell something. Ask a **question** to find out something. Some questions begin with *Are, Can,* and *Do*.

Statements	Questions
They are in 6th grade.	**Are** they in 6th grade?
You can speak French.	**Can** you speak French?
I need a computer.	**Do** I need a computer?

Make Up Questions Copy the chart. Then ask your friends questions that start with *Are, Can,* or *Do*. Finish the questions with words in the chart. Write the names of the classmates who answer "yes."

Are you...	Can you...	Do you...
positive Ramon	ride a bike	read every day
on a sports team	play an instrument	help at home
lazy	speak 3 languages	want to go to college

Practice Copy the statements. Then write them as questions using *Are, Can,* or *Do*.

1. I study for tests.

2. She can play soccer.

3. You are a good singer.

WRITING

SPEAKING/LISTENING

CONDUCT AN INTERVIEW

When you **conduct an interview**, you ask someone questions. Find someone to interview. Then follow these steps.

1 **Write Your Questions** Look at Mr. Socas's questions. Write four or five questions like these. Leave room for the answers.

2 **Ask the Questions** Write down what the person says. Say "thank you" when you are finished.

3 **Share Your Work** Read your interview to the class. Listen while others read their interviews.

Review **questions**. See Handbook page 402.
Learn how to **listen** and **discuss** on pages 373–374.

Language Arts and Content Area Connections

EXPLORE GEOGRAPHY

Compare Puerto Rico and Miami Research Puerto Rico and Miami, Florida. Tell how they are the same and different.

1 **Gather Information** Use books, an atlas, an encyclopedia, or the Internet to research both places. Take notes.

2 **Organize Your Information** Compare the two places.

Venn Diagram

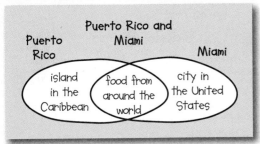

3 **Share Your Diagram** Tell your class what you learned about both places.

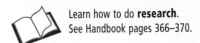

Learn how to do **research**. See Handbook pages 366–370.

STUDY A NEWS STORY

Sometimes writers conduct interviews to get information for a news story. Work with a partner. Study news stories in magazines or newspapers.

Find Quotations Look for a news story with quotations. A **quotation** shows the exact words a person said.

STUDENTS WIN CONTEST

Three Miami students won tickets to the Orange Bowl this week. They won a school writing contest.

"The Orange Bowl is a great football game," said Julie Cata, one winner.

"It is played every New Year's Day in Miami," added her friend Mei Wen.

"They worked hard," said their teacher. **"That is why they won."**

Write Questions List the quotations you found. Think about what questions the writer asked. Write each question by the quotation.

Quotation: "The Orange Bowl is a great football game."

Question: What is the Orange Bowl?

Sammy Sosa, baseball player

Nancy Hom, artist

Sandra Cisneros, author

Albert Einstein, physicist

Gloria Estefan, singer

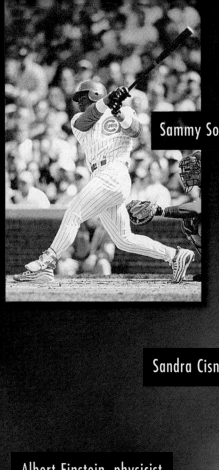

Nadja Halilbegovich, writer

César Chávez, labor leader

Many Kinds of Smart

- How do you express yourself? Can you sing or dance? Do you like to draw or write?

- What do you do well? What is hard for you? How could you get better at the things that are hard for you?

- Every person is good at something different. Why is that important for our world?

THEME-RELATED BOOKS

My Name is Georgia
by Jeanette Winter

The story of a girl who is not afraid to be herself and who grows up to become a famous artist.

Just Like Me
edited by Harriet Rohmer

Fourteen artists use words and pictures to tell about their lives.

NOVEL

**Eye on the Wild:
A Story About Ansel Adams**
by Julie Dunlap

The true story of a boy who doesn't like school but loves to learn. He also loves nature and becomes a nature photographer.

Build Language and Vocabulary

GIVE INFORMATION

Read these sentences. They describe different ways that people use their brain power. In your notebook, copy the sentences that describe you best.

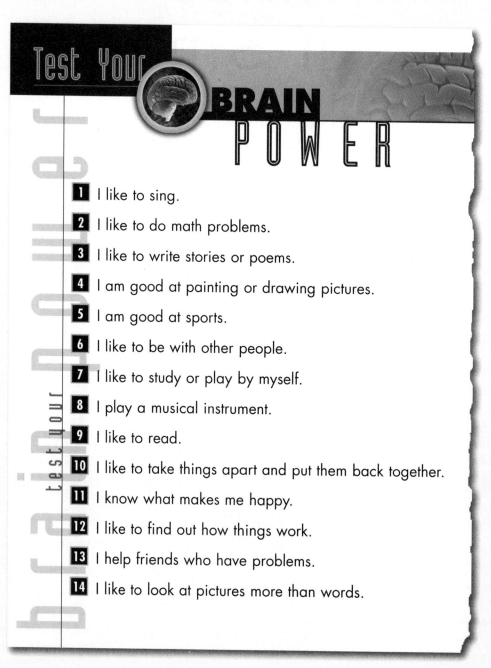

Test Your BRAIN POWER

1. I like to sing.
2. I like to do math problems.
3. I like to write stories or poems.
4. I am good at painting or drawing pictures.
5. I am good at sports.
6. I like to be with other people.
7. I like to study or play by myself.
8. I play a musical instrument.
9. I like to read.
10. I like to take things apart and put them back together.
11. I know what makes me happy.
12. I like to find out how things work.
13. I help friends who have problems.
14. I like to look at pictures more than words.

LEARN ABOUT YOUR BRAIN POWER

Which sentences did you write in your notebook? Check this list. It will tell you what kind of brain power you have.

Talk with some classmates. Ask questions to find out about their brain power.

If you chose:	**You have:**
1 and 8 ➤	Musical Brain Power
2 and 12 ➤	Math Brain Power
3 and 9 ➤	Word Brain Power
4 and 14 ➤	Artistic Brain Power
5 and 10 ➤	Movement Brain Power
6 and 13 ➤	Face-to-Face Brain Power
7 and 11 ➤	On-Your-Own Brain Power

Examples:

How do you use your musical brain power?
How many kinds of brain power do you have?
What sports do you play?

BUILD YOUR VOCABULARY

Brain Power Words Work with a group to make a mind map about one type of brain power.

USE LANGUAGE STRUCTURES ▶ PRESENT TENSE VERBS

Speaking: Give a Report Work with a partner or a group. Choose someone you know or a person shown on page 32. Tell what kind of brain power that person has. Give an example of how the person uses it. You can use words from the **Word Bank**.

Word Bank

dances
draws
paints
plays an instrument
reads
sings
works with numbers
writes

Examples:

Gloria Estefan has musical brain power. She sings.
Sasha has artistic brain power. He draws.

MANY PEOPLE, Many Intelligences

science article
by Joanne Ryder

Prepare to Read

THINK ABOUT WHAT YOU KNOW

Make a Bar Graph Show the kinds of intelligence people in your class have. Then discuss your graphs.

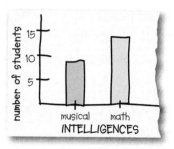

LEARN KEY VOCABULARY

brain power Your **brain power** helps you think, feel, learn, remember, and move.

figure out When you **figure out** something, you learn how to do it.

improve When you **improve**, you get better at something.

intelligence The ability to think, understand, learn, and express yourself is called **intelligence**.

Use New Words in Context Study the new words. Make sentence-starter cards that say *My brain has* and *My brain can.* Then write each new word on a card. Use the cards to make sentences.

LEARN TO MAKE PREDICTIONS

You **predict** before you read. A **prediction** tells what you think you will learn.

READING STRATEGY
How to Make and Check Predictions
1. Look at the pictures and headings in the article.
2. Think about what you will learn. Write your predictions.
3. Read the article.
4. Check your predictions. Were they correct?

Make a prediction chart for "Many People, Many Intelligences." Then read the article to see if your predictions were right.

Many PEOPLE, Many Intelligences

by Joanne Ryder

There are many kinds of brain power and many ways to put it to work. Learn more about the types of intelligence that you already have and those you want to improve.

What Special Intelligence Do You Have?

It takes many people and many kinds of **intelligence** to **put on a play**.

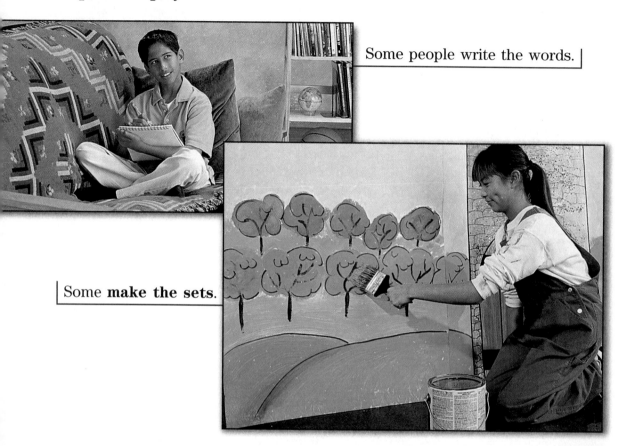

Some people write the words.

Some **make the sets**.

Others are actors and singers.

Some work best alone. Others help everyone to work well together.

....

put on a play act out a story for people to see

make the sets make the pictures and decorations that go on a stage for a play

Everyone is intelligent in different ways. Everyone has different intelligences to use and share.

Word
Are you good at writing or telling stories?
Then you have **word intelligence**.

Musical
Can you play an instrument? Do you like to sing?
Then you have **musical intelligence**.

Math
Are you good at math? Do you like to solve puzzles?
Then you have **math intelligence**.

Artistic
Are you good at making maps or models? Do you like to draw and paint?
Then you have **artistic intelligence**.

Movement
Do you play sports? Do you like to dance?
Then you have **movement intelligence**.

Face-to-Face
Do you like to be with other people?
Then you have **face-to-face intelligence**.

On-Your-Own
Do you understand your feelings? Do you enjoy being alone?
Then you have **on-your-own intelligence**.

BEFORE YOU MOVE ON...

1. **Details** What types of intelligence do people use to put on a play?
2. **Inference** List two intelligences an actor uses. Explain your answers.

Intelligences Go to Work!

Every job uses one or more of the intelligences. Here are some ways people use math **brain power** in their jobs:

- When cashiers **figure out** how to make change, they use math intelligence.

- When carpenters measure boards, they use math intelligence.

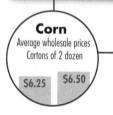

- When farmers **estimate** the value of their crops, they use math intelligence.

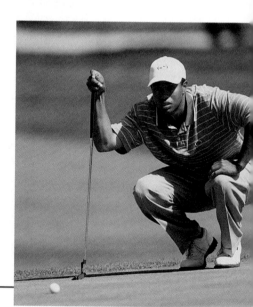

- When professional golfers estimate **distance** and **angles**, they use math intelligence.

---

estimate make a good guess about
distance how far away something is
angles the direction the ball must travel

Exercise Your Intelligence

You may have one or two intelligences you use most often.

But everyone has some of each of the seven intelligences.

You use them everyday—in and out of school.

How many intelligences do you use when you:

- read a magazine?
- play soccer?
- talk with a friend?
- dance to music on the radio?
- go shopping?

Figure out which intelligences are your strongest. Try to do something everyday to **improve** your other intelligences, too. It's **the smart thing to do**!

BEFORE YOU MOVE ON...

1. **Inference** You use your word intelligence to write at school. What other intelligences do you use at school?
2. **Personal Experience** Which of the seven intelligences is your strongest? Which would you like to improve?
3. **Opinion** Do you think it is a good idea to use all your intelligences? Why?

ABOUT THE AUTHOR

Joanne Ryder has strong word intelligence. She has written more than 50 books for children! When she was 10, Joanne discovered the joy of painting pictures with words. Her father helped her discover the world of nature. As a writer, Joanne likes to combine her love of words with her love of nature. Joanne received the American Nature Study Society's Award for her outstanding nature books for children.

....

the smart thing to do a good idea

Respond to the Article
Check Your Understanding

SUM IT UP

Check Predictions Read the predictions you made about the article.

Before You Read	Statements About "Many People, Many Intelligences"	After You Read
F	1. Each person only has one kind of intelligence.	F
T	2. There are six kinds of intelligence.	F
F	3. People who run have math intelligence.	F
F	4. People can strengthen their intelligences.	T

Write each sentence on an index card. Correct the false statements.

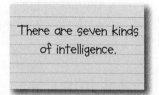

There are seven kinds of intelligence.

Ask Questions Use the back of the card. Write questions you still have about intelligences. Read your questions to the class. Think of a way to find answers.

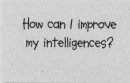

How can I improve my intelligences?

THINK IT OVER

Discuss Talk about these questions with a partner.

1. **Inference** How can you tell the kind of intelligence a person has?

2. **Paraphrase** Tell something you learned about intelligences. Use your own words.

3. **Opinion** Can you say that someone is not intelligent? Explain your answer.

4. **Personal Experience** How can knowing your intelligences help you?

EXPRESS YOURSELF ▶ GIVE INFORMATION

Tell your partner three things you like to do. Describe the intelligences you have. Use sentences like these:

I like to read. I have word intelligence.

Then your partner will tell the class about you:

Juana likes to read. She has word intelligence.

Language Arts and Content Area Connections

MATCH JOBS AND SKILLS

The people on page 40 use their intelligences for their jobs. Find jobs that use your strongest intelligences.

Find Out About Jobs and Skills Think of a job you would like to do. Then list the skills used in the job. A **skill** is the ability to do something well. You can look for information in a book in the library, or talk to someone who has that job.

Make a Tree Diagram Show the job and the skills. Show the intelligence you need for each skill. Share your information with the class.

Tree Diagram

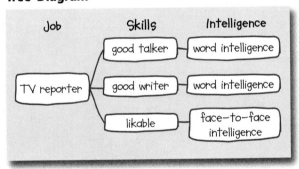

GRAPH INTELLIGENCE TYPES

A **circle graph** shows all of the parts of a whole thing. Use a circle graph to show the intelligences in your class.

1 **Gather Information** Write the strongest intelligence for each student in your class.

2 **Use the Formula** Find the percentages for each type of intelligence.

$$\frac{\text{number of students with math intelligence}}{\text{number of students in your class}} \times 100 = \text{\% with math intelligence}$$

Example:

$$\frac{\text{5 students have math intelligence}}{\text{25 students in my class}} \times 100 = \text{20\% math intelligence}$$

3 **Draw a Circle Graph** Make a section for each percentage. Label each part.

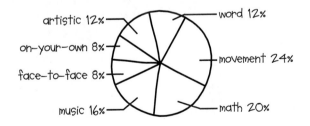

Build Language and Vocabulary
DESCRIBE THINGS

View this painting. Describe what you see.

Vendredi I, Auguste Herbin, acrylic on canvas, completed in 1951. Copyright © 2000.

SEARCH FOR SHAPES

The painting on page 44 has a lot of colorful forms called *geometric shapes*. Draw some of the shapes in your notebook. Work with a group to label the shapes.

BUILD YOUR VOCABULARY

Color, Size, and Shape Words Start a chart like this one in your notebook. Work with the class to describe each of the geometric shapes.

GEOMETRIC SHAPE	Number of Sides	Number of Corners	Type of Line	Color	Size
RECTANGLE	4 (2 long, 2 short)	4	straight	black	big
CIRCLE	0	0	curved	red	medium

USE LANGUAGE STRUCTURES ▶ ADJECTIVES

Speaking: Play a Describing Game Form two teams, Team A and Team B.

- Team A chooses a shape in the painting.
- Team B asks three yes or no questions about the shape. Use words from the **Word Bank**.

    Examples:
    Is your shape big?
    Does it have three corners?
    Is it black?

- Team B tries to guess the shape.
- The team with the most correct guesses wins.

Word Bank

big
corners
curved
dark
light
medium
round
sides
small
straight

ArtSmart

self-portraits
by Nancy Hom
and George Littlechild

Prepare to Read

THINK ABOUT WHAT YOU KNOW

Tell About a Picture Bring a favorite photograph of yourself to class. Show the picture and answer the questions:

- What are you doing in the picture? Where was it taken?
- What does the picture tell about you? What doesn't it show?

accept When you **accept** something, you like it the way it is.

decide When you **decide**, you make up your mind about something.

express You **express** when you show or to tell something.

feature A **feature** is part of your face.

portrait A **portrait** is a picture of a person.

LEARN KEY VOCABULARY

Use New Words in Context Study the new words. Then write the sentences. Choose the correct word to complete each sentence.

1. I want to paint a ___(feature / portrait)___ of myself.

2. I can ___(decide / accept)___ to use pencils or paints.

3. I can draw each ___(portrait / feature)___, like my nose and eyes.

4. A picture is a way to ___(express / decide)___ my ideas.

5. I hope that my teacher will ___(decide / accept)___ my picture.

LEARN TO RELATE CAUSES AND EFFECTS

A **cause** is why something happens. An **effect** is what happens. When you relate causes and effects, you can understand why things happen.

READING STRATEGY
How to Relate Causes and Effects
1. Read the story or article.
2. Look for something that happened. It is the effect.
3. Ask yourself, "Why did that happen?" Your answer is the cause.

Read "Art Smart." Look for causes and effects.

ArtSmart

by Nancy Hom and George Littlechild

Self-portraits are pictures that artists make of themselves. In this selection, two artists use their artistic and word intelligences to present self-portraits.

A Self-Portrait
by Nancy Hom

I like to draw flat shapes that fit together like jigsaw puzzles. My artwork is very simple and graceful, with curves like the edges of clouds. I am like that—soft, gentle, quiet, but strong at the same time. I **express** my strength through **bold** colors and **patterns**. This **portrait** has leaves of **bamboo** in it because bamboo also comes from China. It is strong, but it can bend when it needs to, just like me.

BEFORE YOU MOVE ON...

1. **Details** What plant does the artist say she is like? How are they alike?
2. **Vocabulary** Make a list of the words Nancy used to describe her painting.

bold strong; clear and easy to see
patterns colors or shapes that repeat
bamboo a tall plant with long, stiff stems

ABOUT THE AUTHOR

Nancy Hom is an artist, mother, designer, and the Executive Director of Kearny Street Workshop, an Asian American arts organization. She was born in Toisan, China, in 1949. She grew up in New York City and now lives in San Francisco, California.

A SELF-PORTRAIT

by George Littlechild

Self-Portrait, George Littlechild. Copyright © 1997.

When I was a boy, people knew I was Indian (or First Nations, as we say in Canada) because I had the **features** of my Indian mother. As I got older, people weren't sure anymore. "You sure are **exotic** looking," they told me. "Are you Spanish? Italian? Portuguese?" I was looking more like my white father. But since both of my parents were dead and I was living with my Dutch **foster family**, I was very confused about who I was. No one ever told me then that I was **mixed-blood**.

Sometimes I look Indian now, but sometimes I don't. My looks change according to my **mood**. That's why I've made these four different self-portraits. It took me many years to **accept** my features. Then one day I **decided** that I had to love myself the way I am. I'm a rainbow man, with a half of this and a quarter of that, and a **dash of a mixture of everything**!

BEFORE YOU MOVE ON...

1. **Motive** Why did George paint four self-portraits instead of one?
2. **Inference** George wrote about his different moods. Look at his four pictures. Write words that tell how he felt in each picture.
3. **Personal Experience** George describes himself as a "dash of a mixture of everything." What are you like? Do you have a little bit of many cultures, or just one?

---

exotic different and interesting

foster family family who took care of me

mixed-blood a child who has parents of different races

mood feelings

dash of a mixture of everything little bit of many things mixed together

ABOUT THE AUTHOR

George Littlechild is a painter, printmaker, and mixed-media artist whose works are exhibited in galleries and museums throughout the world. He is a member of the Plains Cree Nation of Canada. George was born in Edmonton, Alberta, in 1958. He now lives in Vancouver, British Columbia.

Respond to the Self-Portraits
Check Your Understanding

SUM IT UP

Relate Causes and Effects Copy and complete these charts.

A Self-Portrait by Nancy Hom

Causes	Effects
Nancy likes to draw flat shapes.	
	Nancy uses bold colors and patterns.
Nancy comes from China.	

A Self-Portrait by George Littlechild

Causes	Effects
	When George was young, people knew he was Indian.
As George got older, he looked more like his white father.	
	George was confused about his identity.
George's looks change with his mood.	

Write Sentences Tell about Nancy or George. Write a sentence that gives a cause and an effect. Use the word *because*.

Example:

Nancy showed bamboo leaves in her portrait **because** she is from China.

THINK IT OVER

Discuss Talk about these questions with a partner.

1. **Inference** What do Nancy and George express in their paintings?

2. **Comparisons** How are the self-portraits the same? How are they different?

3. **Judgment** Which self-portrait describes the artist the best? Explain your answer.

4. **Opinion** Which artist would you like to meet? Why?

EXPRESS YOURSELF

▶ DESCRIBE AND GIVE INFORMATION

Nancy and George added things to their self-portraits that tell about them. Nancy painted bamboo leaves. They show her Chinese culture. Think about something that describes you. Share it with the class and tell how it is like you.

Language Arts and Literature

USE NOUNS IN THE SUBJECT

Learn About Nouns A **noun** is the name of a person, place, or thing. A **common noun** names any person, place, or thing. A **proper noun** names one particular person, place, or thing. Proper nouns begin with capital letters.

Common Nouns	Proper Nouns
girl, doctor	Hannah, Dr. Chen
city, lake	St. Louis, Lake Erie
building, dog	Sears Tower, Lassie

- A **noun** can appear anywhere in a sentence.

  The **painter** puts her **brushes** in the **box**.

- A **noun** is often the **subject** of a sentence. The subject tells whom or what the sentence is about.

  The **painter** puts her brushes in the box.

  The **box** is on the table.

Practice Copy this paragraph. Add a noun to form the subject of each sentence. Then circle all the nouns in the paragraph. List the ones that are proper nouns.

___Ricky___ was born in the Philippines. His _____ moved to the United States last year. Now, _____ is Ricky's favorite class. _____ is his favorite sport. _____ is Ricky's best friend.

CREATE A PORTRAIT GALLERY

Make your own self-portrait. Then write about it.

1. **Create a Self-Portrait** Draw yourself, take a photograph, or use pictures from magazines. Add things that tell about you.

2. **Write a Description** Tell about your self-portrait. Describe what you are doing and the things you show.

3. **Share Your Work** Put up your poster. Go on a tour of the gallery and look at the class portraits.

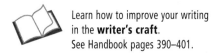

Learn how to improve your writing in the **writer's craft**. See Handbook pages 390–401.

Respond to the Self-Portraits, continued

Content Area Connections

▶ MATHEMATICS
▶ FINE ARTS

IDENTIFY GEOMETRIC SHAPES

A **geometric shape** is a form made of straight lines or curves. Find geometric shapes in the self-portraits.

❶ Learn Geometric Shapes These are some geometric shapes.

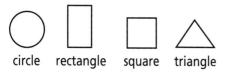

circle   rectangle   square   triangle

❷ Chart Geometric Shapes Copy the chart. Mark the shapes you can find in each portrait. Add information about your own self-portrait.

Artist	◯	▯	▢	△
N. Hom	x			
G. Littlechild	x			
Me				

❸ Share Your List Work with a small group. Describe the shapes you found. Point to the shapes on the self-portraits.

▶ VIEWING/SPEAKING
▶ TECHNOLOGY/MEDIA

RESEARCH A PORTRAIT ARTIST

Give an oral report about an artist like:

Rembrandt   Pablo Picasso
Vincent Van Gogh   Norman Rockwell

Find Information Use encyclopedias, books, or the Internet. Take notes about the artist's life and work. Try these Web sites, but remember that new sites appear every day! Use the artist's name as a key word.

INTERNET

INFORMATION ON-LINE

Web Sites:
➤ **Artists and Museums**
- library.thinkquest.org/17142
- metalab.unc.edu/wm

Give a Presentation Tell about your artist and show a painting or self-portrait. Explain what you like about the art.

Learn how to give an **oral presentation**. See Handbook pages 374–376.

Just Me

poem
by Margaret Hillert

THINK ABOUT WHAT YOU KNOW

Talk It Over Tell about a problem you had with someone. What did the other person think? Do people always see things the same way?

I
me
my
myself

LEARN KEY VOCABULARY

Use New Words in Context Read the vocabulary words. Write new sentences that tell about you.

All About Me

I can taste _____.	My eyes see _____.	I hear myself _____.
a salty peanut some sweet grapes	the blue sky green grass	sing a song talk loudly

LEARN TO READ A RHYMING POEM

When words **rhyme**, they have the same ending sounds. In a **rhyming poem**, the last words in some of the lines of the poem rhyme.

READING STRATEGY

How to Read a Rhyming Poem

1. Look at the end of each line. Which lines rhyme?
2. Read the poem out loud. Listen for rhyming words.
3. Picture what the poet says.
4. Read the poem again. Do you understand it? If not, read it again.

Read "Just Me." Listen for the rhyming words. Think about what the poem means.

Just Me

Nobody sees what I can see,

For back of my eyes there is only me.

And nobody knows how my thoughts begin,

For there's only myself inside my skin.

—Margaret Hillert

back of my eyes in my mind
inside my skin inside me

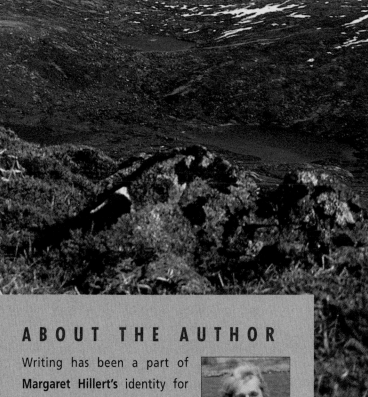

espond to the Poem

THINK IT OVER

Discuss Talk about these questions with a partner.

1. **Inference** What does "there's only myself inside my skin" mean?

2. **Paraphrase** Tell what the poem is about.

3. **Opinion** Do you agree with the poet? Why or why not?

EXPRESS YOURSELF

▶ READ ALOUD A POEM

The way you read a poem aloud makes it sound different. Try these ways:

- Read the poem proudly.
- Read it in a happy way.
- Read it sadly.
- Read it as if you are confused.

Use a tape recorder to tape your reading of the poem. Play it back. How do you sound? How can you improve your reading?

ABOUT THE AUTHOR

Writing has been a part of **Margaret Hillert's** identity for most of her life. In fact, she wrote her first poem when she was in the third grade! Since then, she has written more than 70 books for young people, including poetry like "Just Me." Every poem she creates is unique and special—just like people.

Writing That Describes

A description paints a picture with words. The writer uses colorful details to help you "see" what someone or something is like.

WRITING MODELS

Look at the poem "Discovery." What words does John Wang use to describe himself?

from "Discovery"

> I discover more about myself every day.
> Up to now, I have discovered
> I am this kind of person:
> I am **intelligent.**
> I am **optimistic.**
> I am **positive.**

Look at Nancy Hom's description and portrait. They both show what she is like.

from "Art Smart"

> My artwork is very simple and graceful, with curves like the edges of clouds. I am like that—soft, gentle, quiet, but strong at the same time. I express my strength through bold colors and patterns. The portrait has leaves of bamboo in it because bamboo also comes from China. It is strong, but it can bend when it needs to, just like me.

A Self-Portrait by Nancy Hom

Write Together

1 **Plan the Poem** Your poem will have five lines. Each line will answer one question. Here is a way you can plan the poem:

Line 1	**Who?**	Name of the person
Line 2	**What?**	What the person likes to do
Line 3	**Where?**	Where the person does the activity
Line 4	**When?**	When the person does the activity
Line 5	**Why?**	Why the person does the activity

2 **Brainstorm Ideas** Fill in a 5Ws chart. Look at the two examples.

3 **Write the Poem** Turn your answers into sentences for the poem.

5Ws Chart

Who?	Nancy Hom
What?	draws pictures
Where?	in San Francisco
When?	every day
Why?	to show things she likes

STUDENT WRITING MODELS

Model 1

Nancy Hom
paints beautiful pictures
in San Francisco
every day.
She uses bright colors to show things she likes.

A good description uses **colorful verbs** and **adjectives.**

5Ws Chart

Who?	Nancy Hom
What?	loves to paint bamboo
Where?	from China
When?	as often as she can
Why?	because it is strong like she is

Model 2

Nancy Hom
loves the tall bamboo from China.
She paints it in her pictures
whenever she can
because it is strong like she is.

Writing That Describes, continued

Write on Your Own

WRITING PROMPT

Now write your own poem for your classmates to read. Describe a friend or someone in your family.

PREWRITE

1 **Choose a Person to Describe** Think about people you know. Write their names in a word web.

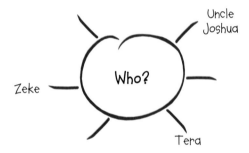

Choose one person to write about. This person is your **topic**.

2 **Get Organized** Make a 5Ws chart about your topic.

5Ws Chart

Who?	Tera
What?	likes music
Where?	in her room
When?	all the time
Why?	makes her feel happy

To Get 💡 Ideas...

Try making a list.
Name someone
- who makes you laugh
- likes the same things you do
- you admire or want to be like
- who does something unusual.

Think About Your Writing

- Are you happy with your topic?
- Do you have enough details to write about? Add more details if you need to.

DRAFT

1 Write Your Poem Use your notes to write sentences and phrases.

2 Choose the Best Details Study these examples.

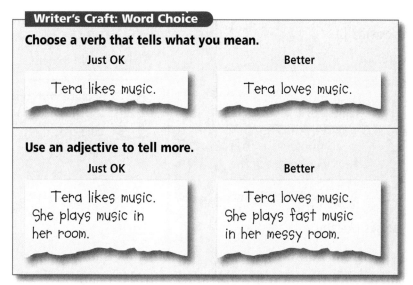

Writer's Craft: Word Choice

Choose a verb that tells what you mean.

Just OK	Better
Tera likes music.	Tera loves music.

Use an adjective to tell more.

Just OK	Better
Tera likes music. She plays music in her room.	Tera loves music. She plays fast music in her messy room.

Choose some words from these lists to help you say just what you mean.

Verbs

likes	laughs	moves	talks
enjoys	smiles	walks	shouts
appreciates	grins	runs	mumbles
loves	giggles	races	whispers
treasures	chuckles	dances	yells
		leaps	
		twirls	

Adjectives

pretty	good	big	strong
attractive	fine	large	tough
lovely	wonderful	huge	powerful
beautiful	super	enormous	mighty
gorgeous	excellent	gigantic	
	first-rate		

Painting is silent poetry, and poetry is painting that speaks.

— Simonedes, a poet in ancient Greece

Think About Your Writing

- Read your draft. Do you like the way it sounds?
- Did you choose the best details?

Writing That Describes, continued

REVISE

1 **Read Your Poem** How does it sound?

2 **Share Your Poem** Have your teacher or a friend read your poem. Ask:
- What do you like best about my poem?
- Did I give a good picture of the person?
- Do I need more colorful verbs or adjectives?

3 **Make Your Changes** Think about the answers to your questions. Then make changes to your poem. Use the revising marks.

Sample of a Revised Line

dances   steady
Ricky ~~moves~~ to the beat.

Revising Marks

∧	Add.
�	Move to here.
⊼	Replace with this.
⌿	Take out.

If you are on a computer, make changes like this.

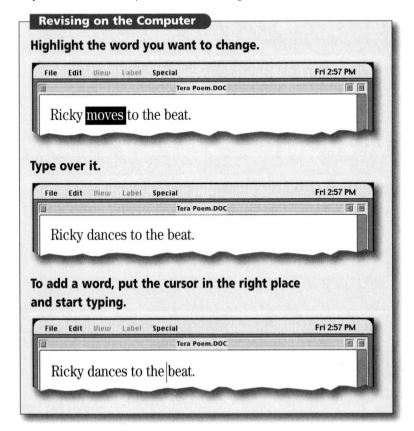

Revising on the Computer

Highlight the word you want to change.

| File Edit View Label Special | Fri 2:57 PM |
Tera Poem.DOC
Ricky **moves** to the beat.

Type over it.

| File Edit View Label Special | Fri 2:57 PM |
Tera Poem.DOC
Ricky dances to the beat.

To add a word, put the cursor in the right place and start typing.

| File Edit View Label Special | Fri 2:57 PM |
Tera Poem.DOC
Ricky dances to the|beat.

Think About Your Writing

- What words or details did you change?
- Did you make your poem better?

> **GRAMMAR IN CONTEXT**

SUBJECTS AND VERBS THAT AGREE

Every sentence has a subject and a verb. The subject and the verb must agree, or tell about the same number of people, places, or things.

> **Examples:** Tera **sings**. Tera and Ricky **sing**.

Study these examples.

Tera

One	More Than One
I **love** music.	We **love** music.
You **love** music.	You **love** music.
Tera **loves** music.	The friends **love** music.
Ricky **loves** music.	They **love** music
The cat **loves** music.	The cats **love** music.

Tera and Ricky

- When you tell about **one other person or thing**, add **s** at the end of the verb.

  > **Examples:** Tera **loves** popular music.
  >
  > This song **makes** her very happy.

- When you tell about **more than one other person or thing**, do not add **s** at the end of the verb.

  > **Examples:** Tera's friends **sing**, too.
  >
  > They all **dance** to the music.

- When you tell about **yourself** or speak directly to another person, do not add **s** at the end of the verb.

  > **Examples:** I **listen** to music.
  >
  > You **like** music, too.

Practice Write each sentence. Use the correct verb.

1. The Beetle Bug Boys ___play / plays___ great music.
2. I ___collect / collects___ tapes by the group.
3. My sister ___know / knows___ all the songs.
4. Sometimes we ___sing / sings___ along.
5. Then my parents ___cover / covers___ their ears!

Writing That Describes, continued

EDIT AND PROOFREAD

1 **Proofread Your Poem** Did you use a capital letter for the person's name? When you find a mistake, correct it. Use the Proofreading Marks.

2 **Check Your Verbs** Do your subjects and verbs agree?

3 **Make a Final Copy** If you are working on a computer, print out the corrected copy of your work. If not, rewrite it and make the corrections you marked.

PUBLISH

Here are some ways to share your writing.

- Print your poem. Add a picture.

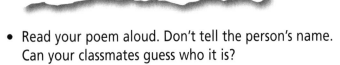

Debbi
cheers for the team
in the gym
every Friday.
She is an energetic person.

- Read your poem aloud. Don't tell the person's name. Can your classmates guess who it is?

- E-mail your poem to the person.

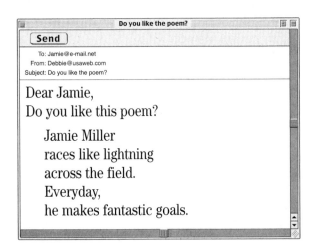

Do you like the poem?		
Send		

To: Jamie@e-mail.net
From: Debbie@usaweb.com
Subject: Do you like the poem?

Dear Jamie,
Do you like this poem?

    Jamie Miller
    races like lightning
    across the field.
    Everyday,
    he makes fantastic goals.

Proofreading Marks

∧	**Add.**
⋏	**Add a comma.**
⊙	**Add a period.**
≡	**Capitalize.**
/	**Make lowercase.**
⌣	**Take out.**
¶	**Indent.**

Think About Your Writing

- Do you like your poem?
  - ☑ Does it describe a person?
  - ☑ Does it tell who, what, where, when, and why?
  - ☑ Are there colorful verbs and adjectives?
  - ☑ Do the subjects and verbs agree?
- What do you like best about your poem? What do you like the least?
- Will this poem go in your portfolio? Why or why not?

A VERY Unique You

1 ▶ Look Back at the Unit

Find Key Ideas In this unit, you read selections about unique people.

Discovery

Could I Ask You a Question?

Many People, Many Intelligences

Art Smart

Work with a group. Copy an important quote from each selection onto index cards. Trade cards with another group. Then talk about each quote. What does it say about identity?

2 ▶ Show What You Know

Sum It All Up Add important ideas about identity to the mind map. Share what you learned with a partner.

Reflect and Evaluate Write sentences to tell:

- what you learned about yourself
- what you learned about others

Put these sentences in your portfolio. Add work that shows what you learned about identity.

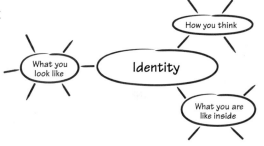

3 ▶ Make Connections

To Your School Make a class mural. Allow space for each student to show something unique and personal.

Ringling Brothers: Astounding Feat of Ernest Clark. Circus poster. Copyright © 1910.

UNITED, WE STAND

The acrobats in this poster depend on each other for their safety. What is it like to count on someone else? Try this: With a partner, sit back-to-back and link elbows. Now work together to stand. What happens if one partner doesn't cooperate? How does it feel to depend on someone else?

THEME 1
Pulling Together
When people pull together to get the job done, that's called teamwork.

THEME 2
Count on Me
Sometimes, our lives depend on being able to count on others.

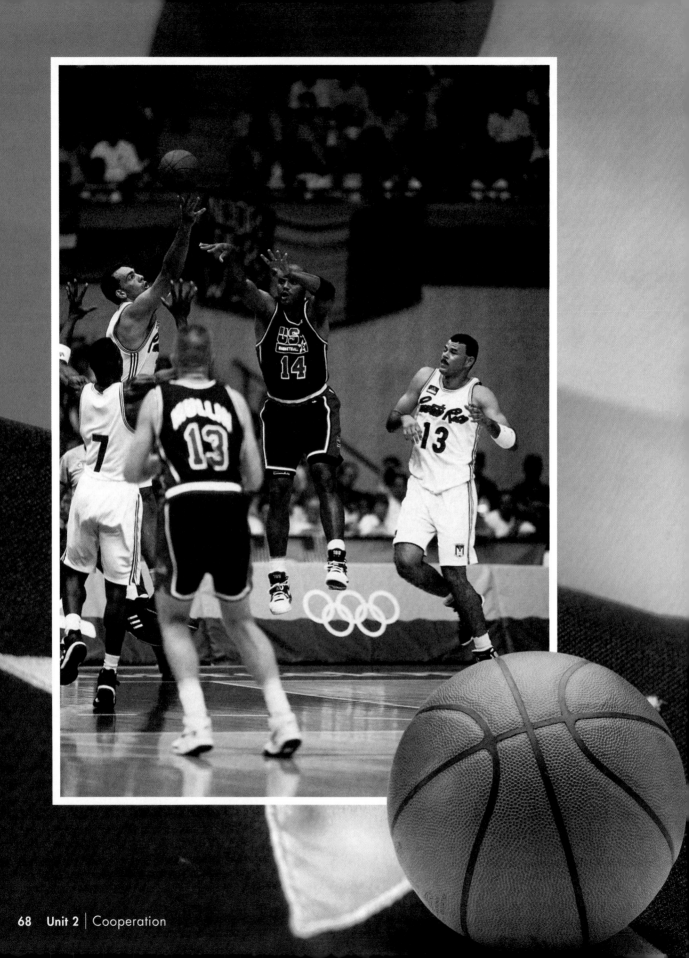

Pulling Together

- How do teammates work together to get a job done?

- Why is it important for every team member to do his or her part?

- When is working as a team easier than working alone?

THEME-RELATED BOOKS

Seven Blind Mice
by Ed Young

In this award-winning book, seven blind mice must work together to solve a riddle.

Raising Yoder's Barn
by Jane Yolen

When lightning strikes Yoder's barn, the whole Amish community comes to help.

NOVEL

**All for the Better:
A Story of El Barrio**
by Nicholasa Mohr

An award-winning author tells the story of how a young girl shows her community the importance of working together.

Build Language and Vocabulary

ENGAGE IN DISCUSSION

Study the photographs and read the saying. What do you think it means?

Many hands make light work.

—*Traditional saying*

LISTEN TO A DESCRIPTION

Listen to a description of the picture on page 70. Then listen again for all the words that name people. Make a web.

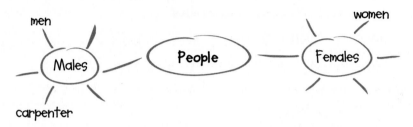

BUILD YOUR VOCABULARY

Pronouns You can use the words in the chart to tell who does something.

In your web, replace the words that name people with pronouns from the chart.

Subject Pronouns

One Person	More Than One Person	Examples
I	We	I listen to the tape. We listen to the tape.
you	you	You look at the picture.
he, she, it	they	He works hard. They work hard.

USE LANGUAGE STRUCTURES   ▶PRONOUNS

Speaking: Draw and Discuss Draw a picture to illustrate one of these traditional sayings. They tell about people working together.

• Two heads are better than one.
• There is strength in numbers.

Form a group with others who illustrated the same saying. Discuss the saying and your pictures. Use pronouns.

> **Example:**
> The friends are working on a hard math problem. **He** is dividing and **she** is subtracting. **They** work together to solve the problem.

TEAMWORK

photo-essay
by Ann Morris

Prepare to Read

THINK ABOUT WHAT YOU KNOW

Role-Play Work with a group. Act out a job that is easier when people work together. Can your classmates guess what it is?

care for People can **care for** each other by loving and helping each other.

cooperate You **cooperate** when you work together.

depend on You **depend on** things or people that you need.

member A **member** is someone who is part of a group.

plan You **plan** when you think about how to do something before you do it.

proud You feel **proud** when you are happy about something you did well.

solve problems When you **solve problems**, you find answers.

team A **team** is a group that works together.

LEARN KEY VOCABULARY

Use New Words in Context Study the new words. Work with a partner to write sentences about team members. Use the new words.

- Team members care for each other.
- They cooperate to get a job done.

LEARN TO IDENTIFY MAIN IDEAS

Key words tell about the most important ideas in a selection. Look for key words as you read. They will help you understand the **main ideas**.

READING STRATEGY
How to Identify Main Ideas

1. Read one part of the selection. Write two or three key words.
2. Look at the key words. Ask yourself: What is the most important idea?
3. Write the main idea.
4. Repeat the steps as you read.

Now read "Teamwork." Find key words that tell the main ideas of the photo-essay.

TEAMWORK

by Ann Morris

In this photo-essay, Ann Morris shows how people all over the world work together to get things done.

A **team** is a group
that works together
or plays together.

Team **members cooperate**
to **get the job done**.
That's called *teamwork*.

A team can be just a few
or a team can
be many.

Even animals can
work in teams.

get the job done do something together, finish the work

Some teams wear **uniforms**.
Others do not.

Teams **plan** together to make things
come out right. Team members
depend on one another. Team
members are **proud** of one another.

Each team member is
part of a whole.

Teamwork makes
the job easier.
Teamwork gets
the job done.

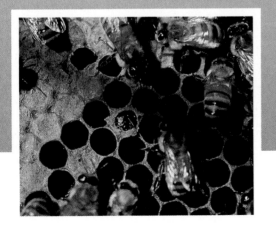

BEFORE YOU MOVE ON...
1. **Viewing/Details** Which teams are wearing uniforms? Which are not?
2. **Personal Experience** Think of a team that you are a part of. Tell a partner about your team.
3. **Viewing/Vocabulary** Look at a picture of one of the teams. Describe how the team members cooperate to do their job.

....

uniforms a set of matching clothing
come out right happen in the way they were planned

Teamwork **75**

nations countries

The best team of all is the family—working together, playing together, **caring for** one another.

And the biggest and most important team is the *world's* family—all the world's **nations** working together to help one another, to **solve problems**, to make peace.

BEFORE YOU MOVE ON...

1. **Vocabulary** The author describes the family team as *the best team*. How does she describe the world's family?
2. **Details** What are some ways that the world's nations work together?
3. **Categorizing** Write a list of teams that work together. Write a list of teams that play together.

ABOUT THE AUTHOR

Ann Morris says she wrote *Teamwork* because "teamwork in school and in life is so important." Ann works with a team of editors, artists, photographers, and others to get her books published. She respects rescue workers who work together to help people in trouble. She also admires teams of people who put on ballets and operas.

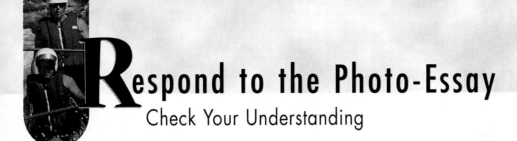

Respond to the Photo-Essay
Check Your Understanding

SUM IT UP

Identify Main Ideas Complete a chart of key words and important ideas from "Teamwork."

Page	Key Words	Important Ideas
74	team, works, plays, members cooperate, get the job done	Teams cooperate in work or play to get a job done.
75		
76		

Add Details to a Paragraph What are the most important ideas of the photo-essay? Work with your class to finish this paragraph:

This photo-essay is about teams. Teams cooperate. They work together to get a job done. Teams also _____

_____

_____ .

THINK IT OVER

Discuss Talk about these questions with a partner.

1. **Theme** What is an important lesson you learned from "Teamwork"?

2. **Personal Experience** What are some teams at your school?

3. **Opinion** Do you like to work alone or with a team? Explain your answer.

EXPRESS YOURSELF

▶ MAKE REQUESTS,
  GIVE AND ACCEPT SUGGESTIONS

When you make a **request**, you ask for something. When you give a **suggestion**, you tell an idea or opinion. Pretend that you and a partner are drawing a map. Practice making requests and giving suggestions politely. Use these sentence starters:

Make Requests	Make Suggestions	Accept Suggestions
May I please	Maybe you could	Thank you for
Would you please	It might be better if	Yes, I agree that

Examples:
- **May I please** use the ruler?
- **It might be better if** you used a red pen.
- **Thank you for** your ideas.

Respond to the Photo-Essay, continued
Language Arts and Literature

⟩ GRAMMAR IN CONTEXT ⟩

USE SUBJECT PRONOUNS

Learn About Subject Pronouns A pronoun takes the place of a **noun**. A subject pronoun is used in the subject of a sentence. It tells who or what is doing something.

> The **girls** are a team. **They** work together.

- Use **I** to tell about yourself. Use **you** to say something directly to another person or persons.

> **I** will wait. **You** can go first.

- Use **he** to tell about a male. Use **she** to tell about a female. Use **it** for a place or thing.

> **Joe** needs help. **He** calls a friend.
>
> **Irene** answers. **She** helps.
>
> **The box** is full. **It** is heavy.

- Use **we** and **they** to tell about more than one person.

> **Rob and I** call. **We** can help.
>
> **Jon and Nia** call. **They** will help, too.

Practice Rewrite the sentences. Use subject pronouns in place of the underlined words.

1. <u>Gabriel</u> is a member of a team.

2. <u>Rita and Carrie</u> play together.

3. <u>The men</u> carry a basket.

4. <u>Susan</u> puts out fires.

⟩ SPEAKING/LISTENING ⟩

PLAY "FINISH MY SENTENCE"

Work with a partner to make sentences about different kinds of teams. Use this sentence frame:

> It takes _____ people on a team
> to _____.

1 **Start a Sentence** One partner fills in the first blank with a number.

2 **Finish the Sentence** The other partner names an activity for that number of people.

Example:
Partner 1: It takes ___four___ people on a team
Partner 2: to ___have a relay race___.

3 **Change Roles** Take turns filling in new numbers and teams. Then share your ideas with the class.

Learn how to be a good **listener**.
See Handbook pages 373–374.

Content Area Connections

MAKE A GOVERNMENT TEAM CHART

The United States government has many teams that work together. Learn about teams like:

- the Supreme Court
- the Senate
- the House of Representatives
- the President's Cabinet

1 Find Information Use the government section in the white pages of a telephone directory. Choose a team from the city, county, state, or federal government. Then use social studies books, encyclopedias, or the Internet to find information. Take notes about each team you find.

2 Organize Your Ideas Use your notes to complete a chart like this:

Government Teams

Team	Members Are Called	Number of Members	What the Team Does
Supreme Court	justices	9	makes decisions about laws

STUDY WILDLIFE TEAMS

Some wild animals and insects live and work in teams. Work with a group to write a report about one kind of wildlife. Choose animals like:

ants	bees	wolves
lions	gorillas	whales

1 Find Information Use print or electronic encyclopedias, science books, or the Internet. Take notes about your team.

2 Write a Report Use your notes to write sentences about how the wildlife team works together. Add pictures of the team at work.

3 Share Your Report Tell about the team. Show your pictures.

A team of ants carries leaves to its nest.

Build Language and Vocabulary

DESCRIBE EVENTS

View the painting. The family works together to make tamales.
Listen to a description of what the family does.

Making Tamales/La tamalada, Carmen Lomas Garza, Acrylic. Copyright © 1990.

LISTEN FOR LOCATION WORDS

Listen to the recording again. Listen for phrases that begin with these words, called **prepositions**. Write the phrases.

Location Words

1. into _____	7. with _____
2. of _____	8. on _____
3. from _____	9. with _____
4. into _____	10. to _____
5. on _____	11. into _____
6. over _____	12. from _____

Compare charts with a classmate. Listen to the recording again if you need to.

BUILD YOUR VOCABULARY

Pronouns You can use these words to show who owns something.

Which person in the picture are these sentences about?

- She has a green bowl in her hands.
- He has a red handkerchief in his pocket.
- They have spoons in their hands.

Possessive Pronouns

One Person	More Than One Person
my	our
your	your
his, her, its	their

USE LANGUAGE STRUCTURES ▶ PRONOUNS AND PREPOSITIONS

Speaking: Describe Events and People Form two teams to play "I Spy." Team 1 chooses someone or something in the picture on page 80. They give three clues that include a possessive pronoun and a preposition. Team 2 guesses.

Example:

Team 1: I spy someone. **His** sweater is brown, **his** hands are **on the table**, and you can't see **his** feet.

Together, we DREAM

poems
by Francisco X. Alarcón

Prepare to Read Poetry

THINK ABOUT WHAT YOU KNOW

Match Dreams A dream is a goal that you have for the future. What is your dream? Write it down or draw a picture of it on a card. Then find a classmate who has a dream like yours.

adobe An **adobe** is a brick made of mud and straw that dries in the sun.

bar A **bar** is a solid object that is longer than it is wide.

entire Something is **entire** when it is complete or whole.

gather When people **gather**, they come together.

layer A **layer** is one thickness of something.

plaster When you **plaster** a wall, you cover it with material to protect it.

reality The way things really are is called **reality**.

require When you **require** something, you need it.

tend When you **tend** something, you take care of it.

weathered Something is **weathered** when it is changed by wind, sun, and rain.

LEARN KEY VOCABULARY

Use New Words in Context Study the new words. Work with a partner to answer the questions. Explain your answers.

1. What is a **bar** of **adobe** made of?
2. Why do you need to **plaster** a new **layer** on a **weathered** house?
3. Why is it better when an **entire** family can **gather** to help?
4. What tools do you **require** when you **tend** a garden?
5. How can you make a dream become **reality**?

LEARN TO VISUALIZE

When you **visualize**, you see a picture in your mind. Visualizing helps you enjoy the feeling of a poem.

READING STRATEGY
How to Visualize

1. Read the entire collection of poems to get the feeling.
2. Go back and read each poem slowly. Look for clear, colorful words.
3. Use the words to make pictures in your mind.

Now read "Together, We Dream." Try to visualize what the poet describes.

Together, we DREAM

by Francisco X. Alarcón

When people share the same dream, wonderful things can happen. Poet Francisco X. Alarcón writes about the dreams that people share.

ADOBES

some of
the oldest
homes

still
standing
in New Mexico

were built
right out
of the Earth

with adobes
that common
people

made
from mud
and straw

spread out
for the sun
to dry

---

built made, put together
mud soft, wet earth
straw the dry stems or stalks of grassy plants
spread out laid on the ground outside

like some
big chocolate
bars

every few
years entire
families

their
neighbors
and friends

would gather
before the rains
to plaster

the weathered
outside adobe
walls

with a new
layer of mud
and straw

adobes—
like people—
require

lots of
attention
and love

BEFORE YOU MOVE ON...

1. **Details** What are adobes made of?

2. **Inference** Why do adobe walls need new plaster "before the rains"?

3. **Opinion** Do you agree with the poet that people "require lots of attention and love"?

attention care

FAMILY GARDEN

in the backyard
of our home
there is a garden

all in our family
do our share
to tend it

Mami loves
to plant and trim
rosebushes

Abuelita keeps
her *yerbabuena*
in a small plot

more than anything
Papi likes
to water everything

the lemon tree
the *calabacitas*
the vegetable rows

and the tomatoes
my sisters grow
every spring

my brothers and I
in turn weed out
and cut the grass

even our puppy
has learned
to plant bones

in this garden
that smiles
like the sun

all in the family
take time to tend
each other's dreams

Mami Mom (in Spanish)

Abuelita Grandma (in Spanish)

yerbabuena mint plant (in Spanish)

plot area of ground for planting

Papi Dad (in Spanish)

calabacitas zucchini squash (in Spanish)

weed out pull out the unwanted plants

COLLECTIVE DREAM

a dream
we dream
alone

reality
we dream
together

BEFORE YOU MOVE ON...

1. **Details** How does each member of the family help with the garden?
2. **Figurative Language** Reread "Collective Dream" and the last three lines in "Family Garden." What reality did the people in "Family Garden" dream together?
3. **Mood** How do these poems make you feel?

....

Collective Dream Dream that belongs to everyone in a group

ABOUT THE POET

Francisco X. Alarcón was born in California, but he grew up in Jalisco, Mexico. One of his best memories about growing up is working in the family garden. "I believe my parents kept this garden for two reasons. One was to have a steady supply of vegetables. The other was to teach me, my five brothers, and two sisters to work together as a team." Today, Francisco X. Alarcón works as a professor and a writer. His work has won many awards.

Respond to the Poems
Check Your Understanding

SUM IT UP

Visualize Copy and complete this chart. Write the title of each poem. Write words from the poem that helped you make pictures in your mind. Then draw what you pictured.

Poem	Key Words	Picture
"Adobes"	oldest homes, New Mexico, built out of the Earth	

Make Comparisons Show your chart to a group. Are your key words and pictures the same? What things look different? Talk about how different pictures can come from the same words.

THINK IT OVER

Discuss Talk about these questions with a partner.

1. **Figurative Language** What does the poet mean when he says that the family garden *smiles like the sun*?

2. **Inference** What did you learn about adobe houses from the poems? Why are some old adobe houses still standing?

3. **Judgment** The poet says that it takes more than one person to make a dream a reality. Is this true? Why or why not?

4. **Personal Experience** Which poem do you like the best? Why?

EXPRESS YOURSELF ▶ DESCRIBE EVENTS

Tell a partner about a time you were on a team. Your partner will ask questions to find out more about the team event. Use questions like these:

• How many people were on the team?

• What did each member do?

• How did working as a team make the job easier?

Language Arts and Literature

GRAMMAR IN CONTEXT

USE PREPOSITIONAL PHRASES

Learn About Prepositions A **preposition** is a short word like *to, on,* or *with.* It is the first word in a **prepositional phrase**. The last word in the phrase is often a noun.

Prepositional phrases add details to a sentence. They may tell about:

- location: **in the garden**
- direction: **into the ground**
- time: **before the rains**

Find Prepositional Phrases Reread the poems. Talk with a partner about how the prepositional phrases help you visualize the poems.

Practice Copy the poetry frame. Study the prepositions. Then complete the prepositional phrases to show location, direction, and time.

> The flowers **in** —————
>
> Turn their faces **to** —————.
>
> They bloom **from** ————— **to** —————
>
> And rise up **from** —————.

SPEAKING/LISTENING

MEMORIZE AND RECITE POETRY

When you **memorize** and **recite** a poem, you say it aloud without looking at the words. Work with a team to memorize and recite "Adobes" or "Family Garden":

- Decide which lines each member will memorize.
- Practice reciting the poem together. Think about the meaning and feeling of the words as you say them.
- Then recite your poem for the class.

REPRESENTING/SPEAKING

CREATE A MULTIMEDIA PHOTO-ESSAY

In a school, many people share the dream of learning. Take photos or make a video of people as they do things like:

study in the library	work on projects
do experiments	use computers

Present your photo-essay to the class. Tell what your pictures show.

Learn how to create a **multimedia presentation**. See Handbook pages 362–363.

Count on Me

- In what ways do people count on other people to survive?

- In what ways do people and animals count on each other to survive?

- How are our lives made better when we have others that we can count on?

THEME-RELATED BOOKS

It's Mine!
by Leo Lionni

In this fable, three selfish frogs learn an important lesson after they count on each other to survive a frightening storm.

My Buddy
by Audrey Osofsky

A boy who uses a wheelchair counts on Buddy, his Service Dog, to help him in many ways. Buddy even goes to school!

Rikki-Tikki-Tavi
by Rudyard Kipling, adapted and illustrated by Jerry Pinkney

In this version of a classic story, a mongoose saves the family that saved its life.

Build Language and Vocabulary

GIVE DIRECTIONS

View this photograph and read the quote. How do people with special needs count on others?

Helen Keller uses a special alphabet to communicate with her teacher, Anne Sullivan. Helen uses her hands to speak to her.

Alone we can do so little,
together we can do so much.

— *Helen Keller*

TAKE A TRUST WALK

Work with a partner. Learn what it is like to count on someone else. One partner will be the guide. The other will keep his or her eyes closed. The guide leads the partner around the room or outside. The guide gives directions: *Walk forward. Stop. Turn left. Go up one step.*, etc. Then, partners can trade places. Discuss what you learned about teamwork and trust.

BUILD YOUR VOCABULARY

Pronouns You can use the words in this chart after a verb or a preposition.

Object Pronouns

One Person	More Than One Person	Examples
me	us	Listen to me. Walk toward us.
you	you	I will guide you.
him, her, it	them	Walk around her. Step over it. Don't trip on them.

Tell the group some of the directions you gave your partner in your "Trust Walk." Use object pronouns.

USE LANGUAGE STRUCTURES ▶ COMMANDS, PRONOUNS

Speaking: Play a Directions Game Form a line of eight to ten people. Choose a leader to give commands. Each command must use an object pronoun. The goal of the game is to move an eraser from the beginning to the end of the line. Try not to repeat any directions. Give everyone a turn as leader.

Examples:
Pass the eraser around **her**.
Throw the eraser over **them**.
Give it to **him**.

A DOG YOU CAN COUNT ON

article
by Caroline Arnold

Prepare to Read

THINK ABOUT WHAT YOU KNOW

Make a Class Web How do people and animals work together as teams? Show some examples on a word web.

LEARN KEY VOCABULARY

blind A **blind** person is someone who cannot see.

command A **command** is an order; it tells what to do.

count on When you **count on** someone, you need that person to help you.

guide dog A **guide dog** is trained to help a person who cannot see.

instructor An **instructor** is a teacher.

partner A **partner** is a person or animal who works with you.

personality Your **personality** is the way you act or what you are like.

skill A **skill** is the ability to do something well.

take care of When you **take care of** something, you give it your time and attention.

training When you get **training**, someone teaches you how to do something.

Relate Words Study the new words. Then write sentences. Use a beginning from column 1 and an ending from column 2.

Beginning
1. A **guide dog** must learn how to
2. A guide dog has special **skills** and
3. Dogs must learn to obey
4. An **instructor** gives the
5. You can **count on** a guide dog

Ending
A. **training** to the team.
B. a gentle **personality**.
C. to be a helpful **partner**.
D. **take care of** a **blind** person.
E. every **command**.

LEARN TO ASK QUESTIONS AND CLARIFY

As you read, you can stop to **ask questions**. This can help you **clarify**, or check your understanding of the main ideas, before you read on.

READING STRATEGY
How to Ask Questions and Clarify
1. Read one part of the article with a partner.
2. Stop at the end of the section. Ask each other questions about what you read.
3. If something is not clear, go back and read that part again. Help each other understand the article.

As you read "A Dog You Can Count On," stop often to ask questions. Make sure you understand each part before you continue.

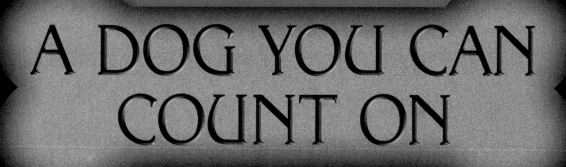

A DOG YOU CAN COUNT ON

from *A Guide Dog Puppy Grows Up*
by **Caroline Arnold**

It takes a lot of training to be a guide
dog for the blind. That's because
guide dog owners really count on
their furry friends. This article
shows how they learn
to work together.

This is the Guide Dog Training Center in San Rafael, California. Hundreds of guide dogs are trained here each year.

Stacy will teach Moe how to work with his new guide dog.

When Moe Enguillado **arrives** to begin his **guide dog** training, Stacy Burrow **greets** him. She is one of his **instructors**. Moe is excited about getting a dog. At the same time, he is a little **worried** about everything he will have to learn.

Stacy knows the dogs very well. Each dog has its own **personality**. After meeting the new students, Stacy carefully **matches each person with** one of the dogs.

---

arrives gets to the place he is going
greets says hello to
worried scared, concerned
matches each person with finds a person who is like each

Moe Enguillado meets Aria, his new guide dog.

"Hello, Moe," says Stacy. "Here's Aria. I **picked** her **especially** for you because you both have **lively** personalities."

Moe **scratches** Aria under the chin. "Hello, Aria," Moe says. "I can't wait to **get to know you better**. We're going to have fun together."

"Yes," says Stacy. "It won't be easy at first. But, one month from now, you two are going to be a **real** team."

Aria sits by Moe's side when he gives the command, "Sit."

BEFORE YOU MOVE ON...

1. **Personal Experience** What kind of dog would match your personality?
2. **Inference** Would you describe Moe Enguillado and Aria as *active* or *quiet*?
3. **Prediction** What do you think Moe and Aria will be able to do after one month of training?

Aria stands by Moe's side when he gives the command, "Heel."

....

picked chose
especially just, only
lively fun, active, busy
scratches rubs, pets
get to know you better learn more about what you are like
real true

They learn how to go around barriers,

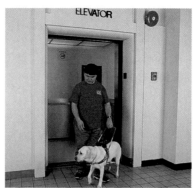

into and out of elevators,

and up and down stairs.

Blind students must learn how to work with their dogs and how to **take care of** them. They learn how to go around **barriers**, into and out of elevators, and up and down stairs. They **enter** offices, grocery stores, and banks. The instructors help the students learn the kind of **skills** and **commands** they will need when they go home with their dogs.

Finally, after four weeks of hard work, the students and their dog **partners** finish their **training**.

As each day goes by, Moe and Aria will **continue to learn** from each other, and they can **look forward to** many happy years together.

BEFORE YOU MOVE ON...

1. **Details** What are some of the things students must learn during their training?
2. **Prediction** How will Moe count on Aria in the years to come?

---

barriers things used to block off an open space for walking

enter go inside

continue to learn keep on learning

look forward to plan to have

ABOUT THE AUTHOR

Caroline Arnold says, "Like many writers of children's books, I began when my children were small." This probably explains why she likes to write for young readers. Some of her books—such as *Why Do We Have Rules?* and *Who Keeps Us Safe?*—explain how people depend on each other in daily life. Caroline Arnold also is the author of the award-winning book, *Saving the Peregrine Falcon.*

Respond to the Article
Check Your Understanding

SUM IT UP

Identify Steps in a Process Put these events from the article in order. Then make a storyboard with a picture and sentence in each box.

- Moe and Aria go home together.
- Moe goes to the training center.
- Moe and Aria learn skills.
- Stacy chooses Aria to be Moe's partner.

Moe goes to the
training center.

Make a Prediction What do you think will happen to Moe and his guide dog? Show your ideas on a new paper. Then share your finished storyboard with a partner.

THINK IT OVER

Discuss Talk about these questions with a partner.

1. **Summary** How do Aria and Moe help each other?

2. **Inference** What special personality does a guide dog need to have?

3. **Comparison** How are guide dogs like pets? How are they different?

4. **Personal Experience** Describe a time that someone helped you do something. How did you feel?

EXPRESS YOURSELF
▶ ASK AND ANSWER QUESTIONS

Play "Hot Seat." One student plays Moe. The class asks Moe questions. The student answers questions as if he or she is Moe.

Choose another student to sit in the "hot seat" and play Stacy.

Respond to the Article, continued
Language Arts and Literature

◗ GRAMMAR IN CONTEXT

USE OBJECT PRONOUNS

Learn About Object Pronouns A pronoun takes the place of a **noun**. An object pronoun comes after a verb or words like *to*, *for*, or *from*.

> A trainer takes the **dogs** to **mom**.
>
> A trainer takes **them** to **her**.

- Use **me** to tell about yourself. Use **you** to say something directly to another person.

> Stacy taught **me**. I can teach **you**.

- Use **him** to tell about a male. Use **her** to tell about a female. Use **it** for a place or thing.

> I see **Abraham**. I call **him**.
>
> We look for **Karen**. We want to see **her**.
>
> She brings the **dog**. We play with **it**.

- Use **us** and **them** to talk about more than one person.

> Henry calls **Eva and me**. He talks to **us**.
>
> Here are **Pam and David**. We can ask **them**.

Practice Rewrite the sentences. Use object pronouns in place of the underlined words.

1. Stacy welcomed <u>Mike and Jane</u>.
2. Stacy gave <u>Mike</u> a gentle dog.
3. Stacy gave <u>Jane</u> a lively dog.
4. The children walked <u>their dogs</u>.

◗ WRITING

WRITE A THANK-YOU LETTER

Pretend you are Moe or his instructor. Write a thank-you letter. Here are some ideas:

- Moe thanks Stacy for training Aria.
- Moe thanks Stacy for her instruction.
- Stacy thanks Moe for coming to the center.

1. **Write the Heading** Include an address and today's date.

2. **Write the Greeting** Write *Dear* and the person's name.

3. **Write the Body** Say "thank you" and tell how you feel.

4. **Write the Closing and the Signature** Write a closing like *Sincerely*, *Yours truly*, or *Your friend*. Then sign your name.

Heading	350 Los Ranchitos Rd. San Rafael, CA 94903 November 5, 2002
Greeting	Dear Moe,
Body	Thank you for giving Aria a good home. You and Aria are a great team. I think you two will be very happy together!
Closing and Signature	Your friend, Stacy

Content Area Connections

SCIENCE

STUDY HUMAN AND ANIMAL TEAMS

Work with a group. Research one human and animal team from a category below:

- **entertainment** — films, the circus
- **transportation** — sled dogs, wagons
- **farming** — teams of horses or oxen
- **rescue work** — snow and earthquake rescue

1 Find Information Use library books, science and social studies textbooks, or the Internet. Take notes about how animals and humans work together.

2 Share Information Make a class chart. List human and animal teams. Tell how they work together.

3 Make a Generalization A **generalization** is a statement you can make after studying many examples. Make a generalization about human and animal teams.

SCIENCE

TECHNOLOGY/MEDIA

RESEARCH BLINDNESS

Work with a team to learn about blindness. Research a topic like:

- **famous people** — Helen Keller, Louis Braille
- **causes of blindness** — diseases, injuries
- **services for the blind** — guide dogs, Braille

1 Find Information Use the library or the Internet. Try these Web sites, but remember that new sites appear every day! Use your topic as a key word.

INTERNET

INFORMATION ON-LINE

Web Sites:
➤ Blindness
- www.keystoneblind.org
- www.nfb.org/kids.htm
- tqjunior.thinkquest.org/5852
- www.guidedogs.com

2 Give an Oral Presentation Work with your group to tell what you learned.

Learn how to do **research**.
See Handbook pages 366–370.
Learn how to use the **Internet**
on pages 364–365.

Build Language and Vocabulary
ASK FOR AND GIVE INFORMATION

View the photos. How are people counting on each other in the rescue scenes?

MAKE RESCUE PICTURES

The pictures on page 102 show a snow rescue. What are other situations where people can be rescued? Brainstorm ideas with your class. Record them on a web. Then choose one rescue situation to draw. Share your picture with the group

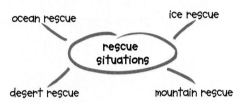

BUILD YOUR VOCABULARY

Survival Words To **survive** means to stay alive. Make a chart like this one. List the things people need to survive. Add your own ideas.

What People Need

shelter	water	food
house	to drink	fruit
tent	to wash	meat
apartment		

USE LANGUAGE STRUCTURES ▶ QUESTIONS AND STATEMENTS

Speaking: Ask and Answer Questions Work with a partner. Take turns asking and answering questions about survival. Use the ideas from your chart.

   Example:
   Question: What kind of shelter do people need to survive?
   Answer: People need a house or tent.

A MOUNTAIN RESCUE

story
by James Ramsey Ullman

Prepare to Read

THINK ABOUT WHAT YOU KNOW

Talk It Over Tell your class about a rescue you have seen or heard about.

LEARN KEY VOCABULARY

Use New Words in Context Study the new words. Act out the action words in a group. Draw pictures of the other words. Then work together to write a sentence for each word.

answer You **answer** when you say or do something after you hear a question or a statement.

brave A **brave** person does not show fear in a difficult situation.

climb When you **climb**, you move yourself up with your hands and feet.

hold on When you **hold on** to something, you do not let go of it.

lower When you **lower** something, you move it downward.

pull When you **pull** something, you move it toward yourself.

remove You **remove** something when you take it away.

silence When everything is quiet, there is **silence**.

tighten When you **tighten** the way you hold something, you grab it harder.

weight A **weight** is something heavy.

LEARN ABOUT PROBLEMS AND SOLUTIONS

In some stories, a character has a **problem**. The **solution** is what the character does to solve the problem. When you find the problem and solution in a story, it helps you understand the most important events.

> **READING STRATEGY**
> **How to Identify Problems and Solutions**
> 1. Read the beginning of the story.
> 2. Ask yourself: What problem does the main character need to solve?
> 3. Find the events that lead to the solution.
> 4. Finish reading the story. Ask yourself: How was the problem solved?

Now read "A Mountain Rescue." Look for the problem at the beginning of the story and the solution at the end.

A MOUNTAIN RESCUE

from *Banner in the Sky* • by **James Ramsey Ullman**

ometimes counting on another person makes the difference between life and death. Sixteen-year-old Rudi Matt is alone on a snow-covered mountain in the Alps. Suddenly, he hears a cry for help. Can a boy save a man's life?

1
DANGER ON A MOUNTAIN

Rudi finds a man who has fallen down a crack in the ice. Together, they
try to think of a way to pull the man up.

The **crevasse** was six feet **wide**
at the top. But Rudi could not tell how
deep it was.

"Hello!" Rudi called. "Hello—"
A **voice answered** from below.

"How far down are you?"

"About twenty feet, I guess."

"How long have you been there?"

"About three hours."

Rudi looked up and down the
crevasse. He was thinking **desperately**
of what he could do.

"Do you have a rope?" asked
the voice.

"No."

"You'll have to get help."

---

crevasse deep crack in the ice
wide long from side to side
deep far down from the top
voice sound made by a person
desperately wildly, hopelessly

Rudi didn't answer. To get down to town would take two hours. To **climb** back up would take three. By that time the man would be frozen to death.

"No," said Rudi, "it would take too long."

There was another **silence**. "I'll think of something," Rudi cried. "I'll think of *something!*"

"Don't **lose your head**," the voice said.

The voice was as quiet as ever. Rudi didn't know who the man was, but he knew he was a **brave** man.

BEFORE YOU MOVE ON...

1. **Details** Why didn't Rudi go to town for help?
2. **Inference** Why did Rudi think that the man was brave?
3. **Prediction** What do you think Rudi will do to help the man?

---

lose your head do something silly or crazy

THE RESCUE

Rudi makes a long rope by tying his clothes to his staff. He and the man work together to pull the man to safety.

———

Rudi drew in a long, slow breath. Lying flat on the **glacier**, he **lowered** the **staff** as far as it would go.

"Can you see it?" he asked

"See what?" said the man.

Obviously he couldn't. Rudi **removed** his jacket and tied it to the staff.

Then, Rudi took his shirt and tied one sleeve to the sleeve of the jacket. As he lay down, the ice **bit into** his **bare** chest.

"Can you reach it?"

"I **can't make it**," said the voice. It was **fainter** than before.

---

glacier large area of ice
staff long walking stick
Obviously Clearly, It was clear that
bit into hurt, cut painfully into

bare uncovered
can't make it can't reach it
fainter quieter, harder to hear

"Wait," said Rudi. He took off his **trousers**. He tied a trouser-leg to the sleeve of the shirt. Then, he lowered the staff and clothes like a **fishing line**.

"Can you reach it now?" he called.

"Yes," the voice answered. "You won't be able to hold me. I'll **pull** you in."

"No you won't."

The pull came. His hands **tightened** on the staff until the **knuckles showed white**. He could hear **scraping** below. The man was **clawing** his boots against the ice-wall.

It seemed like hours. Then at last a head **appeared**.

The climber was close now. But Rudi could **hold on** no longer. His hands were opening. It was all over.

---

trousers pants
fishing line string used to catch fish
knuckles showed white skin over his bones turned white from squeezing

scraping a scratching noise
clawing scratching and climbing with
appeared came into sight, could be seen

And then it *was* over. The **weight** was gone. The man was beside Rudi, turning to him, **staring** at him.

"Why—you're just a boy!" he said in **astonishment**.

....

staring looking with wide open eyes
astonishment surprise, amazement

ABOUT THE AUTHOR

James Ramsey Ullman was a newspaper reporter, a writer, and a mountain climber. He also was part of the first American team to climb Mount Everest. Mr. Ullman used many of his own experiences to help him write his Newbery Honor Book, *Banner in the Sky.* "A Mountain Rescue" comes from that novel.

Respond to the Story

Check Your Understanding

SUM IT UP

Identify Problems and Solutions Copy and complete this chart. Show Rudi's problem and the events that led to the solution.

Problem and Solution Chart

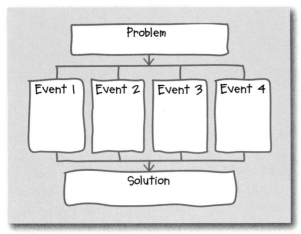

Summarize Use your chart to retell the story. Copy and complete this summary.

> Rudi had to _____.
> First he _____.
> Then Rudi _____.
> The man helped by _____.
> They worked together to _____.
> In the end _____.

THINK IT OVER

Discuss Talk about these questions with a partner.

1. **Character's Feelings** How did Rudi feel when he found the man trapped in the crevasse?

2. **Opinion** Was it a good idea for Rudi to try to help the man by himself? Explain.

3. **Details** What did the man do to help with the rescue?

4. **Personal Experience** Have you ever helped someone in need? What happened? How did you feel?

EXPRESS YOURSELF

▶ASK FOR AND GIVE INFORMATION

Work with a partner. Take turns asking questions about details in the story. For example:

- How wide was the crevasse at the top?
- How far down was the man?
- How long was the man trapped?

Respond to the Story, continued
Language Arts and Literature

▶ GRAMMAR IN CONTEXT

USE SUBJECT AND OBJECT PRONOUNS

Learn about Subject and Object Pronouns A **pronoun** is word that takes the place of a noun. Use a subject pronoun in the subject of a sentence. Use an object pronoun after a preposition or a verb.

Subject Pronouns	Object Pronouns
I	me
you	you
he, she, it	him, her, it
we	us
you	you
they	them

Use Subject and Object Pronouns Work with a partner. Retell "A Mountain Rescue." Use correct pronouns.

Example:

Rudi heard a man call for help. **He** found **him** trapped in the crevasse.

"**I** have to help **him**," Rudi thought.

Practice Rewrite the sentences. Use pronouns in place of the underlined words.

1. Rudi tied his clothes to make a rope.

2. The man climbed toward Rudi.

3. The time seemed like hours.

4. "We did it!" Rudi and the man shouted.

▶ WRITING/SPEAKING

EXTEND THE STORY

Work with a partner to **extend**, or add to, the story. Tell what happened after Rudi saved the man.

1 **Write Your Ideas** How will you and your partner extend the story? Will you write about how the man thanks Rudi? Will you tell how they work together to get off the mountain? Write the new events clearly and in order.

2 **Edit Your Work** Trade papers with another group. Make sure that the events are clear and in order. Check for the correct pronouns. Then make a better final draft.

3 **Share Your Work** Join other pairs of students. Read the stories aloud. Then compare the endings.

 Learn how to improve your writing in the **writer's craft**. See Handbook pages 390–401. Review **pronouns** on pages 414–416.

Content Area Connections

SOCIAL STUDIES

EXPLORE GEOGRAPHY

Learn About the Alps "A Mountain Rescue" takes place in the Alpine Mountains of Switzerland. The **Alps** are mountains that run across several countries in Europe including:

France	Germany	Switzerland
Italy	Austria	Bosnia & Herzegovina
Croatia	Slovenia	Yugoslavia

Create a Map Draw and label the countries the Alps pass through. Then show the path of the mountain range. Label the tallest mountains like Mont Blanc, Piz Bernina, and the Matterhorn.

Make a Fact Sheet Find facts about the Alps. Then answer these questions to display with your map.

- How many miles long are the Alps?
- How many miles wide are they?
- How tall are the highest mountains?

SOCIAL STUDIES

TECHNOLOGY/MEDIA

COMPARE MOUNTAINS

The **Seven Summits** are the tallest mountains on each continent. Work with a group to study a mountain below:

Aconcagua	Elbrus	Puncak Jaya
Kilimanjaro	Everest	Vinson Massif
McKinley		

Find Information Use encyclopedias, atlases, or the Internet. Take notes about the mountain's location, height, and when it was first climbed.

Try these Web sites, but remember that new sites appear every day! Use the mountain's name as a key word.

INTERNET

INFORMATION ON-LINE

Web Sites:
➤ Mountains
- www.eblast.com
- www.peakware.com

Combine Information Make a class chart to compare the seven mountains your class studied.

Learn how to make a **chart**.
See Handbook pages 340–341.

Writing That Informs and Explains

**Expository writing gives information about an idea or event.
The writer includes important details to help explain the information.**

WRITING MODEL

Look at these sentences and photographs from "Teamwork."
What words give you information about teamwork? How do the
photographs help explain the information?

from **"Teamwork"**

Team members cooperate
to get the job done.
That's called teamwork.

A team can be just a few . . .
or a team can be many.

Even animals can
work in teams.

Write Together

1 **Plan the Chart and Summary** The chart will show
- **What** we did
- **Why** we did it
- **When** we did it
- **Where** we did it
- **How** we did it
- **How** we felt about it

2 **Brainstorm Ideas** Fill in the chart. Look at the example.

3 **Write the Summary** Use the chart to write a summary.

STUDENT WRITING MODEL

Our class had a beach cleanup to make Seaside Park cleaner and safer. We went to the beach on Friday afternoon. We divided the class into teams, and each person got a job to do. Then we picked up empty soda cans and old crumpled papers. Finally we loaded up five big bags of garbage. We were proud of our work. We were excited to tell our friends and family about it.

Experience Chart

What we did beach cleanup
Why we did it to make the beach a cleaner, safer place
When we did it Friday afternoon
Where we did it Seaside Park
How we did it on teams, each person had a job
How we felt about it proud, excited to tell others

The events follow a logical order. **Time order words** show the steps.

Details help to make the story more interesting.

Writing That Informs and Explains, continued

Write on Your Own

Learn to write by doing it.
— P. D. James

WRITING PROMPT

Now explain your part in the group activity. Write a summary for your family or friends to read.

PREWRITE

1 **Show What You Did** Draw pictures of how you did your job.

I went to the beach. | I looked at the trash. | I wrote down the kinds of trash.

2 **Get Organized** Make an experience chart about your topic.

Experience Chart

What I did	recorded the kinds of trash
Why I did it	I was the team recorder.
Where I did it	Seaside Park
When I did it	Friday afternoon
How I did it	wrote the name of each item
How I felt about it	like to write, important job

Think About Your Writing

• Did you fill in all the details on your chart?

• Are there more you want to add?

DRAFT

1 **Write Your Summary** Use your chart to write your summary.

2 **Choose the Best Details** Use words that are specific.

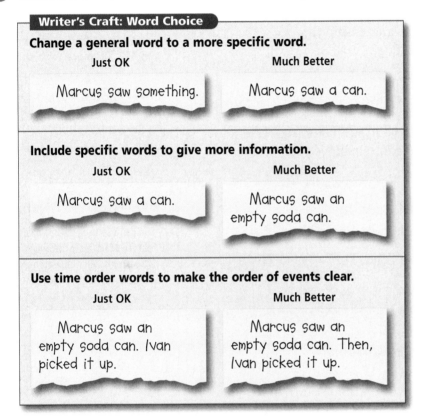

Writer's Craft: Word Choice

Change a general word to a more specific word.

Just OK	Much Better
Marcus saw something.	Marcus saw a can.

Include specific words to give more information.

Just OK	Much Better
Marcus saw a can.	Marcus saw an empty soda can.

Use time order words to make the order of events clear.

Just OK	Much Better
Marcus saw an empty soda can. Ivan picked it up.	Marcus saw an empty soda can. Then, Ivan picked it up.

Time Order Words

first
next
then
last
finally
before
after
while
when

Collect specific words in categories you are writing about.
Use them to add details.

Talent Show
juggle
play the violin
dance
sing

Litter
paper plates
old newspapers
candy wrappers
fast food containers

Lunch Room Decorations
student artwork
curtains
table centerpieces
anti-litter posters

Think About Your Writing

- Read your draft. Do you like the way it sounds?
- Are there more specific words to explain what you did?

Writing That Informs and Explains, continued

REVISE

1 **Read Your Summary** Does it make sense?

2 **Share Your Summary** Have a classmate read your summary. Ask:
- What part do you think is the most interesting? What part could be more interesting?
- Did I tell about events in the right order?
- Do I need to add more specific details?

3 **Make Your Changes** Think about your classmate's answers to your questions. Then make changes to improve your summary. Use the Revising Marks.

Sample of a Revised Summary

My job in the beach cleanup was Recorder.
I wrote the name of ~~stuff~~ litter we found. For
example, Marcus saw an empty soda can. I wrote soda can on my notepad. Ivan picked it up.

Revising Marks

∧	Add.
↶	Move to here.
⋏	Replace with this.
⌣	Take out.

Key In TO Technology

You can use the cut-and-paste feature of your word-processing program. It will help you move words or sentences from one place to another.

Think About Your Writing

- What words did you change?
- What details did you add?
- Do you like the way your summary sounds now?

> GRAMMAR IN CONTEXT

PRONOUNS

A noun is the name of a person, a place, a thing, or an idea. A pronoun takes the place of a noun.

	PRONOUNS	EXAMPLE
I	Use **I** to talk about yourself.	**I** can help in the cleanup.
You	Use **you** to talk to one or more other people.	Carlos, **you** can count the cans. Sam and Teresa, **you** can take the cans to the recycle center.
He	Use **he** to talk about a boy or man.	**William** collected the trash. **He** collected the trash.
She	Use **she** to talk about a girl or woman.	**Sara** carried the bag. **She** carried the bag.
It	Use **it** to talk about a place or thing.	**The bag** was heavy. **It** was heavy.
We	Use **we** to talk about other people and yourself.	**María and I** took notes. **We** took notes.
They	Use **they** to talk about other people or things.	**The notes** were helpful. **They** were helpful.

Practice Read each pair of sentences. Write the second sentence and add the correct pronoun.

1. My friends and I had a neighborhood cleanup. ___I / We___ collected litter from the streets and sidewalks.
2. Lisa and Tim took the trash to the dump. ___He / They___ made three trips.
3. Sylvia got some flower seeds. ___He / She___ planted them next to the sidewalk.
4. All the parents admired our work. ___They / We___ were proud of us.
5. My mother had a party for us. ___She / It___ made cookies and lemonade.

Writing That Informs and Explains, continued

EDIT AND PROOFREAD

1 **Proofread Your Summary** When you find a mistake in spelling, punctuation, or capitalization, correct it. See pages 431–439 in the Handbook for help. Use the Proofreading Marks.

2 **Check Your Pronouns** Do the pronouns tell about the right person? Do they tell about the right number of people?

3 **Make a Final Copy** If you are working on a computer, print out a final copy of your work. If not, rewrite it and make the corrections you marked.

PUBLISH

Choose a way to share your summary. Here are some ideas.

- Submit your summary to your school newspaper. Add a title. Include your name.

Seaside School News

Park Cleanup
by Christina Villegas

Last Wednesday, our class cleaned up Seaside Park. We divided the class into teams, and each team got a job to do. One team picked up anything that was plastic. Another team collected empty soda cans. Another team gathered pieces of paper. Everything we

The park looks so clean now!

found filled six garbage bags! At the end we were so tired, but we were proud of our work. Now we can enjoy the park even more.

- Read your summary to your family, friends, or classmates. Answer any questions they may have.

- Design a scrapbook page. Attach your summary. Add pictures. Then, make a class scrapbook.

Proofreading Marks

∧	Add.
⩜	Add a comma.
⊙	Add a period.
≡	Capitalize.
/	Make lowercase.
﹌	Take out.
¶	Indent.

Think **About Your Writing**

- Do you think your summary is interesting?
  - ☑ Does it include the important ideas and details?
  - ☑ Does it explain what happened in the correct order?

- Do the pronouns tell about the right people?

- What do you like best about your summary?

- Will this summary go in your portfolio? Why or why not?

United, We Stand

▶1 Look Back at the Unit

Rank Team Goals This unit showed many kinds of teams.

| Teamwork | Together, We Dream | A Dog You Can Count On | A Mountain Rescue |

Work with a team of students. Write the title of each selection on an index card. Think about a team from each selection. On the back of each card, list the team's goals, such as *saves lives*, *does a job*, *has fun*. Now decide which team has the most important goal. Rank the teams from 1 to 4.

▶2 Show What You Know

Sum It All Up Add ideas about cooperation to the mind map. Share what you learned with a partner.

Cooperation

Looks Like	Sounds Like	Feels Like

Reflect and Evaluate Finish these sentences:

- People cooperate when they _____.
- Cooperation is important because _____.

Put these sentences in your portfolio. Add work that shows what you learned about cooperation.

▶3 Make Connections

To Your Community Invite a team of community workers to your school. Or, plan a trip to see the team at work. Learn about how they work together.

*Fate chooses our relatives;
we choose our friends.*

—J. DeLille

Making Connections

List the important people in your life. Put an *R* next to names of relatives. Put a *P* next to professional people, such as your doctor. Put an *F* next to names of friends. Are the people on your list mostly from one group? Or, do you have people in all groups? Talk with a partner about why each person is important to you.

Finding Friendship

- What makes a good friend? How can you be a good friend to others?

- What does friendship mean to you? Why is it important?

- How do you make new friends? How do you keep them?

THEME-RELATED BOOKS

You're Not My Best Friend Anymore
by Charlotte Pomerantz

Even best friends have arguments. In this story, Molly and Ben learn how to work out a disagreement and stay friends.

Robin Hood and Little John
by Barbara Cohen

Can enemies become friends? That's how a famous friendship begins in this story. It's been told since the Middle Ages!

Mrs. Katz and Tush
by Patricia Polacco

A special friendship that lasts for years begins when Larnel gives Mrs. Katz a homeless kitten.

Build Language and Vocabulary

EXPRESS FEELINGS

Read these proverbs. Then listen to a short story about a good  friend. Which friendship proverb does this story remind you of?

FRIENDSHIP

A good friend shields you
from the storm.

—Chinese proverb

As for clothes,
the newer the better;
as for friends,
the older the better.

—Korean proverb

Real friends will share even
a strawberry.

—Slovakian proverb

Who is mighty? One who
makes an enemy into a friend.

—Jewish proverb

MAKE A FRIENDSHIP FLOW CHART

How do people become friends? Share your ideas with the class. Then, make a chart like this one. Write about the way you made friends with someone you know.

A Friendship Flow Chart

| Two people smile at each other. | They sit together in class. | They work on a class project together. | They have fun together after school. |

BUILD YOUR VOCABULARY

Friendship Words Good friends do special things for each other. They understand each other's feelings. Work with a group to brainstorm a mind map about how good friends act and feel.

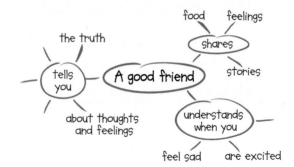

USE LANGUAGE STRUCTURES ▶ PAST TENSE VERBS

Speaking: Tell a Friendship Story Tell the story of how you made friends with someone. Explain how you felt. Use past tense verbs.

Example:
Once I **went** to a new school. I **felt** lonely because I **had** no friends. On my first day, I **saw** a tall girl. She **smiled** at me. That **made** me feel good. Later, we **were** on the same basketball team in gym class. I **passed** her the ball, and she **made** a basket. After that, I **knew** we would be friends.

THE QUALITIES of FRIENDSHIP

fables
by Aesop

Prepare to Read

THINK ABOUT WHAT YOU KNOW

Talk It Over Honesty is one important quality of friendship. Talk about other qualities you look for in a friend.

---

dance When you **dance**, you move your body to music.

jealous A **jealous** person wants what someone else has.

kindness A **kindness** is something good that you do or say.

show off When you **show off**, you show others how well you can do something. People show off to get attention.

terrified When you are **terrified**, you feel very scared.

trap A **trap** is used to catch animals.

LEARN KEY VOCABULARY

Use Words in Context Study the new words. Then write each sentence. Add the best word to complete each sentence.

1. My friend and I decided to sing and ___dance___ in a contest.

2. She was not scared, but I was _____.

3. I felt like an animal caught in a _____!

4. She began to _____ her dance steps for the judges.

5. I felt _____ when she won first prize.

6. The judges showed _____ and gave me a prize for my singing.

LEARN TO IDENTIFY SEQUENCE

In stories, events happen in an order called **sequence**. Knowing the sequence of events helps you understand the story.

> ### READING STRATEGY
> **How to Identify Sequence**
> 1. Read the story.
> 2. Ask yourself: What happened first? What happened next?
> 3. Put the events in order. Use order words like: *first, next, then, finally.*

Read "The Qualities of Friendship." Think about the sequence of events.

THE QUALITIES of FRIENDSHIP

BY AESOP

Fables are stories that teach a lesson, or *moral*. These fables about friendship were first told in ancient Greece by Aesop, a famous storyteller. Do you think these lessons are still important, more than a thousand years later?

The Mouse and the Lion

A lion was sleeping in his cave. He awoke when he felt something **scurry by**. The lion was surprised to see a small mouse. **In a flash**, he trapped the mouse under his huge paw.

"Oh, great lion," the **terrified** mouse cried, "if you **free me**, I'll never forget your **kindness**. Someday, I could help you."

The lion roared with laughter. "You tiny mouse," he said, "how could you help me? You're even too tiny to eat. I shall let you go." And he did.

---

scurry by run past him very quickly
In a flash Very quickly
free me let me go

Then one day, the lion was caught in a hunter's **trap**. **In spite of his strength**, the lion could not **escape**. The mouse heard the lion's roars. He **rushed** to the lion's side. Without saying a word, the mouse began to **gnaw at** the ropes. Soon, the lion was free.

"Thank you, little friend," the **grateful** lion said to the mouse. "I never would have guessed that such a small friend could be such a big help."

Moral:
A friend returns one kindness with another.

BEFORE YOU MOVE ON...

1. **Details** Why did the lion think that the mouse could not help him? Was he right or wrong? Explain.
2. **Vocabulary** Make a list of story words that mean "move quickly." Add other words you know that describe the way things move.
3. **Personal Experience** This fable is about friends helping friends. How has a friend helped you?

In spite of his strength Even though he was so strong
escape get away, run away
rushed ran very quickly
gnaw at chew on, bite on
grateful thankful

The Monkey and the Camel

One day, the **beasts** of the **desert** had a party. All the animals were pleased when the monkey arrived, for she was a great dancer. "**Dance** for us, Monkey," the animals **begged**.

So Monkey danced for them. She **put on a great show**. The animals clapped. They **praised** her **lively kicks** and her quick steps. But the camel was **jealous**. He wanted the animals to clap for him. He wanted them to praise *his* dancing.

---

beasts wild animals
desert dry, sandy land
begged asked over and over again

put on a great show pleased them with her dancing
praised said how much they liked
lively kicks fast, jumping dance steps

So, to everyone's surprise, Camel began to dance. His tail went up. His head went down. One leg went one way. One leg went another. He looked so silly, all the animals started to laugh. At last, Camel kicked in too many **directions** at once. His legs got **all tangled up**. He fell flat on his face. The animals pointed and **made fun of** him. "That's what you get for trying to **show off**!" they said, and they **drove him away** with their laughter.

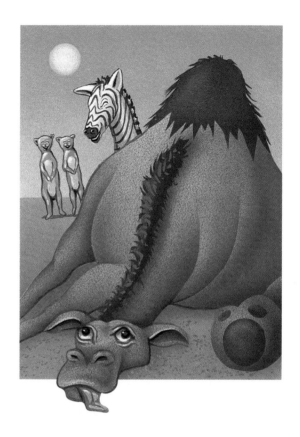

Moral:
The fastest way to lose friends is to try to be something you are not.

directions different ways
all tangled up twisted together
made fun of laughed at
drove him away made him leave

BEFORE YOU MOVE ON...

1. **Details** What did the animals like about the way Monkey danced?
2. **Inference** Camel could not dance well because of his long legs. What other animals could have trouble dancing? Why?
3. **Opinion** Do you think the other animals were fair to Camel? Explain.

ABOUT THE AUTHOR

Aesop lived more than 25 centuries ago. He was born a slave around the year 600 BCE. Aesop became famous for the stories he told. His master, Iadmon, set him free from slavery. Aesop's stories were first written down about 200 years after he died.

Aesop, Diego Velázquez, oil on canvas, c. 1639–1640. Museo del Prado, Madrid, Spain.

Respond to the Fables
Check Your Understanding

SUM IT UP

Show Sequence Make a storyboard for the first fable. Draw pictures and write words to describe the order of events. Then make another storyboard for the second fable.

Storyboard

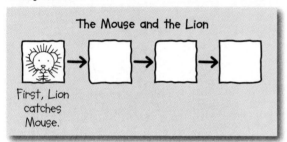

Make a Group Storyboard Make big pictures from your small drawings. Each person in your group will draw one picture. Put them in order. Draw arrows to show sequence. Write a sentence about each picture.

Retell the Fables Use the storyboards to tell the fables in your own words. Show each picture and tell how each character feels about the events.

THINK IT OVER

Discuss Talk about these questions with a partner.

1. **Author's Purpose** Why does Aesop write about animals? Do his fables have good messages for people, too?

2. **Judgments** The animals made fun of Camel. Discuss good and bad ways to share your feelings about a friend.

3. **Opinion** Which fable do you like better? Why?

4. **Personal Experience** How do you show your friendship to others?

EXPRESS YOURSELF
▶ ASK FOR AND GIVE ADVICE

Pretend you are Camel. You want to get attention from the other animals. Ask a partner for ideas. Then pretend your partner is Camel. Give advice about how to get attention.

Language Arts and Literature

USE ACTION VERBS

Learn About Action Verbs An action verb tells what the subject does. The **tense** of a verb shows when an action happens.

- Use a **present tense verb** if the action is happening now or if it happens all the time.

- Use a **past tense verb** if the action happened earlier, or in the past.

Present Tense Verbs	Past Tense Verbs
Lion **traps** Mouse.	Lion **trapped** Mouse.
Mouse **helps** Lion.	Mouse **helped** Lion.
Monkey **dances**.	Monkey **danced**.

Use Verbs in Sentences Work with a partner. First your partner does something and uses a present tense verb to describe the action. Then you use a past tense verb to tell what your partner did. Take turns.

Example:
Partner 1: I **clap** my hands.
Partner 2: You **clapped** your hands.

Practice Write the sentences. Change the present tense verbs to past tense verbs.

1. The mouse surprises the lion.
2. The lion roars with laughter.
3. A hunter traps the lion.
4. The mouse rushes to the lion.
5. The little mouse gnaws the ropes.

IDENTIFY PLOT AND CHARACTER

Learn About Plot and Character The **plot** tells the events that happen in a story. The events follow a sequence from beginning to end. Stories also have **characters**. Aesop's characters are all animals.

Learn to Map a Story A **story map** shows how the characters and the plot work together in a story. Copy and complete this map for "The Lion and the Mouse."

Story Map

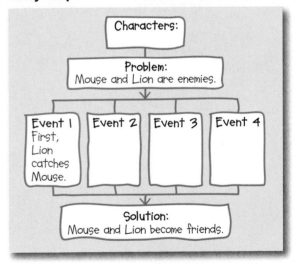

Practice Now make a story map for "The Monkey and the Camel."

Respond to the Fables, continued

Content Area Connections

STUDY AESOP AND HIS WORLD

Work with a group to research Aesop and ancient Greece. Choose one of these projects:

- **Make a Map** Show where Aesop lived. Use an encyclopedia or an atlas of the ancient world. Label islands, seas, cities, and towns. Show your map to the class.

- **Write a Biography** A **biography** tells about a person's life. Learn more about Aesop. Use library books, encyclopedias, and the Internet to find information. Write a biography to show what you learned.

STUDY AESOP'S FABLES

Search for more fables by Aesop. Find one to illustrate. Then present your fable to the class.

1 **Find Aesop's Fables** Look in books or on the Internet. Find a fable you like and print it. Try these key words and Web sites to begin your search, but remember that new sites appear every day!

INTERNET

INFORMATION ON-LINE

Key Words:
Aesop
fables

Web Sites:
➤ Fables
- www.dusklight.com
- www.pacificnet/~johnr/aesop

2 **Present the Fable** Illustrate the fable. Then present the fable and art to the class.

Learn how to use the **Internet**.
See Handbook pages 364–365.

We Could Be FRIENDS

poem
by Myra Cohn Livingston

Prepare to Read Poetry

THINK ABOUT WHAT YOU KNOW

Idea Exchange Who calls you on the telephone? Can telephones help friendships? Share your ideas with the class.

goof around When friends **goof around**, they play together and have fun.

supposed to be The way things are **supposed to be** is how they should be.

LEARN KEY VOCABULARY

Relate Words Study the new words. Work with a partner to make a chart. Add your own ideas. Then share your chart with the class.

Friends are supposed to be	Friends goof around when they
honest	ride bikes

LEARN TO MAKE COMPARISONS

Make **comparisons** to see how things are the same and different.

READING STRATEGY
How to Compare Experiences
1. When you read about a person, think about what the person says or does.
2. Ask yourself: Does the person act or think the same way I do? How is the person different from me?
3. Ask yourself: How would I feel or act in the same situation?

As you read "We Could Be Friends," compare your experiences with the narrator's experiences. Do you make friends in the same way?

WE COULD BE FRIENDS

We could be friends
Like friends are supposed to be.
You, picking up the telephone
Calling me

    to come over and play
    or take a walk,
    finding a place
    to sit and talk,

Or just goof around
Like friends do,
Me, picking up the telephone
Calling you.

    —Myra Cohn Livingston

Respond to the Poem

THINK IT OVER

Discuss Talk about these questions with a partner.

1. **Inference** Who is *you* in the poem? Why is the telephone important to the two friends?

2. **Personal Experience** How do you communicate with friends?

3. **Opinion** Do friends have to like the same things? Explain.

EXPRESS YOURSELF

▶ MAKE COMPARISONS

What do you like to do for fun? Write four things in a list. Then find two students who like some of the things you like. Find two students who like different things. Tell the class what you found.

ABOUT THE POET

Myra Cohn Livingston (1926–1996) was an award-winning poet. She wrote many books of poetry for children and adults, some on the theme of friendship. In "We Could Be Friends," she shows that it's up to each of us to take the first steps toward friendship. "It is not 'you picking up the telephone calling me' but 'me picking up the telephone calling you,'" she said. She wrote the poem for people who have friends and people who are still searching for them.

Build Language and Vocabulary

EXPRESS LIKES AND DISLIKES

Listen to this traditional song; then try singing it.
After you know the song, sing it as a round
with two or more groups.

Make New Friends

Make new friends
and keep the old.
One is silver
and the other gold.

A circle is round—
it has no end.
That's how long
I want to be your friend.

—Traditional

MAKE A FRIENDSHIP CHART

There are many kinds of friends—not just old and new ones! Make a chart. Show the kinds of friends you have in the first column and list their names in the second.

Category	Friend's Name	My Friend Is Like
School Friend	Mei	
Family Friend		
Childhood Friend		
Sports or Hobby Friend		
Neighborhood Friend		

BUILD YOUR VOCABULARY

Friendship Words In the third column of your chart, tell about each friend. Use the **Word Bank** to get ideas.

As you work through this unit, you can add different kinds of friends. Also add more words to tell what you like best about each one.

Word Bank

brave
creative
friendly
funny
good at sports
good dancer
good listener
happy
problem-solver
smart
strong

USE LANGUAGE STRUCTURES ▶ VERB + INFINITIVE

Speaking: Express Likes and Dislikes Use the information from your friendship chart to tell about a friend. Tell what you like about your friend and what you don't like. Tell your story to a partner. Then, tell it to the class.

Example:
Jean-Claude was my childhood friend. He was good at sports. I liked to play soccer and ride bikes with him. Sometimes he liked to be bossy. I didn't like that. Since I moved to Miami, we like to write letters to each other.

My Best Friend

autobiography
by Eloise Greenfield and
Lessie Jones Little

Prepare to Read

THINK ABOUT WHAT YOU KNOW

Quickwrite Imagine a day with a friend. What would you do? Where would you go? Write sentences that tell about your day.

LEARN KEY VOCABULARY

best friend A **best friend** is the friend you like the most.

crazy about When you are **crazy about** something, you really love it.

every chance we got When we did something **every chance we got**, we did it whenever we could.

go out of my way When I choose to take a longer way, I **go out of my way**.

go over You **go over** to a place when you visit.

had our lives all planned out We knew what we wanted to do in the future; we **had our lives all planned out**.

stop to worry When you **stop to worry** about something, you take time to think about it.

talk and talk When people **talk and talk**, they talk for a long time.

that was all there was to it When you were sure of how something would be, you could say, "**that was all there was to it.**"

Use New Words in Context Study the new words. Then take turns reading this dialogue with a partner.

> **Friend 1:** Do you have a **best friend**?
>
> **Friend 2:** Lei was my friend in China. We were **crazy about** the same things. I used to **go out of my way** to **go over** to his house.
>
> **Friend 1:** Have you talked to Lei since you moved here?
>
> **Friend 2:** We called each other **every chance we got**. We would **talk and talk** about the future. We **had our lives all planned out**.
>
> **Friend 1:** Did you **stop to worry** about your friendship when you moved to the United States?
>
> **Friend 2:** No. We were best friends and **that was all there was to it**.

LEARN ABOUT MAIN IDEAS AND DETAILS

The **main idea** of a story is the most important idea. **Details** give examples and information to help you understand the main idea.

READING STRATEGY
How to Relate Main Ideas and Details
1. Read the selection.
2. Look for the most important idea.
3. Look for details that tell about the main idea.

Now read "My Best Friend." Look for the main ideas and details.

My Best Friend

from *Childtimes*
by Eloise Greenfield and
Lessie Jones Little

Lessie Jones Little was born
in Parmele, North Carolina, in
1906. In many ways, growing up
at the beginning of the century
was different from growing up
today. Women did not have full
voting rights. Black people did not
have all the same rights as white
people. Yet, best friends back then
did a lot of the same things they do
today. They spent time together
and shared their dreams.

LILLIE AND LESSIE

For best friends Lillie and Lessie, even simple things were fun.
That's because they did them together.

Lillie Belle Draper was my **best friend**. We played together **every chance we got**. When Mama would send me to the store or to the post office, I'd **go out of my way** to go past Lillie's house, and I'd stand at her gate and call, "Hey Lil-lie!" And she'd answer, "Hey Les-sie!" She'd come out to the gate and we'd **talk and talk** until I knew **I had better get going**.

Pattie Ridley Jones, Lessie's mother (above right), with Lessie's sister Lillie Mae (1928).

....

I had better get going it was time to go

Lessie and Lillie had fun making frog houses with dirt.

Lillie's married sister, Isabel, lived next door to me, and when Lillie would come in the summer to spend the day with her, I'd **go over**, and we'd sit on the bottom step of **Isabel's front porch** with our **bare feet** on the ground. We'd draw pictures in the dirt while we talked and rub them out with our hands. Or we'd **rake** the cool, **damp** dirt on top of our feet and pack it down tight, then slide our feet out, leaving a little **cave** we called a frog house. And all the time, we'd be just talking.

Isabel's front porch the part of the house outside Isabel's front door
bare feet feet with no shoes or socks
rake pull together, gather

damp not very wet, moist
cave open area under the ground

HAPPY TIMES

The girls took lots of long walks. They talked about
books and boys and music.

Sometimes we'd go walking down the **railroad track**. I'd take my **bucket** with me so I could fill it with the nuggets of **coal** that had fallen from passing trains, and take them home to use in the stove. Lillie would help me, but the bucket didn't always get filled because we stopped so much to talk.

We'd sit on the **silky gray rails** and stretch our legs out toward the **weeds** and tall grass and talk about things like books or boys. And we talked about music a lot. Both of us were **crazy about** the piano. We wished we could play like some of the people we'd seen.

Jelly Roll Morton (above) was a famous jazz pianist in the early 1900s.
Many people were crazy about his music.

....

railroad track iron track, path for a train
bucket metal or plastic container with a handle, used to
carry water or other things

coal a black mineral formed in the earth and used for fuel
silky gray rails train tracks
weeds wild plants that grow in many places

I thought everything Lillie did was pretty. The way she walked, **swinging along**, **throwing one foot out** a little more than the other, as if she were **walking to a bouncy kind of music**. The poems she wrote, poems about trees and other growing things, and birds. The way she sang, **leaning** her head back with a **faraway look** in her eyes, as if she were in love with the words and the music, and making the sounds come out so easily.

BEFORE YOU MOVE ON...

1. **Details** Where did Lessie's family get some of the coal to use in their stove?

2. **Evidence and Conclusion** Lessie said that "everything Lillie did was pretty." What were some of the "pretty things" that Lessie liked about Lillie?

....

swinging along moving her arms and legs back and forth

throwing one foot out stepping with one foot out

walking to a bouncy kind of music hearing happy music as she walked

leaning tilting, holding at an angle

faraway look dreamy expression

GROWING UP TOGETHER

Lessie and Lillie shared a goal of going to college together.

Lillie and I **had our lives all planned out**. We were going to be schoolteachers. I was going to be just like Miss Estee Riddick, **stick** a pencil in my hair and walk up and down the **classroom aisles** calling out spelling words to my students. I would pronounce each syllable of every word just the way Miss Estee did. But first we were going to college. We were going to Hampton **Institute** and **be roommates**, and we would make ninety-five to a hundred in all of our **subjects**.

I was a few years older than Lillie was, but we didn't **stop to worry** about how we would manage to go to college at the same time. We were going to be roommates at Hampton Institute, and **that was all there was to it**. After all, we were best friends.

....

stick put
classroom aisles rows between the desks in our class
Institute School, College
be roommates live together
subjects classes

BEFORE YOU MOVE ON...

1. **Setting** What can you find in the words or pictures to tell you that the story happened long ago?
2. **Prediction** The story ends here. What do you think will happen to the two friends in the future?

ABOUT THE AUTHORS

After graduating from high school, **Lessie Jones Little** and her best friend Lillie did not go to the Hampton Institute as they had planned. However, Lessie did work as a teacher. She also married Lillie's cousin, Weston. They had five children, including a daughter, Eloise.

Eloise Greenfield grew up to become a well-known author of children's books. Many of her books have won awards. *Childtimes*, which Eloise wrote with her mother, won the Coretta Scott King Honor Award.

Respond to the Autobiography
Check Your Understanding

SUM IT UP

Relate Main Ideas and Details Study the tree diagram for pages 144–145 of "My Best Friend." Then make diagrams for Parts 2 and 3.

Tree Diagram for Part 1

Main Idea	Details
Lillie and Lessie were best friends	They liked to play together.
	They visited each other.
	They made frog houses together.
	They liked to talk and talk.

Write a Paragraph Use the tree diagram for Part 1 to write your paragraph. Follow these steps:

- Write a **topic sentence** to tell the main idea.
- Write details to support the main idea.
- Write a **concluding sentence** to sum up your paragraph.

> Lessie and Lillie were best friends. They liked to play together. They visited each other every chance they got. They made frog houses together. They liked to talk and talk. They had fun being best friends.

Now write paragraphs for Parts 2 and 3. Use your tree diagrams for ideas.

THINK IT OVER

Discuss Talk about these questions with a partner.

1. **Opinion** Would Lessie be a good friend? Why or why not?

2. **Author's Purpose** Why do you think Lessie wrote her autobiography?

3. **Comparisons** How would Lillie and Lessie's story be different if they grew up today? How would it be the same?

4. **Personal Experience** Do you have your life all planned out, like Lessie and Lillie did? Explain.

EXPRESS YOURSELF
▶ EXPRESS LIKES AND DISLIKES

Think about the qualities you like and dislike in a best friend. Share your ideas with the class. Then make a large class T-chart. Write the qualities that most people said.

Respond to the Autobiography, continued
Language Arts and Literature

▶ GRAMMAR IN CONTEXT

USE LINKING VERBS

Learn About Linking Verbs A linking verb connects the subject of a sentence to a word in the predicate. The **predicate** tells what the subject is, has, or does.

The word in the predicate can describe the subject.

Lessie **was** happy.

Or, the word in the predicate can be another way to name the subject.

Lessie **was** a good friend.

All the forms of the verb **be** are linking verbs.

Present Tense	Past Tense
I **am** happy.	I **was** sad.
He **is** funny.	She **was** mad.
We **are** friends.	They **were** sisters.

Use Linking Verbs With a partner, make up sentences about today and the past. Use *am*, *is*, *are*, *was*, and *were* in your sentences.

Example:
Today I **am** a good student. Last year, I **was** lazy.

Practice Copy these sentences. Add *am*, *is*, *are*, *was*, or *were* to finish each sentence.

1. In the past, Lessie _____ a teacher.

2. Today, Lessie _____ a writer.

3. Years ago, the girls _____ neighbors.

▶ LITERARY ANALYSIS
▶ WRITING

WRITE ABOUT A FRIENDSHIP

Learn About Point of View Every story has a **narrator**, who tells the story. In "My Best Friend," Lessie is the narrator. She is part of the story and uses words like *I*, *me*, *my*, and *we*. This is called **first-person point of view**.

Example:
Lillie Belle Draper was **my** best friend.

In "The Qualities of Friendship," Aesop is the narrator. He is not part of the story and uses words like *he*, *she*, *it*, and *they*. This is **third-person point of view**.

Example:
A lion was sleeping in **his** cave.

Organize Your Ideas Think about a friend and the things you do together. Use a graphic organizer to record your ideas.

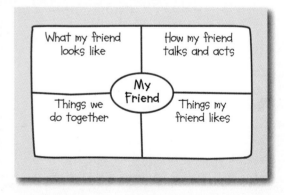

What my friend looks like	How my friend talks and acts
Things we do together	Things my friend likes

(center: My Friend)

Write About Your Friendship Choose a point of view. Then use it to describe your friendship.

Content Area Connections

COMPARE GENERATIONS

"My Best Friend" shows what life was like in 1906. How has the world changed? Interview an older person about life in the past. Interview a friend about life today. Then compare the information.

1 **Prepare Your Questions** Write questions about topics like:

music	fashion	famous people
jobs	school	entertainment

Examples:
What kinds of music did you like as a child?
What clothes did people wear?

2 **Conduct the Interviews** Ask your questions politely. Write the answers. Be sure to say "thank you" when you are finished.

3 **Organize Your Information** Make a chart. Compare what life was like in the past with how life is now.

Topic	Then (19__)	Now (20__)
music	classical, folk	country, rap, hip hop,
fashion		

4 **Share What You Learned** Tell your class about your interviews. Listen to your classmates. What discoveries did they make?

Learn how to **listen** and **discuss**. See Handbook pages 373–376.

Talk with an adult about life in the past.

The Family (La familia), José Clemente Orozco, mural. Copyright © 2000.

Across Generations

- What are your special talents? Who else in your family has talents like yours?

- What are your physical features? Who else in your family has features like yours?

- How have earlier generations changed your world? How can you change the world for the generations that will follow you?

THEME-RELATED BOOKS

In My Family/En mi familia
by Carmen Lomas Garza

Paintings and short descriptions present scenes from life in a Mexican American family.

Honoring Our Ancestors
edited by Harriet Rohmer

Fourteen artists use words and pictures to honor members of their families.

NOVEL

Yang the Youngest and His Terrible Ear
by Lensey Namioka

The youngest child of four tries to fit in with his family. It's hard to when everyone else is musical!

Build Language and Vocabulary

GIVE INFORMATION

Listen to this song; then sing along. 📼

Family Tree

Before the days of Jell-O
lived a prehistoric fellow
who loved a maid and courted her
beneath the banyan tree.
And they had lots of children,
and their children all had children,
and they kept on having children
until one of them had me.

Chorus

My grandpa came from Russia,
my grandma came from Prussia,
they met in Nova Scotia,
had my dad in Tennessee.
Then they moved to Yokohama
where Daddy met my mama.
Her dad's from Alabama
and her mom's part Cherokee.

Chorus

—Tom Chapin

Chorus

We're a family and we're a tree.
Our roots go deep down in history.
From my great-great-granddaddy
reaching up to me,
we're a green and growing family tree.

MAKE A FAMILY TREE

Read the second verse of "Family Tree." Use the information to complete a family tree like this one:

Family Tree

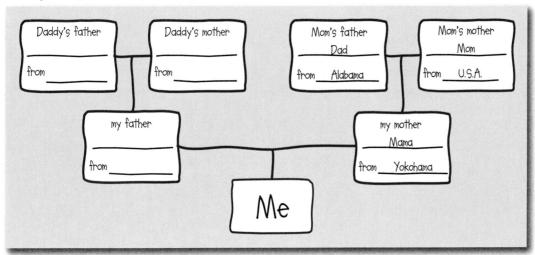

BUILD YOUR VOCABULARY

Family Words Now, make a tree of your family or the people you live with. Show as many people as you can. Use words from the **Word Bank** to label your family tree. As you work through this unit, continue adding the names of other family members.

USE LANGUAGE STRUCTURES ▶ PAST TENSE VERBS: *was/were*

Speaking: Tell About Your Family Use the information from your family tree to tell the class about your family history.

Example:

My grandpa was from Cuba, and my grandma was from the Dominican Republic. They were in Puerto Rico when they met. My dad was born in San Juan.

Word Bank

aunt
cousin
dad
daddy
father
grandfather
grandma
grandmother
mama
mom
mother
nana
papa
pop
uncle

HONORING *Our* Ancestors

family portraits
by Stephen Von Mason,
Helen Zughaib,
and Enrique Chagoya

Prepare to Read

THINK ABOUT WHAT YOU KNOW

Share Ideas What does it mean to honor someone? Talk about the people you honor and how you honor them.

advise You **advise** someone when you tell what you think he or she should do.

ancestor An **ancestor** is a family member who lived before you.

dedicate When you **dedicate** your work to someone, you make it for that person.

education You get an **education** when you learn.

leader The **leader** of a group tells the others what to do.

pioneer The first person to go some place new or do something new is a **pioneer**.

source of The **source of** something is where it comes from.

support Strength and encouragement are examples of **support**.

LEARN KEY VOCABULARY

Relate Words Study the new words. Then draw eight boxes with a new word in the center of each box. Write words that go with the new word in the corners of each box.

how to paint   read

education

school   learn to cook

LEARN TO PARAPHRASE

When you **paraphrase**, you use your own words to say the same thing as the author. Paraphrasing can help you understand what you read.

READING STRATEGY
How to Paraphrase
1. Read a sentence.
2. Ask yourself: What does the sentence mean?
3. Say it in your own words.

Now read "Honoring Our Ancestors." Stop to paraphrase each difficult sentence.

HONORING
Our Ancestors

George Crespo, oil paint on burlap; frame is cedar wood and twine. Copyright © 1999.

Three artists describe the paintings they created to honor members of their families.

by Stephen Von Mason
Helen Zughaib
Enrique Chagoya

I HONOR
My Ancestors

by Stephen Von Mason

Pharoah Jackson Chesney

Cornelius Grant Mason, Jr.

Jordan Douglass Chavis, Jr.

This painting is for my **ancestors**. On the left is my great-great-great-grandfather, Pharoah Jackson Chesney. He was a **pioneer**—one of the first **settlers** of Knoxville, Tennessee. He lived to be 120 years old.

On the right is my uncle, Jordan Douglass Chavis, Jr. He was a **famous musician**, the **leader** of a big band called "The Tennessee Collegians" from Tennessee State University. He was a musical pioneer. He started Tennessee State's music **department**.

In the center is my father, Cornelius Grant Mason, Jr., in the clothes he wore when he was a **student pilot** in the late 1940s. He, too, was a pioneer—part of the first group of Black pilots in America.

THE ARTIST
Stephen Von Mason is a painter, printmaker, and fine art framer. He lives in Oakland, California.

---

settlers people who build and live in a new town
famous musician person known for making music
department section (of a school)
student pilot person who is learning how to fly an airplane

Within the painting:

SVMASON

1898

Jordan Douglass "Chick" Chavis Jr.

...Played Carnegie Hall along side...Billie Holiday and Lester Young...

Cornelius Grant Mason Jr.

A Student Pilot...

...Maxy McCleron...Leola Carter...

PARENTS

Cornelius Grant Mason Jr.
m. Josephine Beechum-Mason...deceased
m. Loistean Mason Ed.D.

AUNTS and UNCLES

Jordan Douglass Chavis Jr.   Ervin Edward Mason
Katherine M. Mason-Chavis   Angie Snodgrass-Mason

GREAT GRANDPARENTS

Tip Chesney and Uretha B. McFeeter-Chesney

GREAT. GREAT. GREAT. Grandparents

Isaac Burke and Amanda Sharp-Burke
...was a Blacksmith from Algiers, Algeria-N. Africa

Stephen Von Mason, oil on rag paper. Copyright © 1999.

BEFORE YOU MOVE ON...

1. **Details** What did Stephen's three ancestors do?
2. **Viewing and Describing** Look carefully at the painting. Tell your partner what you see.

I HONOR
My Grandmother

by Helen Zughaib

Miriam Sultani Zughaib

This is Teta, my Lebanese grandmother. (Teta means "grandmother" in Arabic.) She grew up in Syria and Lebanon and came to America after World War II. The man in the picture frame is Teta's husband, my grandfather. When I was a child, I loved going to Teta's house—it was so warm and always **smelled delicious**. Teta would **pinch my cheek** and say, "I love you, I love you, I love you!"

Scraps of cloth, thread and yarn were everywhere. Teta was a wonderful **seamstress**. The clothes she made were beautiful and so unusual that you never knew what she would put together. I learned about colors and patterns from Teta.

She would sit with me for hours, teaching me how to **knit and crochet**. While we were knitting, she would share stories about her childhood. She was an educated woman, which was very **unusual** in those days. She often **advised** me to "put **education** in your heart, not boys!" Well, thanks to you, Teta, I put art in my heart, too.

THE ARTIST
Helen Zughaib is a painter. She lives in Washington, D.C., with her two cats, Noodle and Chunky Beef.

---

smelled delicious had a smell of good things to eat
pinch my cheek squeeze my cheek between her fingers
Scraps of cloth Little pieces of fabric
seamstress woman who makes clothes, woman who sews
knit and crochet make clothes using special needles and yarn
unusual different, special

Helen Zughaib, gouache and ink on board. Copyright © 1999.

BEFORE YOU MOVE ON...

1. **Details** What did Teta do well?

2. **Inference** What did Helen learn from Teta?

Honoring Our Ancestors **161**

I HONOR
My Father and Mother

by Enrique Chagoya

A wedding photo of Enrique's parents— Enrique Chagoya Galicia and Ofelia Flores de Chagoya

I **dedicate** this drawing to my parents because they were my most important **source of** love and **support** when I was growing up.

My father gave me my first drawing and painting lessons and taught me **color theory** when I was seven years old. I remember when I first saw him drawing **landscapes** and animals. I thought his hand was magical. Ever since then, I've always wanted to do the same thing.

My mother **had a big heart**, not only for our family, but for many people who knew her. She **went out of her way** to help people in need and never expected anything back.

I drew the shape of my mother's body using the words "nunca me digas adiós." That's Spanish for "never tell me good-bye." She never wanted to say good-bye to me when I left Mexico. Instead, she said, "See you later." When she died four years ago, we told each other, "See you later."

THE ARTIST
Enrique Chagoya teaches painting, drawing, and printmaking at Stanford University. He was born in Mexico City and now lives in San Francisco, California.

....

color theory how to mix and use colors

landscapes pictures of trees, mountains, and rivers; scenes that show what the land looks like

had a big heart had a lot of love, was very kind

went out of her way did whatever she could

Enrique Chagoya, pencil and acrylics on paper. Copyright © 1999.

1. **Vocabulary** With a partner, list words from the article that tell about art. Can you add more?

2. **Personal Experience** What words would you use to draw the shape of your mother or father?

Respond to the Family Portraits
Check Your Understanding

SUM IT UP

Identify Cause and Effect An **effect** is something that happens. A **cause** is the reason it happens. Use the word *because* before a cause. Use the word *so* before an effect.

I went home **because** I missed my family.
effect · cause

I missed my family, **so** I went home.
cause · effect

Complete this summary. Write the missing cause or effect.

> Three artists painted family portraits. Stephen Von Mason honored his ancestors because <u>they were pioneers</u>. Helen Zughaib's grandmother taught her about art, so she _____. Enrique Chagoya painted his parents because _____.

Paraphrase the Summary Copy and complete the paraphrase. Add facts about Helen Zughaib and Enrique Chagoya.

> Three artists made pictures of their relatives.
> Stephen Von Mason's ancestors were pioneers,
> so he drew them in his painting.

THINK IT OVER

Discuss Talk about these questions with a partner.

1. **Comparisons** How are the three pictures alike? How are they different?

2. **Opinion** Which artist's story did you like most? Why?

3. **Judgment** What is the best way to honor someone?

4. **Personal Experience** What is something you have learned from your ancestors?

EXPRESS YOURSELF ▶ DESCRIBE THINGS

Work with a partner to study one of the portraits. Write notes that describe the portrait. List things you see. List colors and shapes. Write about where things are placed. Then use your notes to describe the painting.

Language Arts and Literature

USE CONTEXT CLUES

Learn About Context Clues Sometimes you can figure out the meaning of a new word by studying context clues. A **context clue** is a hint that you get from the words around the new word.

Find Context Clues Tell the meaning of *seamstress*. What words gave you context clues?

> Scraps of cloth, thread and yarn were everywhere. Teta was a wonderful **seamstress**. The clothes she made were beautiful. . .

Context clues: *The clothes she made, Scraps of cloth, thread and yarn*

Meaning: a woman who sews

Practice Write the meaning and context clues for the underlined words.

1. A portrait of my mother is on the wall. It looks just like her.

2. My mother is very talented. She writes poetry, plays the piano, and draws.

3. On her birthday, we will honor her with a party. It will be a fun celebration.

4. I am happy to have such a remarkable mother. She is wonderful and special.

WRITE A DEDICATION

A **dedication** is a way to honor someone special. Dedicate a portrait to someone in your family.

1 Make a Portrait You can:
- draw or paint a picture
- take a photograph
- use old photographs to make a collage.

2 Write a Dedication Tell why you want to honor this person.

> I dedicate this _____ to _____
> because _____
> _____

3 Share Your Work Present your portrait to the class. Read your dedication aloud. Tell about the person you want to honor.

Learn how to give an **oral presentation**. See Handbook pages 374–376.

Respond to the Family Portraits, continued
Content Area Connections

SOCIAL STUDIES

TECHNOLOGY/MEDIA

RESEARCH AN ANCESTOR'S COUNTRY

Compare an ancestor's life in a different country with your life in the United States.

Gather Information Use your own experience or interview a relative. Find an article or search the Internet. Try the Web sites below, but remember that new sites appear every day! Use the country's name as a key word.

INFORMATION ON-LINE

Web Sites:
➤ **Geography**
  • www.geographia.com
  • www.emulateme.com

Make Comparisons Make a Venn diagram to compare the countries.

Learn how to make **diagrams**.
See Handbook pages 343–344.

FINE ARTS

TECHNOLOGY/MEDIA

MAKE A MULTIMEDIA PRESENTATION

Celebrate your class's families in a creative way.

1 **Make a Poster** Use a large piece of paper. In the center, put a portrait and dedication that honors your ancestors. Add art that describes your family.

2 **Add Music** What music does your family like? Choose a favorite song to play.

3 **Add Photographs** Use a camera or a video camera. Record activities like:
  • your family singing a song
  • interviews with family members
  • your family having fun.

4 **Have a Celebration** Invite your families to your class. Show off your work.

Learn how to make a **multimedia presentation**.
See Handbook pages 362–363.

Everybody Says

poem
by Dorothy Aldis

Prepare to Read Poetry

THINK ABOUT WHAT YOU KNOW

Share Opinions Do people say you look "just like" someone? How does it make you feel? Do you want to look like someone else? Share your thoughts with your classmates.

everybody Everyone or every person is **everybody**.

image If you are the **image** of someone, you look a lot like him or her.

look just like When you **look just like** a person, you look the same as the person.

LEARN KEY VOCABULARY

Use New Words in Context Study the new words. Then write each sentence. Write a new word on the red line. Write the name of a relative or other person on the black line.

1. _____Everybody_____ says I look like my ___father___.

2. My mother says I am the _____ of _____.

3. Some day I want to _____ _____.

LEARN ABOUT POETRY

Poems have special **characteristics**, or qualities. They help to give poetry a unique sound. Understanding these characteristics can help you enjoy poetry more.

READING STRATEGY

Characteristics of Poetry

1. When words have the same ending sounds, they **rhyme**.

2. When the number of syllables in the words of a poem has a regular pattern, the poem has **rhythm**.

3. Saying a word again and again is called **repetition**.

Now read "Everybody Says" aloud. As you read, listen for rhyming words, rhythm, and repetition.

Everybody Says

Everybody says
I look just like my mother.
Everybody says
I'm the image of Aunt Bee.
Everybody says
My nose is like my father's
But I want to look like ME!

—Dorothy Aldis

Respond to the Poem

THINK IT OVER

Discuss Talk about these questions with a partner.

1. **Character's Motive** What does the speaker in the poem want?

2. **Personal Experience** The speaker says: "I want to look like ME!" Do you feel the same? How do you show the world who you are?

▶ WRITING/SPEAKING

WRITE A POEM

Use "Everybody Says" as a model poem about yourself.

Model Poem

> Everybody says
> I look just like _____.
> Everybody says
> I'm the image of _____.
> Everybody says
> My _____ is like _____.
> But I want to look like _____!

Try to make your poem rhyme.
Try to give your poem rhythm.
Then recite your poem for the class.

ABOUT THE POET

Dorothy Aldis (1896–1966) may have gotten her love of writing from her father. He was a newspaper man. During her lifetime, Ms. Aldis wrote many novels and books of poetry for young readers. She received the Children's Reading Round Table award for her outstanding work in children's literature. Her work is still read and loved by many.

Build Language and Vocabulary
DEFINE AND EXPLAIN

Some physical traits, or features, are inherited from your parents. The shape of your earlobe is an inherited trait. What shape is your earlobe? One of your parents probably has the same trait!

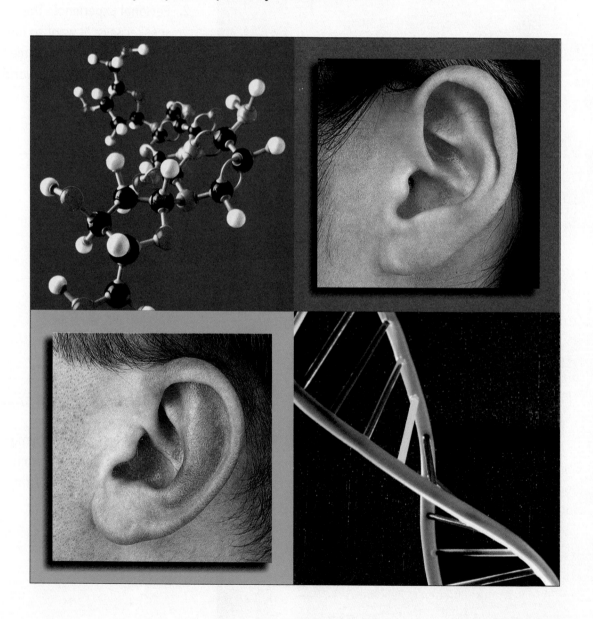

MAKE A TALLY CHART OF PHYSICAL TRAITS

Learn about inherited traits. Take a survey of
the people in your class. Find out how many:
- can curl their tongue into a long tube shape
- can roll their tongue sideways
- have attached earlobes
- have free earlobes.

Record your findings on a tally chart like
this one. Ask your family the same question.
Share the information in class.

Can curl tongue	HH HH HH
Can roll tongue	HH II
Have attached earlobes like this:	IIII
Have free earlobes like this:	HH HH HH

BUILD YOUR VOCABULARY

Words About Traits Read the definition of the word *inherit*.

> **inherit** *verb* When you **inherit**
> something, you receive it from your
> parents or ancestors.

Now work with the class to brainstorm a list of features or traits you have
inherited from your parents or other family members. As you work through this
unit, add to your list.

USE LANGUAGE STRUCTURES ▶ PRESENT AND PAST TENSE VERBS

Writing and Speaking: Define and Explain Work with a partner. Define
physical traits and *character traits*. Give examples of each type of trait.
Share your definitions and examples with the class.

Example:
Your physical traits are the way you look.
You inherit physical traits from your parents.
Sarita inherited green eyes from her grandmother.

Grandfather's NOSE

science article
by Dorothy Hinshaw Patent

Prepare to Read

THINK ABOUT WHAT YOU KNOW

Share Information How are you like others in your family? Talk about how you look and act like your family.

combination A **combination** is a mix or a blend.

family resemblance People in some families look like each other. They have a **family resemblance**.

gene A **gene** is a part of a cell that tells your body how to form and grow.

genetics The science of **genetics** studies genes and how they are passed from parent to child.

identical twins Two babies born at the same time are called **twins**. **Identical twins** have the same genetic information.

inherit When you **inherit** something, you get it from your parents or ancestors.

relative A **relative** is a person in your family.

trait A **trait** is a person's way of looking or being.

LEARN KEY VOCABULARY

Use New Words in Context Study the new words. Then write these sentences. Write **T** for true. Write **F** for false.

___T___ 1. You can **inherit** a **trait** from a **relative**.

_____ 2. You can share a **family resemblance** with a friend.

_____ 3. **Identical twins** have the same **combination** of genes.

_____ 4. Scientists who study **genetics** learn about parts of a **gene**.

LEARN TO READ NONFICTION

Many articles are nonfiction. **Nonfiction** gives facts and information. Reading nonfiction is a good way to learn.

> ### READING STRATEGY
> #### How to Read Nonfiction
> 1. Look at the article before you read. Read the title and headings. Look at the pictures and captions.
> 2. Write your questions about the topic.
> 3. Read and take notes.
> 4. Read your notes and think about what you learned.

Now read "Grandfather's Nose" and follow the steps for reading nonfiction.

Grandfather's NOSE

by Dorothy Hinshaw Patent

Has anyone ever told you that you have your father's eyes or your mother's hair? In this article, science writer Dorothy Hinshaw Patent explains how we get some of these "special gifts" from our parents.

What Is Genetics?

Do you look like your mother or father? Do people mix you up with your brother or sister? People usually do look like their **relatives** in some ways. They have a "**family resemblance**."

How is a grandfather's nose or a mother's red hair **passed along** to a daughter or grandson? That is, how are these features inherited? When you **inherit** something, you receive it from your parents.

Scientists try to understand how we inherit family **traits**, or characteristics. They call their work *genetics* (jen-NET-icks). Genetics is the science that studies how traits are inherited.

....

passed along given

What kind of family resemblance do you see in this family?

Scientists study how traits are inherited.

BEFORE YOU MOVE ON...

1. **Details** What do scientists learn about when they study genetics?
2. **Personal Experience** What kind of "family resemblances" does your family have?

So Many Genes

Genes are the basic **units of inheritance.** Humans have about 50,000 different genes. Even though there are family resemblances, everyone looks different because there are so many ways the genes can be combined. This is one reason why **identical twins** are so **remarkable**.

Identical twins result when a fertilized egg divides into two separate **cells** that don't stick together. Each of the cells then goes on to **develop into a complete embryo**, a very young baby developing inside its mother. Both twins have exactly the same genes, since they come from the same fertilized egg. That is why they look identical.

The Development of a Single Baby and of Twins

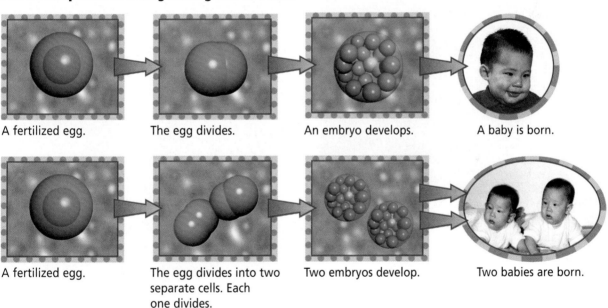

A fertilized egg. → The egg divides. → An embryo develops. → A baby is born.

A fertilized egg. → The egg divides into two separate cells. Each one divides. → Two embryos develop. → Two babies are born.

---

units of inheritance pieces of information
passed from your parents' cells to yours

remarkable amazing, special

cells tiny parts that make up living things

develop into a complete embryo grow into
an unborn baby

BEFORE YOU MOVE ON...

1. **Cause and Effect** Why do most people look different from one another?

2. **Paraphrase/Viewing** Reread paragraph two (above) and look at the flow chart. In your own words, tell how identical twins are formed.

So Many Differences

The possible **combinations** of genes are almost **countless**. Even though there are now over six billion people on Earth, no two of them look exactly alike, except for identical twins. Each human being is different from everyone else. People may say you have your grandfather's nose, but no one just like you has ever lived. And no one just like you will ever live again.

BEFORE YOU MOVE ON...

1. **Details** About how many people are there on Earth now?
2. **Personal Experience** What is something about you that is different from everyone else? Is it something you like, or something you'd like to change? Explain.

Each human being is unique.

....

countless too many to count

ABOUT THE AUTHOR

In the past 25 years, **Dorothy Hinshaw Patent** has written more than 100 science books for children and young adults. "I have tremendous respect for the minds of children," she says. "They're capable of learning so much. They're like sponges: they just soak stuff up." Dr. Patent dedicated her book, *Grandfather's Nose*, to "the teachers who gave me a love of genetics."

Respond to the Article
Check Your Understanding

SUM IT UP

Relate Main Idea and Details Work with a group. Copy the paragraph. Then use your notes to finish the summary.

> Genetics studies __how traits are inherited__. Parents pass their genes to their _____. Genes tell the body to develop certain traits. Humans have about _____ genes. There are many, many possible combinations of genes. That is why each person is _____. Only _____ have the same genes.

Write Sentences Tell what you learned from the article. Tell what you still want to learn.

Example:
Our looks are inherited from our parents.
What other traits are inherited?

THINK IT OVER

Discuss Talk about these questions with a partner.

1. **Inference** The author says: "No one just like you has ever lived." What does she mean?

2. **Judgment** Can identical twins have different personalities? Explain.

3. **Personal Experience** What three traits do you want your children to inherit from you?

4. **Opinion** Some day human parents may be able to choose traits for their children. Is this a good idea? Why or why not?

EXPRESS YOURSELF ▶ DEFINE AND EXPLAIN

Work with a partner to define the term *family resemblance*. Then read your definition to the class. Give an example of a resemblance in your own family.

Respond to the Article, continued
Language Arts and Literature

USE NEGATIVE SENTENCES

Learn About Negative Sentences Use a **negative word** like one of these to make a sentence mean "no":

no	nothing	never	none
not	nobody	no one	nowhere

Examples:

No one just like you has ever lived.
Not all twins are exactly alike.

Do not use two negative words in the same sentence.

anyone
She does not look like ~~no one~~ else.

Make Up Negative Sentences Ask a friend a question that starts with: *Do you*, *Can you* or *Have you*. Your friend will answer with a negative sentence. Then change roles.

Example:
You: Do you like milk?
Your partner: I do **not** like milk.

Practice Write these as negative sentences.

1. Anna looks like her relatives.

2. All twins are exactly alike.

3. We inherit traits from our friends.

WRITE LABELS

Think of your family or look at the photographs of families in this unit. Find traits that family members share.

1 **Make Your Drawing** Draw a picture of yourself or a child on page 168, 173, or 174.

2 **Find Similarities** Find features that look like the other family members.

Examples:
The boy has dark eyes like both parents.
I have straight hair like my father.

3 **Add Labels** Write family traits next to your drawing. Draw lines to connect the words to the part of the picture they describe.

Content Area Connections

STUDY GENETICS

Parents pass traits to their children. Each parent has two genes for each trait. The parents each pass one gene for each trait to their child.

1 **Learn about Punnet Squares** A **Punnett square** shows all the ways parents' genes can be combined in their children.

Punnett Square 1

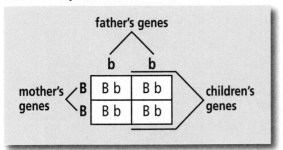

This Punnett square shows how the trait for eye color is passed from parents to children. The father has two genes for blue eyes (**bb**) and the mother has two genes for brown eyes (**BB**). The Punnett square shows that each child will have one **B** gene and one **b** gene.

2 **Learn About Dominant and Recessive Genes** **Dominant genes** block **recessive genes** from being inherited. In Punnett Square 1, each child has one gene for blue eyes (**b**) and one gene for brown eyes (**B**). The gene for brown eyes is dominant. Since all four children have at least one **B** gene, they all will have brown eyes.

3 **Complete a Punnett Square** What happens when two parents have mixed genes? Copy and complete Punnett Square 2. How many children will have brown eyes? How many children will have blue eyes?

Punnett Square 2

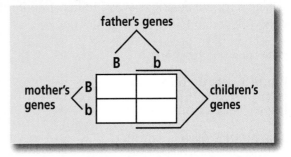

Writing for Personal Expression

Writers tell us their thoughts and feelings in expressive writing.

WRITING MODELS

Read these sentences from "My Best Friend." How does the writer feel about Lillie? How do you know?

from "My Best Friend"

I thought everything Lillie did was pretty. The way she walked, swinging along, throwing one foot out a little more than the other, as if she were walking to a bouncy kind of music.

Here Helen Zughaib describes a visit to her grandmother. What helps you understand how Helen feels?

from "Honoring Our Ancestors"

When I was a child, I loved going to Teta's house—it was so warm and always smelled delicious. Teta would pinch my cheek and say, "I love you, I love you, I love you!"

Write Together

① **Brainstorm Ideas** Make a list of people to write about. Choose one person to be your topic.

② **Get Ready to Write** Before you write, always think about:

- What you are writing, or the **form**
- Who will read your work, or the **audience**
- What you are writing about, or the **topic**
- Why you are writing, or the **purpose**

Fill out an **FATP** chart to get ready to write.

③ **Plan and Write the Paragraph** A paragraph has one main idea. All the details in the paragraph go with the main idea. Make a chart like the one below. Then use your chart to write the paragraph.

FATP Chart

HOW TO UNLOCK A PROMPT
Form: _paragraph_
Audience: _students in room 24_
Topic: _Lola_
Purpose: _to express how we feel about her_

STUDENT WRITING MODEL

Main Idea
Lola moved away, but we are still good friends.

Detail
We can send e-mails.

Detail
We can send pictures.

Detail
We can call her every week.

A Good Friend

Lola moved away, but we can still be friends. We can send e-mails to each other. It's always great fun to read what Lola has to say. We can send pictures of our class. We can call her every week. I hope that we will stay friends forever!

Writing for Personal Expression, continued

Write on Your Own

WRITING PROMPT

Now write your own paragraph. It can tell about a person or an experience. Express your feelings about the topic. Then, share your writing with classmates.

PREWRITE

1 **Choose a Topic** Think about people and experiences that have been special to you. Choose one as your topic. Then fill out an **FATP** chart to help guide your writing.

2 **Get Organized** Make a main idea chart. Add details about your thoughts and feelings.

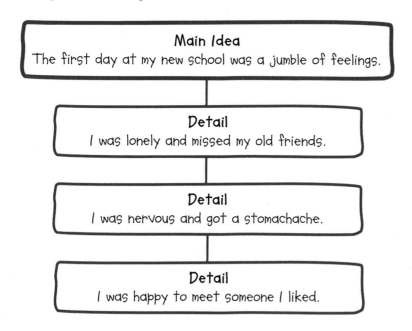

Main Idea
The first day at my new school was a jumble of feelings.

Detail
I was lonely and missed my old friends.

Detail
I was nervous and got a stomachache.

Detail
I was happy to meet someone I liked.

FATP Chart

HOW TO UNLOCK A PROMPT

Form: paragraph

Audience: classmates

Topic: my first day at a new school

Purpose: to share the feelings I had that day

Think About Your Writing

- Are you happy with your topic?
- Do you want to share your feelings about it?
- Will your topic be interesting to your audience?
- Do you have enough details to write about?

DRAFT

1 Write Your Paragraph Use your main idea chart to help you write an expressive paragraph.

2 Use Examples and Details Study the sentences below.

I write to clear my own mind, to find out what I think and feel.

— V.S. Pritchett

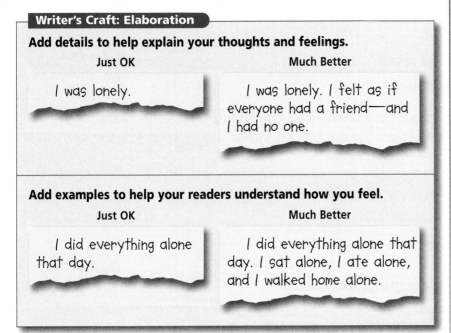

Writer's Craft: Elaboration

Add details to help explain your thoughts and feelings.

Just OK	Much Better
I was lonely.	I was lonely. I felt as if everyone had a friend—and I had no one.

Add examples to help your readers understand how you feel.

Just OK	Much Better
I did everything alone that day.	I did everything alone that day. I sat alone, I ate alone, and I walked home alone.

Read these lists. Each names a feeling and gives three examples of when you might feel that way. Think of more examples that go with your topic.

Happy
got good grades
had fun at sports
met a new friend

Sad
left a place I like
summer was over
just heard bad news

Nervous
took a test
gave an oral report
met new people

Excited
got chosen for a team
my artwork got displayed
scored my first goal in soccer

Think About Your Writing

- Read your draft. Do you like what you wrote?
- Did you include examples to explain how you felt?

Writing for Personal Expression, continued

REVISE

1 **Read Your Paragraph** Does it express your thoughts and feelings?

2 **Share Your Paragraph** Have your teacher or a friend read your paragraph. Ask:

- Is the topic of my paragraph clear?
- Do you understand how I felt?
- Have I left out any important details?
- Are there interesting details I could add?

3 **Make Your Changes** Think about the answers to your questions. Then make changes to your paragraph. Use the Revising Marks.

Sample of a Revised Sentence

I talked to a girl. (revised to: I talked to a quiet girl with a friendly smile.)

If you are using a computer, make changes like this.

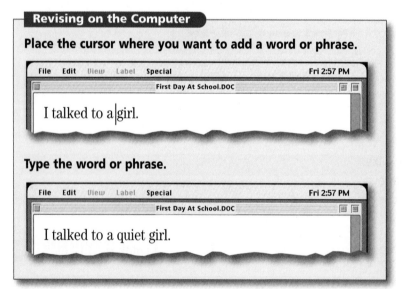

Revising on the Computer

Place the cursor where you want to add a word or phrase.

| File | Edit | View | Label | Special | | Fri 2:57 PM |

First Day At School.DOC

I talked to a|girl.

Type the word or phrase.

| File | Edit | View | Label | Special | | Fri 2:57 PM |

First Day At School.DOC

I talked to a quiet girl.

Think About Your Writing

- What details and examples did you add?
- Did they make your paragraph more interesting?

> GRAMMAR IN CONTEXT

PAST TENSE VERBS

The tense of a verb shows when an action happens. Use a past tense verb if the action happened earlier, or in the past.

Examples: My family **moved** to Texas last week.
I **walked** to school yesterday.

- The past tense form of a regular verb ends in **-ed.**

Follow these rules to add **-ed:**

Spelling Rules

For most verbs, just add **-ed**.	**start**	I **started** at a new school last week.
	stay	I **stayed** in the hall at first.
For verbs that end in silent **e**, drop the **e** and add **-ed**.	**like**	I **liked** my teacher right away.
If the verb ends in one vowel and one consonant, double the final consonant and add **-ed**.	**tap**	I **tapped** my foot because I was so nervous.
For verbs that end in a consonant and **y**, change the **y** to **i** and add **-ed**.	**study**	We **studied** math before lunch that day.

- **Irregular verbs** do not end with **-ed** to show past tense. They have special forms like the examples at the right. See Handbook pages 424–425 for more examples.

Some Irregular Verb Forms

Present	Past
do	did
feel	felt
fly	flew
get	got
go	went
know	knew
make	made
run	ran
see	saw
take	took
tell	told

Practice Write each sentence. Put the verb in the past tense.

1. I ___(go)___ to my new school.
2. Everything ___(seem)___ to go wrong.
3. I ___(drop)___ all my books in the hall.
4. I ___(study)___ different subjects in my old school, so I couldn't do the science.
5. Finally, at lunch, some kids ___(ask)___ me to sit with them.
6. I really ___(like)___ them. I ___(know)___ everything would be okay.

Writing for Personal Expression, continued

EDIT AND PROOFREAD

1 **Proofread Your Paragraph** When you find a mistake in capitalization, punctuation, or spelling, correct it. See pages 431–439 in the Handbook for help. Use the Proofreading Marks.

2 **Check Your Verbs** Have you used past tense verbs to describe things that happened in the past? Did you follow the spelling rules for past tense verbs?

3 **Make a Final Copy** If you are working on a computer, print out a final copy of your work. If not, rewrite it and make the corrections you marked.

PUBLISH

Here are some ways to share your writing.

- Write your paragraph on a large index card. Place it on a bulletin board for others to read.

> I miss my family back home in Mexico. Here in the USA I have only one aunt and a baby cousin nearby. In Mexico, all my family and friends lived near me. I had lots of cousins who were also thirteen. We had so much fun together!
>
> by Magdiel Ramírez

- Read your paragraph aloud to some friends. Ask whether they learned something new about you.

- Type your paragraph on the computer and view it in different kinds of type. Print it in the one you like best.

Proofreading Marks

∧	Add.
⩜	Add a comma.
⊙	Add a period.
≡	Capitalize.
∕	Make lowercase.
⤳	Take out.
¶	Indent.

Think About Your Writing

- Are you pleased with your paragraph?

  ☑ Does it express your thoughts or feelings?

  ☑ Do you state the main idea clearly and include details to support it?

  ☑ Did you include enough examples?

  ☑ Did you use past tense verbs and spell them correctly?

- What do you like best about your paragraph?

- Will this paragraph go in your portfolio? Why or why not?

Making Connections

1 Look Back at the Unit

Rate Selections In this unit, you read about friendship and family.

The Qualities of Friendship

My Best Friend

Honoring Our Ancestors

Grandfather's Nose

Work with a partner. Write the title of each selection on an index card. Rate each selection with stars. If you liked the story, draw 5 stars. If you didn't like it, draw fewer stars. Now write on the back of the card. Tell one thing you liked about the selection. Then describe a relationship in it.

2 Show What You Know

Sum It All Up Add new ideas to your mind map about relationships. Talk with a partner. Tell why people have close relationships. Explain how relationships can change.

Reflect and Evaluate Write a sentence. Describe something you learned about relationships. Add this statement to your portfolio. Add work from the unit that shows what you learned.

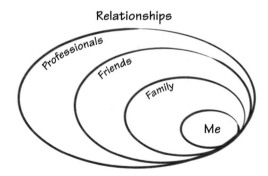

3 Make Connections

To Your Community Build a new relationship by finding a pen pal. Write letters or send e-mail to someone in your school, in your community, or around the world.

UNIT 4 Community

Seeing the World Through Pictures, Robert Silvers, photomosaic. Copyright © 1997.

Communities Count

Write these headings: Earth, Sea, and Sky.
Now take one minute to study the picture of
planet Earth. List as many of the things in the
tiny photos as you can for each category. Next, do
this activity with a group of classmates. What did
you learn about working together? How does
working together make a difference?

189

Thinking Ahead

- Who is responsible for taking care of our planet?

- What are some of the problems facing our planet? What are some solutions?

- How can we work together in our communities to keep our planet healthy?

THEME-RELATED BOOKS

ACTIVITY
COLLECTION

The Giving Tree
by Shel Silverstein

A simple story of a tree who gives all it can to make a person happy.

Nature's Green Umbrella Tropical Rain Forests
by Gail Gibbons

This book looks at plant and animal life in tropical rain forests, and describes the importance of this ecosystem.

50 Simple Things Kids Can Do to Save the Earth
by The EarthWorks Group

If you want to protect our planet, this book is full of lots of easy things you can do to help!

Build Language and Vocabulary
MAKE COMPARISONS

View this photograph and read the quote. What effect could clearing the forest have on the next seven generations?

We must consider the impact of our decisions on the next seven generations.

—*from the Great Law of the Iroquois Confederacy,*
16th Century

MAKE A COMPARISON CHART

Compare the pictures on pages 190 and 192.
Then brainstorm words to describe each one.
Record them in a chart. Discuss how tree-cutting
can affect the next seven generations.

Before	After
green forest	burned trees
homes for birds	smoke
beautiful	ugly

BUILD YOUR VOCABULARY

Nature Words Trees are an important part of our Earth. Read this definition
to learn what trees and other special parts of our planet are called.

> **nat·u·ral re·sourc·es** *noun*
> **Natural resources** are the minerals, air,
> plants, animals, and water that are part of our
> planet. Natural resources come from the earth.

Now, think of as many natural resources as you can and list them. Add to your
list as you go through this unit.

USE LANGUAGE STRUCTURES ▶ FUTURE TENSE VERBS

Speaking: Compare Possibilities for the Future Choose a natural resource
from your list. Think about what the resource will mean for the next seven
generations. Write a sentence to tell what will happen if we do not take care of
that resource. Write another sentence to tell what will happen if we do take care
of that resource. Share your sentences with the group. Compare the possibilities.

Example:
If we cut down all the trees, the soil will wash away.
If we take care of the trees, we will have clean air and
beautiful forests.

Common Ground

persuasive essay
by Molly Bang

Prepare to Read

THINK ABOUT WHAT YOU KNOW

Share Ideas You share things like rooms, food, telephones, and the television with your family. How do you decide how to share these things?

benefit When you **benefit** from something, you are helped by it.

common If something is **common**, it may be shared.

common ground Land shared by everyone is **common ground**.

commons A **commons** is a piece of land that is shared by the whole town.

forest A **forest** is a large area with many trees.

fossil fuel A **fossil fuel** is a source of energy found in the earth. Coal, oil, and natural gas are **fossil fuels**.

natural resource A **resource** is something people use. A **natural resource** comes from the earth.

sustain When you **sustain** something, you keep it going.

village A **village** is a small community.

villager A **villager** is a person who lives in a village.

LEARN KEY VOCABULARY

Relate Words Study the new words. Sort them into groups. Draw a circle and label each group. Think of more words to add.

Places
to Live

(village
forest)

Words That
Look Alike

(village
villager)

Natural
Resources

(forest
water)

LEARN TO MAKE A K-W-L CHART

A **K-W-L chart** helps you connect new information to what you already know. It also helps you think about what you want to learn before you read.

K	W	L

READING STRATEGY
How to Make a K-W-L Chart

1. Look at the essay. Think about the topic.
2. Write what you **know** about the topic under **K**.
3. Write what you **want to learn** under **W**.
4. Read the essay. Write what you **learned** under **L**.

Make a K-W-L chart. Follow the steps in the Reading Strategy as you read "Common Ground."

Common Ground

The Water, Earth, and Air We Share

by Molly Bang

Our Earth has many wonderful natural resources. In this essay, Molly Bang describes how these resources can be destroyed and presents a persuasive argument for working together to take care of them. If communities don't care for our resources, there will be nothing left for future generations.

1

THE VILLAGE COMMONS

Hundreds of years ago, people made a plan to share land for their animals in a way that was fair for everyone.

*L*ong ago, a **village** was built around a **commons**. The commons was "**common ground**" which belonged to everyone in the village. All the **villagers** could bring their sheep to the commons to **graze**. But there was a problem.

A villager who owned many sheep used more of the commons than a villager who owned a few sheep, or one, or none at all. And because the **common** grass was free, people put as many sheep to graze there as they could. Soon there were too many sheep.

There was not enough grass for all of them. This was not good for the commons, or for the sheep, or for the villagers. So the people did one of two things.

Some people stayed in the village, but they made a plan together. They **agreed** to keep the commons **lush and green**, and to do a better job of sharing it. Each person could only put one sheep on the commons.

Everyone had to follow this rule. Other people chose to move away. There was always someplace else to go.

---

graze eat grass
agreed decided together
lush and green healthy and beautiful

BEFORE YOU MOVE ON...

1. **Cause and Effect** What problem was caused by having too many sheep on the commons?

2. **Opinion** Do you think the villagers' plan for using the commons was fair? Why or why not?

3. **Inference** Why did some of the villagers move away?

The commons was "common ground."

There was not enough grass for all the sheep.

They agreed to do a better job of sharing it.

THE WORLD TODAY

Today, our common resources are being used up.

*T*oday the world is much like that village. Now our commons are our parks, **reserves**, and **natural resources**, and the waters and air of the whole world. Today we have almost the same problem that the villagers had.

Today each fisherman tries to catch as many fish as he can from the common sea. This way, the fisherman has more fish to sell—**in the short run**. But soon there are fewer and fewer fish. This is not good for the fish, the sea, or for the people.

Today each **lumber company** wants to cut down as many trees as it can, to sell for wood, paper, and **fuel**. The more trees the lumber company cuts down, the more money it makes—in the short run. But after cutting down so many trees, there are fewer and fewer **forests**. This is not good for the trees, or for the **forest creatures**, or the forest **soil**.

BEFORE YOU MOVE ON...

1. **Vocabulary** *In the short run* means "now." What do you think *in the long run* means?
2. **Details** The villagers almost used up all the grass on the commons. List two resources that we are in danger of using up today.
3. **Cause and Effect** What would happen if we used all the fish and trees now?

---

reserves land that is saved for a special reason
in the short run now, at the present time
lumber company company that cuts down trees for use in making products
fuel something used to give heat and power
forest creatures animals that live in the woods
soil dirt, ground, earth

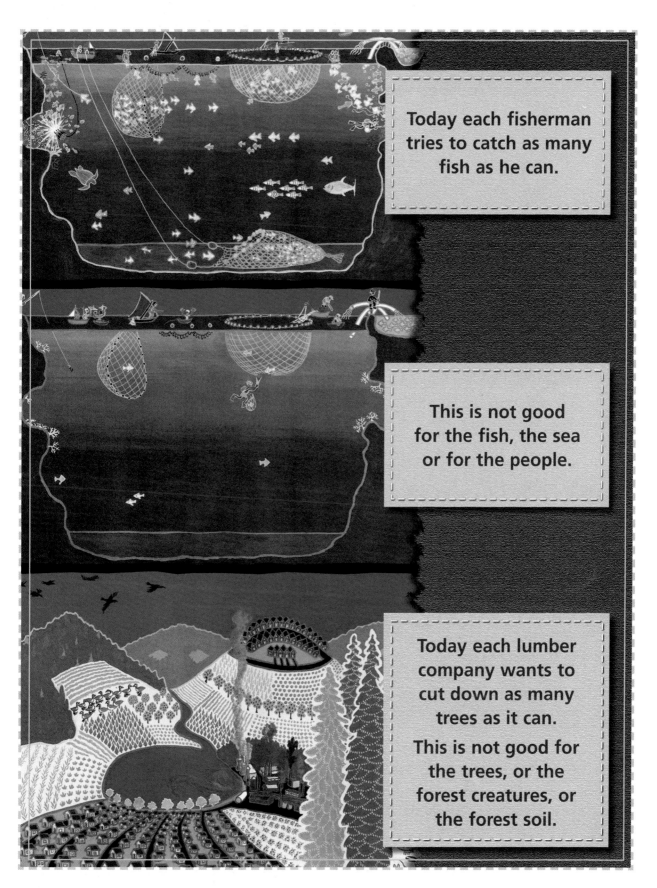

Today each fisherman tries to catch as many fish as he can.

This is not good for the fish, the sea or for the people.

Today each lumber company wants to cut down as many trees as it can.

This is not good for the trees, or the forest creatures, or the forest soil.

3

PLANNING FOR THE FUTURE

If we want to preserve our natural resources for
future generations, we must plan together *now*.

We use our common **oil**, **gas**, and **coal** to heat our houses and run our cars. Companies use them to make plastics and other chemicals. In this way, we can stay warm, travel long distances, and visit stores full of amazing things to buy—in the short run. But some day, these **fossil fuels** will be used up.

We all need water for drinking, cooking, and washing. Farms need water for crops and livestock.

And businesses need water to cool equipment and clean up **wastes**.

So we pump as much of our common water as we can. This works pretty well—in the short run.

But over time, the wells **run dry**, and the wastes **pollute the water**. There is not enough clean water for all the people, the farms, and the businesses.

Fresh water, fossil fuels, forests, fish—one by one, we are destroying the natural resources that **sustain** our lives.

So then here is our common question:

If our country, our companies, and each one of us **benefit** more in the short run from using as many natural resources as we can, then what will stop us from destroying our whole world— our common ground?

We need to answer this question TOGETHER, because today we are different from those long-ago villagers in one very important way . . .

---

oil liquid found in Earth that can be used for fuel

gas vapor—like air or steam—found in Earth that can be used for fuel

coal black mineral that is burned to make heat or energy

wastes garbage and other unwanted materials

run dry have no more water

pollute the water make the water dirty

We use our common
oil, gas, and coal
to heat our houses
and run our cars.
But someday,
these fossil fuels
will be used up.

We pump as much
of our common
water as we can.
But over time,
the wells run dry.

Now we don't have any place else to go.

BEFORE YOU MOVE ON...

1. **Details** How do we use natural resources like water and fossil fuels today?

2. **Inference** What does the author mean when she says that we don't have any place else to go?

3. **Author's Purpose** Why do you think Molly Bang wrote this story?

ABOUT THE AUTHOR

Molly Bang has written and illustrated more than 20 books for young readers. She enjoys learning stories from around the world, and has lived in Mali, Japan, and India. Molly Bang was inspired to write *Common Ground* after talking with a group of geologists—scientists who study the earth. She was so concerned by what she learned from them that she wrote *Common Ground* that very evening! She believes that people must plan ways to take care of the Earth's resources now—before it's too late.

Respond to the Essay
Check Your Understanding

SUM IT UP

Connect New Information to What You Know Follow these steps to complete your K-W-L chart:

- Read the **K** column. Correct any mistakes.
- Read the questions under **W**. Write any answers you learned under **L**.
- Write new things you learned under **L**.
- What questions do you still have? Think of ways to find answers.

Evaluate the Essay Look at your K-W-L chart and think about the essay. Then copy and complete these sentences.

The author, wants us to _____.
The essay is good because _____.
The essay would be better if _____.

THINK IT OVER

Discuss Talk about these questions with a partner.

1. **Inference** The author suggests that we must plan together to save our world. Who does she mean by "we"?

2. **Personal Experience** What natural resources are important where you live? How can you help save these resources?

3. **Opinion** What will the world be like in 100 years?

EXPRESS YOURSELF
▶ DEFINE AND EXPLAIN

Work in a group. Discuss a problem that can happen when people use natural resources. Brainstorm ways to solve the problem. Then share your group's ideas with the class.

Problems:

- We need lumber to build houses, but our forest has lost too many trees.
- We need energy for cars and heat, but we are using up our fossil fuels.

Respond to the Essay, continued
Language Arts and Literature

USE ADJECTIVES THAT COMPARE

Learn About Adjectives That Compare
Adjectives can help you make comparisons. To compare two things, add **-er** to the adjective. To compare three or more things, add **-est**.

> The pine tree is **tall**.
>
> The oak tree is **taller** than the pine.
>
> The redwood is the **tallest** of the three.

For long adjectives, use **more** and **the most** to make comparisons.

- To compare two things, use **more**:

  The oak is **more beautiful** than the pine.

- To compare three or more things, use **the most**:

  The redwood is **the most beautiful** tree of all.

Make Comparisons Act out a feeling with two friends. For example, one of you can act happy. The next can act happier, and the third, the happiest of all. Ask classmates to make comparisons to describe your actions.

Practice Write the sentences. Choose the correct adjective to complete each sentence.

1. Brazil has the (big) rain forests in the world.

2. Rain forests are (wet) than regular forests.

3. Rain forest animals are the (interesting) animals in the world.

WRITE AN OPINION PARAGRAPH

What resources are used in your lunch? Save your non-food trash from lunch. Make a chart to show what you found.

Do Research Paper, plastic, and metal are made from natural resources. Use an electronic or print encyclopedia to learn which resources are used to make them. Make a chart like this:

I found:	It is made of:	Natural resources:	Can it be recycled?
a napkin	paper	wood	yes
a straw	plastic		

Write a Paragraph Give your opinion about the use of natural resources in your lunch. Then explain your ideas.

Learn how to improve your writing in the **writer's craft**.
See Handbook pages 390–401.

Content Area Connections

▶ SCIENCE

STUDY ENVIRONMENTAL PROBLEMS

How can we save natural resources? Work with a group. Study a problem that threatens a natural resource like:

acid rain	air pollution
water pollution	loss of forests

① Gather Information Research your topic in the library or on the Internet. Take notes as you read.

② Find Solutions How can people help? Brainstorm ideas with your group.

③ Organize Information Make a chart to show what you learned.

Environmental Problems and Solutions

Problems	Causes	Effects	Solutions
air pollution	smoke from fires and cars makes the air dirty	people get sick	don't burn trash, carpool

Learn how to do **research**.
See Handbook pages 366–370.

▶ SCIENCE

EXPLORE RECYCLING

We can **recycle** used natural resources to make new things. For example, we can recycle paper so that new trees do not need to be cut down. Most products made of glass, aluminum, paper, and plastic can be recycled.

Look for recyclable materials in your school and at home. List the things your class found. Discuss how your class can help recycle natural resources.

▶ FINE ARTS

PICTURE THE ENVIRONMENT

Study the environmental collage on page 188. How do you see the world? Make a collage. Use pictures of the environment. You can:

- use magazine and newspaper pictures
- download pictures from the Internet
- create your own pictures.

Put the pictures together in a creative way. Then share your work with your classmates.

Build Language and Vocabulary

EXPRESS OPINIONS • PERSUADE

View this cartoon and read the joke. What is the real message in this joke?

MAKE A MIND MAP

Do you agree that "guarding the environment" is important? What are some of
the natural resources that we should protect? Use the pictures in this unit for
ideas. Then record your ideas on a mind map. Share your ideas about why each
resource is important.

BUILD YOUR VOCABULARY

Words About the Environment Read this definition to learn a word about
caring for our natural resources.

> con·ser·va·tion *noun*
> **Conservation** is careful planning to stop natural
> resources from being destroyed or ruined.

What are some ways that conservation can help us take care of our natural
resources? Add your ideas to your mind map.

USE LANGUAGE STRUCTURES ▶ VERBS: *should, must, can*

Writing: Express Your Opinion Think of a way to conserve natural resources.
Use it to make a poster. Use *should*, *must*, or *can* to write a caption to persuade
people to take care of that resource.

Examples:
We **can** pick up trash to help keep our beaches clean.
We **must** recycle paper to help save trees.

PROTECTING
our planet

songs
by Raffi

Prepare to Read Songs

THINK ABOUT WHAT YOU KNOW

Brainstorm Ideas Make a class list of ideas for cleaning up your school. What can students do alone? How must adults help?

crystal clean When something is **crystal clean**, it is clear and pure.

earth/Earth The ground or dirt is **earth**. The planet we live on is called **Earth**.

life Something that has **life** is alive. **Life** can also mean living things.

nation People who live in one country form a **nation**.

planet A **planet** is any one of the large objects in space that travel around the sun.

rain forest A **rain forest** is an area covered by trees that gets at least 100 inches of rain each year.

source of power A **source of power** is where energy comes from.

stream A **stream** is a small river of moving water.

up to me When something is **up to me**, I am the one who should do something.

valley A **valley** is the land between hills or mountains.

LEARN KEY VOCABULARY

Relate Words Study the new words. Then look at the table of contents. Tell a partner what each chapter title means in your own words.

The Planet Earth

LEARN TO PREVIEW AND MAKE PREDICTIONS

When you **preview**, you look at a selection before you read. You figure out what it is about. **Previewing** helps you to **predict** what you may read.

READING STRATEGY
How to Preview and Predict

1. Look at the titles and illustrations. Ask yourself: What do they tell me about the subject?
2. Think about the author. Ask yourself: What do I know about this author? How does the author feel about this subject?
3. Write predictions about what you will read.

Before you read "Protecting Our Planet," predict why Raffi wrote these songs. Then read to see if your predictions are correct.

PROTECTING
our planet

by Raffi Cavoukian

In this collection of songs, popular singer Raffi describes our beautiful planet, as well as some of the threats facing our world today. His songs call on us to work in our communities to protect the wonders of our natural world.

OUR WONDERFUL WORLD

The world we live in is full of natural beauty
and resources for all of us.

One Light, One Sun

One light, one sun.

One sun lighting everyone.

One world turning.

One world turning everyone.

One world, one home.

One world home for everyone.

One dream, one song.

One song heard by everyone.

One love, one heart.

One heart warming everyone.

One hope, one joy.

One love filling everyone.

One light, one sun.

One sun lighting everyone.

One light warming everyone.

One sun lighting everyone. The sun gives light to everyone who lives on Earth.

One world turning everyone. As the Earth turns, everyone on the planet turns, too.

joy strong feeling of happiness

Big Beautiful Planet

Chorus:

> There's a big, beautiful planet in the sky.
>
> It's my home, it's where I live.
>
> You and many others live here, too.
>
> The Earth is our home; it's where we live.

We can feel the power of the noonday sun—

A blazing ball of fire up above—

Shining light and warmth enough for everyone:

A gift to every nation from a star.

Chorus

We can feel the spirit of a blowing wind—

A mighty source of power in our lives—

Offering another way to fill our needs:

Nature's gift to help us carry on.

Chorus

BEFORE YOU MOVE ON...

1. **Author's Style** Why does Raffi repeat the word *one* in his song "One Light, One Sun"?

2. **Theme** What is Raffi's message to community members with these two songs?

3. **Comparisons** What is the message in these songs? What is different?

---

noonday sun sun at noon, when it reaches its highest point in the sky

blazing brightly burning, shining

spirit of a blowing wind strength of moving air

mighty great, strong

Offering Giving

fill our needs give us what we need to live

carry on go on, keep living

Pollution threatens to destroy our natural resources
and our health.

Clean Rain

Clean rain, crystal clean rain.
Clean rain.

I remember the days when the rain fell clean
Into the valleys and into the streams,
Clean through the air and clean to the Earth.
They say that the rain fell clean.

Rain on the land and rain in the water,
Clean fell the rain from the skies above.
The rain brought life, life in every drop,
The rain that we used to know.

Clean rain, crystal clean rain.
Clean rain.

the rain fell clean the water in the rain was clean
when it came down
life in every drop each drop of rain helped living
things grow

I remember the days when the rain fell clean
Into the valleys and into the streams,
Clean through the air and clean to the Earth.
They say that the rain fell clean.

There's life in the woods and life in our waters,
Moving in the beauty of this Earth that we love,
And praying for the day when the rain falls clean
Like the rain we used to know.

Clean rain, crystal clean rain.
Clean rain.

BEFORE YOU MOVE ON...

1. **Author's Point of View** Raffi writes about the clean rain that fell in the past. What do you think Raffi thinks about the rain that falls today?

2. **Inference** What happens when the rain that falls is not clean?

3. **Tone** How do you think Raffi felt when he was writing this song? Explain.

3

COMMUNITIES CAN CREATE CHANGE

Communities must join together to protect the plants and animals
of our planet from destruction.

Evergreen, Everblue

Evergreen, everblue,

As it was in the beginning,

We've got to see it through.

Evergreen, everblue.

At this point in time

It's up to me, it's up to you.

Amazon is calling, "Help this planet Earth,"

With voices from the jungle,

   "Help this planet Earth."

Hear the tree that's falling:

   "Help this planet Earth."

Rainforests are crying,

   "Help this planet Earth to stay

Evergreen, everblue,

As it was in the beginning,

We've got to see it through."

Evergreen, everblue.

At this point in time

It's up to me, it's up to you.

....

see it through do everything we can to get the result
we want

At this point in time Right now, At this moment

Ocean's wave is rumbling, "Help this planet Earth,"

With voices from the seaway, "Help this planet Earth."

Water's for the drinking: "Help this planet Earth."

Beluga whales are singing, "Help this planet Earth to stay

Evergreen, everblue,

As it was in the beginning,

We've got to see it through."

Evergreen, everblue.

At this point in time

It's up to me, it's up to you.

Right now is when we're needed.

We can all do something.

The young, the old together.

The more we get together,

The more we help this planet Earth.

continued next page

....

seaway oceans

So come all united nations, help this planet Earth.

Children of one mother, help this planet Earth.

With love for one another, help this planet Earth.

For our sons' and daughters' future, help this planet Earth to stay

Evergreen, everblue,

As it was in the beginning,

We've got to see it through.

Evergreen, everblue.

At this point in time

It's up to me, it's up to you.

BEFORE YOU MOVE ON...

1. **Classify** List things from the song that should stay "evergreen" and "everblue."
2. **Figurative Language** How are humans "children of one mother?" What "mother" is Raffi describing?
3. **Author's Purpose** Why do you think Raffi wrote this song?

ABOUT THE SONGWRITER

Raffi Cavoukian was born in Egypt in 1948. His first language was Armenian, his family language. Raffi learned English at the age of 10, when his family moved to Canada.

Today, Raffi is a popular entertainer. He uses his songs to express his love of nature and his wish to preserve it.

"I believe that we can rescue our beleaguered planet only through a change of heart and mind," says Raffi. "My new music celebrates our power to act together to preserve the beauty and bounty of the Earth for our children's future."

---

united nations countries that agree to work together

Respond to the Songs
Check Your Understanding

SUM IT UP

Check Predictions Review your predictions. Why did you think Raffi wrote these songs? Were your predictions correct?

Raffi wants to **persuade**, or encourage, people to take care of the Earth. Think about what Raffi wants people to do in each song.

Analyze Persuasive Techniques Raffi uses different ways, or **techniques**, to persuade his readers to take care of the Earth. Think of words and phrases to add to the chart.

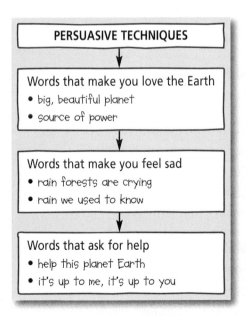

PERSUASIVE TECHNIQUES

↓

Words that make you love the Earth
• big, beautiful planet
• source of power

↓

Words that make you feel sad
• rain forests are crying
• rain we used to know

↓

Words that ask for help
• help this planet Earth
• it's up to me, it's up to you

Evaluate the Songs Did Raffi's techniques persuade you to take care of the Earth? Tell why or why not.

THINK IT OVER

Discuss Talk about these questions with a partner.

1. **Summarize** What part of the environment is each song about? How are the songs alike?

2. **Inference** How can you tell that Raffi cares about the Earth?

3. **Opinion** Can these songs change peoples' ideas about our environment?

4. **Personal Experience** What questions would you like to ask Raffi?

EXPRESS YOURSELF ▶ RECITE

Work with a group. Choose a song to **recite**, or say out loud. Decide who will read each part of the song. Decide which parts the whole group will read together. Practice reading. Then recite your song for the class. Use your voice to make the words persuade.

Respond to the Songs, continued
Language Arts and Literature

(GRAMMAR IN CONTEXT)

USE INDEFINITE PRONOUNS

Learn About Indefinite Pronouns When you don't know the name of a specific person, place, or thing, use an **indefinite pronoun**.

Some Indefinite Pronouns

person	anyone	someone	everyone
place	anywhere	somewhere	everywhere
thing	anything	something	everything

Examples:

Everyone can help save the planet Earth.
We should help **anywhere** we can.
Is there **something** you can do?

Use Indefinite Pronouns How can you and your classmates help this planet Earth? Finish these sentences:

• Something I can do is . . .

• Everyone should . . .

• Anyone can . . .

Practice Write the sentences. Use an indefinite pronoun to complete each sentence.

1. _____ can help save the planet.

2. What is _____ you can do to help?

3. _____ can help by saving water.

4. Try to recycle _____ you go.

5. Do _____ you can to keep Earth "evergreen, everblue."

(LITERARY ANALYSIS)
(WRITING/REPRESENTING)

WRITE A HAIKU POEM

A **haiku poem** tells one idea about nature. Write your own feelings about nature.

❶ **Learn the Haiku Pattern** Each haiku has seventeen syllables in three lines.

Line 1 5 syllables	Crys tal clear rain drops
Line 2 7 syllables	Gone from the val leys and streams
Line 3 5 syllables	A tear falls for you

❷ **Write Your Draft** Create a poem about nature. Use the haiku pattern.

❸ **Edit Your Poem** Trade poems with a partner. See if you understand the poem. Check to see that the poem matches the haiku pattern. Give your partner ideas about how to make the poem better.

❹ **Make a Final Draft** Make a new copy of your haiku poem. Write neatly or use a word-processing program on a computer. Add pictures of nature.

Learn how to use a **word-processing program**.
See Handbook pages 354–361.

STUDY REPETITION AND AUTHOR'S STYLE

Learn About Repetition When writers use **repetition**, they say words or phrases more than once. Repetition shows the author's important ideas.

In "Evergreen, Everblue," Raffi wants people to protect our planet. He repeats the phrase "Help this planet Earth" to make his point.

Find Repetition Look back at the songs in "Protecting Our Planet." What words are repeated? How does repetition help you remember Raffi's main points?

Practice Copy the poem. Add a repetitive phrase.

> Drivers are driving everywhere,
> Their smog pollutes the nice, fresh air.
> Try to find a different way to go —
> Try a bike or the bus.
>
> _____
>
> _____

WRITE A FRIENDLY LETTER TO RAFFI

Work with a partner. Tell Raffi what you learned from his songs. Be sure to tell:

- which song you like the most
- your ideas about the environment
- how you will help the Earth.

Write a Letter Use this model:

Heading

Cabrillo Middle School
1423 Veteran Avenue
Los Angeles, CA 90010
March 19, 2004

Greeting

Dear Raffi,

Body

    Our class read four of your songs. Our favorite is "Big Beautiful Planet" because it talks about how much we need the sun and the wind. We care about our environment, too. We are going to pick up trash at our school.
    Thank you for writing your songs.

Closing and signature

Sincerely,
Binh and Tony

Send Your Letter Use this address:

c/o Troubadour Records
1078 Cambie Street
Vancouver, BC
Canada V6B 5L7

Respond to the Songs, continued
Language Arts and Literature

LEARN ABOUT PROPAGANDA

Propaganda techniques try to make you feel or think a certain way. Advertisements use propaganda techniques because they want you to buy what they are selling.

- A **glittering generality** says that the product is special. Some ads may say:
  New! and *Improved!*

- The **bandwagon technique** says that everyone buys the company's product. They may say:
  Everyone should have this!

- Companies use **name calling** to show that they are better than others. For example:
  Other brands are more expensive.

① **Identify Propaganda Techniques** Work with a partner. Find propaganda techniques in the ad.

② **Study Modern Propaganda Techniques** Find examples of propaganda techniques in magazines, newspapers, or television commercials. Make a T-chart to list the techniques that you find. Give examples of each technique.

③ **Give an Oral Presentation** Show the advertisement to the class. Talk about the propaganda techniques you found. Tell if the advertisement made you want to buy the product.

Learn how to make a **chart**.
See Handbook page 341.
Learn how to give an **oral presentation** on pages 374–376.

Content Area Connections

SCIENCE

TECHNOLOGY/MEDIA

RESEARCH ENDANGERED SPECIES

Endangered species are animals that are disappearing from our planet. Work with a group to study animals that are in danger today.

1 **Find Information** Use science books, magazines, encyclopedias, or the Internet. Take notes. Try these Web sites, but remember that new sites appear every day!

INFORMATION ON-LINE

Web Sites:
▶ **Endangered Species**
 • www.sprint.com/epatrol
 • www.epa.gov/kids
 • www.amnh.org/exhibitions/endangered

2 **Organize Your Information** Make a chart.

Endangered Species	Where They Live	Why They Are Endangered	How People Can Help
Bengal Tigers	India, China, Siberia,	hunting, fewer forests	save forests

3 **Prepare Your Presentation** Tell your class about the endangered species you studied. Use drawings and maps to show information. Then listen to the other groups in your class. Add their information to your chart.

4 **Write a Persuasive Statement** Study your chart. Then write about how people can help animals that are in danger.

Learn how to do **research**.
See Handbook pages 366–370.
Learn to use the **Internet** on pages 364–365.

Dealing With Disasters

- How do people in communities help each other every day?

- When disaster strikes, how do the contributions of each individual help the whole community recover?

- When is it important to help out in your community—every day, or when disaster strikes? Why?

THEME-RELATED BOOKS

Hurricane!
by Jonathan London

The sky grows dark and the wind begins to blow. A family in Puerto Rico hurries to a shelter until an unexpected hurricane is over.

Flood
by Mary Calhoun

A family, facing the threat of flood, is determined to save their home. Then the levy breaks and they must flee to save their lives.

...If You Lived at the Time of the Great San Francisco Earthquake
by Ellen Levine

How did the 1906 earthquake sound? How did it feel? This book answers these and other questions.

Build Language and Vocabulary

GIVE AND CARRY OUT COMMANDS

Listen to this poem about an earthquake.
Then, recite it with the class.

When the Ground SHAKES

When the ground shakes along the street
There's something happening beneath your feet.
Earth layers are shifting,
Slipping,
Sliding,
Bumping together.
Shock waves are rising!

When the ground shakes beneath your feet
There's something happening above the street.
Everything's rattling,
Crashing,
Cracking,
Moving around.
An earthquake's happening!

— Sheron Long

BRAINSTORM IDEAS

What should you do when an earthquake happens? Record your ideas in a list and discuss each of them.

> **What To Do During an Earthquake**
>
> - get under a table
> - go outside in the open
> - stay away from windows and other glass

BUILD YOUR VOCABULARY

Words About Earthquakes You never know when an earthquake will happen, but it is a good idea to be prepared. Add a column to the chart with ideas about how to prepare for an earthquake. Then, add another column with ideas about ways to help after an earthquake. Use words from the **Word Bank**.

Word Bank

batteries
clothing
food
mess
plan
shelter
supplies
water

How To Prepare for an Earthquake	What To Do During an Earthquake	How To Help After an Earthquake
• make a plan to meet family members • keep candles, flashlights, and batteries in the house	• stand in a doorway • get under a table • go outside in the open • stay away from windows and other glass	• give extra clothing to shelters • serve food at a shelter • help clean up the mess

USE LANGUAGE STRUCTURES ▶ COMMANDS

Speaking and Listening: Role-Play Disaster Responses Work with a group. Choose one person to be an earthquake expert. The expert will give the group commands about what to do before, during, or after an earthquake. Use ideas from the chart. The other group members will act out each command.

> **Examples:**
> Make a plan to meet family members before an earthquake.
> Stand in a doorway during an earthquake.
> Give extra clothing to shelters after an earthquake.

EARTHQUAKE AT DAWN

play
by Kristiana Gregory

Prepare to Read

THINK ABOUT WHAT YOU KNOW

Idea Exchange Work with a group to study the diagrams on the next page. Discuss how earthquakes happen with your group.

---

epidemic An **epidemic** is a sickness or disease that spreads quickly.

restore power When you **restore power**, you get the electricity to work again.

rise When things begin to **rise**, they start to get up.

ruins Fallen buildings, damaged roads, or bridges that cannot be fixed are called **ruins**.

separate When something is **separate**, it is by itself.

sewer A **sewer** is an underground tunnel that carries wastes from houses and buildings.

supplies Materials that people need are called **supplies**.

take good care of When you **take good care** of someone, you give that person special attention.

tent city A **tent** is a shelter made of cloth. A **tent city** is a large area with many tents.

threatened If you are **threatened**, you are warned that something bad may happen.

LEARN KEY VOCABULARY

Relate Words Study the new words. Then copy the web below. Work with a group to sort the new words into the web.

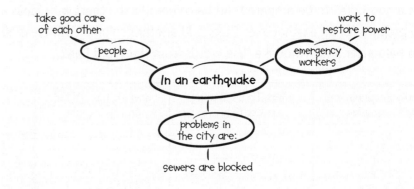

LEARN ABOUT PLAYS

A **play** is a story that is acted out. The written form of a play is the **script**. The script tells the actors what to say and do.

> ### READING STRATEGY
> **How to Read a Script**
> 1. **Acts** and **scenes** show the time and setting of the action.
> 2. **Stage directions** tell the players what to do.
> 3. **Speaker words** tell who is speaking.
> 4. **Dialogue** is words the characters say.

Now read "Earthquake at Dawn." Picture the stage. Imagine the players speaking. Imagine them acting out the stage directions.

The Making of an Earthquake

❶

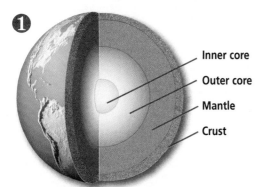

The Earth is made of layers.

- Inner core
- Outer core
- Mantle
- Crust

❷

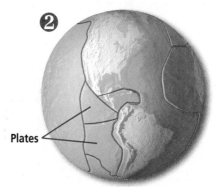

Plates

Earth's crust is made up of large blocks of rock called *plates.*

❸

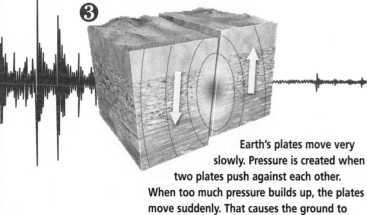

Earth's plates move very slowly. Pressure is created when two plates push against each other. When too much pressure builds up, the plates move suddenly. That causes the ground to shake. We feel this shaking as an earthquake.

❹

Earthquakes can damage or destroy buildings, roads, and bridges.

❺

The force of an earthquake is measured on a seismograph machine using the Richter scale.

Earthquake at Dawn   **227**

EARTHQUAKE AT DAWN

A PLAY IN ONE ACT
by
Kristiana Gregory

Twenty-two year old photographer Edith Irvine, her father, and her traveling companion, Daisy Valentine, travel from their home in Stockton, California, to San Francisco. There, the young women plan to board a ship to Australia to exhibit Edith's work. They arrive in San Francisco on April 18, 1906, just in time to experience a powerful earthquake. As they wander the streets of the city, they are separated from Edith's father and soon become involved in helping victims of the disaster.

SETTING

TIME:
MORNING OF APRIL 18, 1906

PLACE:
CITY OF SAN FRANCISCO, CALIFORNIA, AFTER AN ENORMOUS EARTHQUAKE

CHARACTERS

EDITH IRVINE:
A 22-YEAR-OLD PHOTOGRAPHER PREPARING FOR A TRIP TO AUSTRALIA

DAISY VALENTINE:
EDITH'S 15-YEAR-OLD TRAVELING COMPANION

CITIZENS OF SAN FRANCISCO:
MR. AND MRS. SOMERS, STORE OWNERS
MARY EXA, FRIEND OF THE SOMERS
MR. AND MRS. WESTLAKE, AN ELDERLY COUPLE

1

HELPING HANDS

Edith and Daisy meet some earthquake victims and help with a rescue.

❧ Begin Scene 1 ❧

A grocery store with broken windows is at the center of the stage. The front wall of the store has fallen down, so the inside can be seen.

*[Enter Edith and Daisy, walking though the **ruins** of the city. Their clothes are torn and dirty.]*

Mrs. Somers: *[from door of grocery store]*

Someone, please!

Daisy: Look, over there, the woman by the grocery store. See her? In the **nightdress** and garden boots. She's holding a baby.

Mrs. Somers: Thank goodness for you girls. *[pulls Edith and Daisy into her store]* My poor husband is in our store, **stuck** up to his neck in dried beans. **What a mess** everything is. The young lady who lives with us, Mary Exa, is trying to dig him out.

Daisy: Haw! Oh, forgive me . . . *[then quietly to Edith]* . . . but a man buried in beans is the funniest thing I've ever heard!

Edith: Hush up now, Daisy. Let's help the poor **fellow**. He may be hurt, you know.

Mrs. Somers: It was that last **shock** that did it. **Eight-fourteen sharp**, and everything that didn't fall the first time fell then. Mercy!

---

nightdress clothing for sleeping, women's pajamas
stuck trapped, unable to move
What a mess How dirty, How untidy

fellow man
shock small earthquake
Eight-fourteen sharp At exactly fourteen minutes after eight o'clock

[Edith and Daisy join Mary Exa. They begin digging into the beans with their hands to free Mr. Somers.]

Edith: Hoist!

Mary Exa: Here he comes! Uh!

Mr. Somers: *[brushing himself off]* Ladies, I thank you. I seem to be fine. Are you all right, dear?

Mrs. Somers: Yes, baby Timothy and I are fine, but I have never seen such a mess in my life!

Edith: Allow me to **introduce myself**. I'm Edith Irvine and this is **my traveling companion**, Daisy Valentine. We were **to set sail** for Australia this afternoon. The **docks** are such a mess, I doubt that any ships will sail. Now, I guess we'll be going back home to Stockton.

Mrs. Somers: *[looking at the girls kindly]* How dreadful for you. But mercy, where are my manners? You must be hungry. Let's see what we can offer you. Edith and Daisy, will you take baby Timothy while we look through this mess for something we can eat? Mary, see what you can find.

....

Hoist Lift
introduce myself tell you who I am, tell you my name
my traveling companion the friend I am traveling with

to set sail going to travel on a boat
docks place where the ships load and unload goods and people

Edith: [holding the baby up and at arm's length] Daisy, I think the baby **needs changing**. But I'm smelling something else. I smell smoke.

Mr. Somers: Look, over there, toward the **harbor**! Can you see all those **plumes** of smoke? . . . nine . . . ten . . . eleven . . . Eleven separate fires . . . Chief Sullivan's going to be busy this morning!

Mary Exa: [proudly] Chief Sullivan has an **outstanding fire department**. San Francisco will **be safe in his hands**.

Mr. Somers: Oh yes, dear, no worries. [pulling two wooden chairs out to the sidewalk and motioning for his wife and Edith to sit]

Daisy: Oh, look. There's a sign on that pole down the street. Edith, let's go see what it says.

[Edith hands the baby to Mrs. Somers. She and Daisy exit the stage.]

End Scene 1

BEFORE YOU MOVE ON...

1. **Inference** When Edith and Daisy meet Mrs. Somers, she is wearing a nightdress. What do you think she was doing when the earthquake happened?
2. **Details** Why can't Edith and Daisy sail to Australia as they had planned?
3. **Cause and Effect** What might cause a fire to start after an earthquake?

---

needs changing needs to have his diaper changed, has a dirty diaper

harbor place where ships stay when they are not sailing

plumes long, vertical clouds

outstanding fire department excellent team that puts out fires

be safe in his hands not be in danger because he is in charge

The mayor tries to keep the city under control.
His message scares Edith and Daisy.

Begin Scene 2

A street corner with a telephone pole.

[Enter two men carrying hammers and signs. Edith and Daisy then enter as the men begin to nail the signs to the telephone pole.]

Daisy: *[grabs Edith's arm]* What do those signs say? The ones those men are nailing on the telephone pole.

Edith: *[reads aloud]* **SEWERS** BLOCKED. DON'T USE TOILETS. **EPIDEMIC THREATENED. OBEY ORDERS** OR GET SHOT.

[men exit stage]

Daisy: Do you think they're serious?

Edith: *[laughing]*: Of course not. There's not a man alive who would shoot a lady for doing what she needs to do.

Daisy: What does this one say, Edith?

Edith: It's from the mayor of San Francisco. **Basically** it says, oh dear, oh dear . . . !

Daisy: Edith! What?

Edith: It says that soldiers and police are **authorized** to KILL any and all persons caught **looting** or **committing** any other crime . . . and the gas and lighting companies won't **restore power** until the mayor says to. Dear me. Isn't this **illegal**?

[sound of gunshot]

Daisy: *[alarmed]*: Oh!

Edith: There's trouble somewhere. Let's get back to Mrs. Somers' house!

[Edith and Daisy rush off stage.]

End Scene 2

BEFORE YOU MOVE ON...

1. **Details** What warnings were posted after the earthquake?
2. **Character's Motive** At first Edith laughs about the warning signs. Why does she change her mind?
3. **Inference** Why do you think the mayor threatens to shoot people who don't follow the rules?

OBEY ORDERS Do what you are told, Follow instructions
Basically The main thing
authorized given permission

looting stealing
committing carrying out, doing
illegal against the law, not allowed

San Francisco, California. April 18, 1906. Soldiers walk past burning buildings and ruins.

Aftershocks continue. Edith, Daisy, and their new friends decide to join the people in the park.

———

Begin Scene 3

Inside the upstairs apartment above the Somers' grocery store.

[Mr. and Mrs. Somers and Mary Exa are pulling blankets and mattresses off beds.]

Edith: *[offstage]* Hello, where is everybody?

Mrs. Somers: We're here, upstairs. We're just getting some things. Mr. Somers, please carry that **mattress** and those blankets out to the yard.

[Mr. Somers exits with mattress and blankets. Edith and Daisy enter.]

Mrs. Somers: Ladies, please **take no offense** if I offer you a fresh change of clothes. *[hands clothes to Edith and Daisy]* There is a clean blouse for each of you, and two clean **petticoats**. **Unfortunately**, there is only one **spare** hat.

[Another powerful jolt strikes. Everybody falls to the ground, hands over head.]

Mrs. Somers: Oh, my! More glass is breaking . . . watch out!

Edith: *[hugs Daisy]* Are you all right? Hurry. Let's **change into** these clothes while we can. Here you go, Daisy. You take this lovely hat. You look so good in blue. It seems silly to worry about our clothing at a time like this, but I do feel better somehow.

---

mattress pad to sleep on—usually on a bed
take no offense do not be angry with me
petticoats skirts to wear under dresses

Unfortunately Sadly
spare extra
change into put on, get dressed in

[*Edith and Daisy go behind a screen, change clothes, and return.*]

Mary Exa: I don't think it's safe to go down into the store right now . . . things keep shaking so . . . but Mr. Somers did bring up some fruit. We have no water to drink, but these oranges will help our **thirst**. Here . . .

   [*Mary hands out oranges.*]

[*Enter an elderly couple.*]

Mrs. Somers [*greeting the couple*]: Hello! Daisy and Edith, these are our neighbors, Mr. and Mrs. Westlake!

Mrs. Westlake: We've had **a terrible time**. Our **canaries flew off** when their **cages** fell over. We barely saved the cat before the chimney crashed onto our bed. I **hollered** to the Davenports, but they didn't answer. Not a word. Oh dear . . . I'm afraid something **horrible** has happened to them.

[*Enter Mr. Somers.*]

Mr. Somers: We have to get out of here. The city is burning. Every **jolt brings down** more buildings. I don't think the store is safe anymore.

Mr. Westlake: We saw people **heading for** Golden Gate Park. They are using whatever they have to **set up** a **tent city**.

---

thirst need to drink something
a terrible time bad experiences
canaries flew off pet birds flew away
cages wire houses for birds
hollered called out, yelled

horrible very bad, awful
jolt brings down aftershock knocks down
heading for going to, moving towards
set up put up, build

Mrs. Somers: Yes. That's the safest place to be. Maybe we'll find water there.

Edith: Daisy and I will go, too. We'll help you carry whatever we can.

Mr. Somers [*taking charge*]: It's **settled**, then. We'll go to Golden Gate Park!

[*All exit except Daisy.*]

Daisy [*to audience*]: Edith and I did finally return to our home in Stockton. Her father got home safely, too. The people of San Francisco **took good care** of each other until more help arrived. **Communities from all over the nation** sent food and **supplies**.

Nearly all of the city burned to the ground, but not for long! Within weeks, a new San Francisco began to **rise** out of the ashes.

[*Exit Daisy.*]

The End

---

settled decided, agreed on
Communities from all over the nation People in towns and cities all across the country

---

BEFORE YOU MOVE ON...

1. **Details** How did the Somers family and the girls help each other?

2. **Comparisons** Why was it safer to stay in the park than in the store?

3. **Figurative Language** What do you think Daisy meant when she said that a new San Francisco began to rise out of the ashes?

ABOUT THE AUTHOR

Kristiana Gregory has been a reporter, editor, and children's book reviewer. Her books, *Earthquake at Dawn* and *Jenny of the Tetons*, were chosen as Notable Children's Trade Books for Social Studies. Kristiana lives in California and has experienced dozens of earthquakes. She hopes that by learning about the past, her readers will be able to help their communities prepare for the future.

Respond to the Play
Check Your Understanding

SUM IT UP

Analyze Characters and Setting "Earthquake at Dawn" takes place in 1906. What clues from the script and the illustrations show this? Make a chart like the one below.

How Do You Know It Was 1906?	
How people dress	women wear petticoats
How people talk	
How the city looks	

Rewrite the Play Imagine that the story happened today. Choose a scene from the play to rewrite. Where would it take place? How would people talk? What commands would they give? How could they help each other? Remember to include stage directions and other parts of a script.

Evaluate Literature Talk with a partner about how the time and place cause the plays to be different. Write a sentence or two to summarize your ideas.

THINK IT OVER

Discuss Talk about these questions with a partner.

1. **Literary Analysis** Imagine what the play would be like as a short story. Which would you like better?

2. **Generalization** Read this saying: "Disaster brings out the best in some people, the worst in others." What does this mean? Use details from the play to explain.

3. **Cause and Effect** What problems do earthquakes cause?

4. **Personal Experience** Have you ever been in a disaster? Describe your experience.

EXPRESS YOURSELF
▶ GIVE AND CARRY OUT COMMANDS

Form groups. A volunteer pretends to be a character in the play in a Hot Seat!

- The rest of the group acts as the director and tells the character what to do.

- The character carries out the commands.

Respond to the Play, continued
Language Arts and Literature

GRAMMAR IN CONTEXT

USE HELPING VERBS

Learn About Helping Verbs Some verbs are made up of more than one word. The last word is called the main verb. It shows the action. The verb that comes before the main verb is the helping verb. Here are some helping verbs.

can	could	may	might
must	should	will	would

Examples:

An earthquake can cause great damage.
People must cooperate in an emergency.

In a negative sentence, the word *not* comes between the helping verb and the main verb.

The ships may not sail today.

Use Helping Verbs Write the helping verbs listed above on cards. Put the cards in a pile. With a group, take turns choosing a card. Use the word in a sentence to tell or ask something about an earthquake.

Practice Copy these sentences. Add a helping verb to complete each sentence.

1. Damaged buildings _____ fall down.

2. Everyone _____ go to a safe place.

3. _____ the people find water to drink?

4. Other cities _____ come to help.

5. The city _____ rise from the ashes.

LITERARY ANALYSIS
WRITING

WRITE A LITERARY CRITIQUE

When you **critique** a character, you tell what is good and bad about the character. Critique the characters in the play.

❶ **Set the Standards** What traits are important to have in a disaster? Write the traits in your chart.

❷ **Critique the Characters** Give each character a grade for each trait.

Literary Report Card

name	courage	generosity
Edith Daisy Mrs. S.	A+	

❸ **Write a Paragraph** Critique one character. Explain what you liked and didn't like about the character. Give examples from the story.

Content Area Connections

MAKE A TIME LINE

In **historical fiction**, some people and events were real. Other parts could have happened. Find examples of these.

1 Find Information Look for facts about the San Francisco earthquake that happened on April 18, 1906. Use history books, encyclopedias, and the Internet.

You can try these sites for information:
• www.sfmuseum.org
• quake.wr.usgs.gov/more/1906
• www.exploratorium.edu/covis/earthquake

2 Organize Your Information Take notes about what happened during and after the earthquake. Put your facts in the order they happened.

3 Make a Time Line Write the historical events in one color. Add the events of the play in a different color. What parts of the play were real and what were imaginary?

Time Line

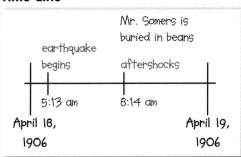

SCIENCE

TECHNOLOGY/MEDIA

CREATE AN EARTHQUAKE DATA CHART

Learn about recent earthquakes.

Gather Information Use newspapers or the Internet. Take notes about three earthquakes. Try these Web sites to begin your search, but remember that new sites appear every day!

INTERNET

INFORMATION ON-LINE

Web Sites:
➤ **Current Earthquakes**
  • www.discovery.com
  • www.planetdiary.com

Make a Chart Compare the earthquakes. List the location, date, size, and damage for each earthquake. Share your chart with the class.

Learn how to make **charts**.
See Handbook pages 340–341.

Build Language and Vocabulary
ELABORATE

View this picture. How do these people help during a disaster in their community?

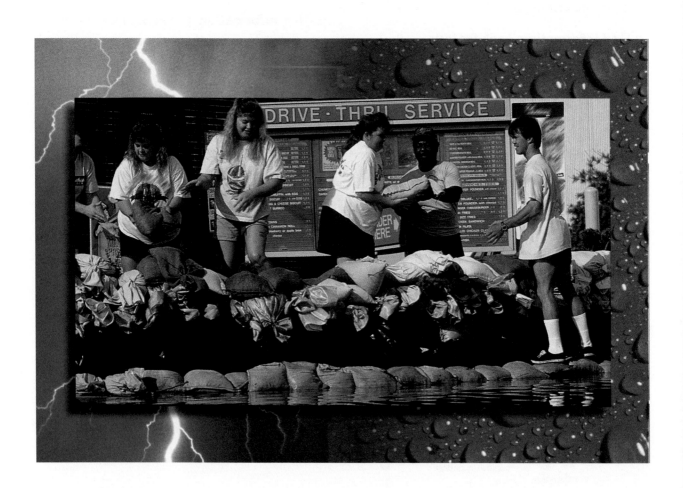

RECORD DETAILS

Look at the picture on page 240 with a small group. Each person plays an important part in building the wall of sandbags. Write a sentence to describe what is happening in the picture.

People work to stack the sandbags.

Compare sentences. Look at the details in each person's sentence. Notice the differences.

BUILD YOUR VOCABULARY

Words and Phrases Look again at one sentence your group wrote. Add details to tell more about the picture.

- Add an **adjective** to tell what something is like.

  People work to stack the heavy sandbags.

- Add an **adverb** to tell how, when, or where something is done.

  People work quickly to stack the heavy sandbags.

  This adverb tells **how**.

- Add a **prepositional phrase** to give more information. Some phrases, like this one, tell where someone is.

  People near the water work quickly to stack the heavy sandbags.

USE LANGUAGE STRUCTURES ▶ ADJECTIVES, ADVERBS, PREPOSITIONS

Writing: Elaborate Copy this paragraph. Add adjectives, adverbs, and prepositional phrases to tell more about the picture. Use the **Word Bank** to help you get ideas.

    People form a line. Some people fill bags with sand. Some people pass the sandbags. Some people stack the sandbags. A wall of sandbags is forming. The wall helps to stop the water. The volunteers work to build a taller wall.

Word Bank

Adjectives
heavy
muddy

Adverbs
carefully
quickly

Prepositions
by
on top of

WHEN DISASTER STRIKES

news articles
by Richie Chevat

Prepare to Read

THINK ABOUT WHAT YOU KNOW

Make a Word Web Work with your class to complete the word web about disasters.

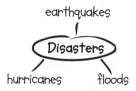

LEARN KEY VOCABULARY

aid Money, food, and supplies for people who need help is called **aid**.

damage Harm and destruction are kinds of **damage**.

evacuee A person who must move away from a disaster is called an **evacuee**.

recovery When something gets back to normal after a problem, it is called **recovery**.

relief worker A **relief worker** is someone who helps people after a disaster.

rescue worker A **rescue worker** tries to save people in emergencies.

shelter People can stay in a **shelter** when they have no home.

struggle When you **struggle**, you try hard to do something.

survivor Someone who is still alive after a disaster is called a **survivor**.

wreckage What is left after things are destroyed or ruined is called **wreckage**.

Use New Words in Context Study the new words. Use these ideas to write a paragraph about a disaster and how people struggle to rebuild.

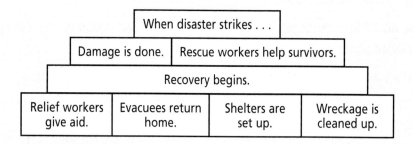

Example:

When disaster strikes, damage is done. Rescue workers help survivors.

LEARN TO READ FOR INFORMATION

When you read nonfiction, you can use photos, maps, and diagrams to find information. These pictures help you understand information.

READING STRATEGY
Where to Find Information
- A **photo** is a picture of someone or something real.
- A **caption** describes what is in a photo or picture.
- A **map** shows where events happen.
- A **diagram** is a drawing that explains information.

Now read "When Disaster Strikes." Use the information in photos, captions, maps, and diagrams to help you understand the articles.

WHEN DISASTER STRIKES

By RICHIE CHEVAT

Natural disasters can occur at any time, in any place around the world. When natural disasters strike, communities pull together to help each other and to rebuild. Sometimes, people of the world act together as a global community when disaster strikes. These events, taken from newspaper articles, tell about three real-life disasters.

Earthquake in Taiwan, 1999

2:00 A.M.

Massive Quake Rocks Taiwan — Hundreds Feared Dead

A huge earthquake **rocked** the island of Taiwan just before 2 a.m. It sent twelve-story buildings crashing to the ground. Hundreds are **feared dead** and hundreds more are trapped in the **rubble**.

The quake measured 7.6 on the Richter scale and may be the strongest quake ever to hit this area. **Power is out** in many places. Government officials **call for calm** and **warn of continuing aftershocks**.

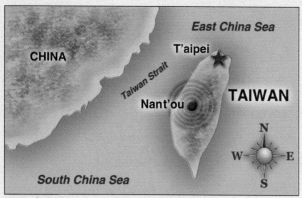

Site of the September 21 earthquake

6:00 A.M.

Taiwan Quake Kills More Than 1,400

The **death toll** from today's early morning earthquake stands at 1,450. **Rescue workers** fear it will go even higher. Hundreds of people are still trapped in wrecked buildings. Dozens of aftershocks, several as strong as a major earthquake, make rescue work dangerous. Everywhere, rescuers are working to dig out **survivors** Cranes and bulldozers are being used.

Often, friends and neighbors are using their bare hands to remove the rubble.

A 12-story building lies on its side after an earthquake jolted Taiwan.

---

rocked shook, moved

feared dead thought to be dead

rubble ruins of destroyed buildings

Power is out There is no electricity, Electric power is not working

call for calm ask people to be calm

warn of continuing aftershocks let people know there may be more earthquakes

death toll number of people who died

11:00 A.M.

Rescue Effort Grows

As many as 3,000 people were trapped in fallen buildings after a pre-dawn earthquake. Rescue teams **comb through** the **wreckage** to find those still trapped. Trained dogs are searching the rubble. Survivors are still being pulled from under the **concrete.**

"My wife was buried under **debris** for nine hours. Luckily, she was pulled out alive," says a 59-year-old grocer from the town of Puli.

Tens of thousands of people are on the streets, afraid to return to their homes. **Soup kitchens** are being set up in parks. Countries around the world—including the United States, Germany, and Japan—offer to send **aid**. A team from Turkey is **rushing to the scene**. Aftershocks keep coming. The terrible search for survivors continues, but it seems that the worst is over.

> ### POINT-BY-POINT
>
> #### HOW COMMUNITIES RESPOND TO DISASTERS
>
> **After an Earthquake:**
>
> - The government calls for calm.
> - Community members and rescuers search for survivors.
> - The international community sends aid.

BEFORE YOU MOVE ON...

1. **Vocabulary** The article reports that hundreds of people were killed. List other words from the article that tell numbers of things.
2. **Cause and Effect** Why does the death toll rise as the days go by?
3. **Details** Why was it difficult for rescue workers to help the people who were trapped?

---

comb through search carefully in
concrete strong, hard building material, made from cement and minerals
debris rocks and rubble created by the earthquake

Soup kitchens places where food is served for free to people who need it
rushing to the scene coming to the disaster site as quickly as possible

Hurricane in the Caribbean, 1998

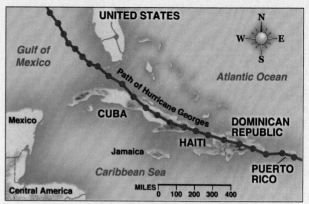
The path of Hurricane Georges

MONDAY, SEPTEMBER 21, 1998

Hurricane Georges Hits Puerto Rico

Hurricane Georges slammed into the island of Puerto Rico at around 6 p.m. today. Winds **reached** over 115 miles per hour. Airplanes flipped over like toys. Trees were **uprooted** and flew through the air like missiles. Over 80 percent of the island is without electricity. Seventy percent of all homes are without water.

Inside a Hurricane

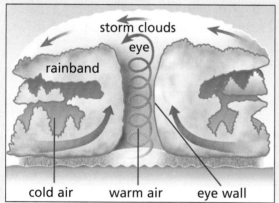

Low pressure in the eye of a hurricane pulls in cooler air, creating a powerful storm with winds over 74 miles per hour.

TUESDAY, SEPTEMBER 22, 1998

Georges Blasts Dominican Republic — Rescue Efforts Begin

Hurricane Georges spreads its destruction to the Dominican Republic. **Mudslides** and **flooding** kill over 200 people. More than 100,000 people are left **homeless**.

Meanwhile, rescue workers bring aid to Puerto Rico. More than 20,000 people **crowd into shelters** in San Juan and other cities.

FRIDAY, SEPTEMBER 25, 1998

Hurricane Relief Underway

Rescue workers in the Dominican Republic and Haiti **struggle** to bring food, water, and shelter to people. House

---

reached got as fast as
uprooted pulled from the ground
Mudslides Rushing rivers of mud and rain

flooding water overflowing the banks of rivers
homeless without homes, with nowhere to live
crowd into are pushed together in

after house **lies in ruins** or without a roof.

"There's no water. There's no power. There is nothing," says Domingo Osvaldo Fortuna as he fills a plastic jug with water from the garbage-filled Ozama River in Santo Domingo.

Aid from the United States begins to arrive. A French cargo plane brings **relief workers**, food, and medicine. Sixty-three firefighters from New York help to search for survivors.

Sunday, September 27, 1998

Hurricane Continues — Tons of Food On the Way

Tons of food and supplies begin to arrive in the Dominican Republic and Haiti. Volunteers fly in with tons of bottled water and enough **plastic sheeting** to repair 15,000 houses. Members of the U.S. military carry aid to towns **cut off by** flooding and mudslides.

Although it will take weeks or even years for the islands to **repair** the **damage**, **recovery** has slowly begun.

POINT-BY-POINT

HOW COMMUNITIES RESPOND TO DISASTERS

After a Hurricane:

- Emergency shelters are set up for people who are left homeless.
- Rescue workers bring food, water, and medicine to disaster victims.
- Rescue workers search for survivors.
- The international community sends aid to help victims recover and rebuild.

BEFORE YOU MOVE ON...

1. **Vocabulary** What words or phrases describe the strength of the hurricane?
2. **Cause and Effect** What problems did the hurricane cause?
3. **Details** How did other countries help the people on the islands?

---

lies in ruins sits on the ground in pieces
Tons Several thousands of pounds
plastic sheeting waterproof covering

cut off by unable to have contact with the outside world because of
repair fix, correct

Flood in the American Midwest, 1997

FRIDAY, APRIL 11, 1997

Red River Keeps Rising While Volunteers Build Levees

Swollen by melting snow and spring rains, the Red River continued to rise today. It has already reached 39 feet in Fargo, North Dakota, about 80 miles downstream from Grand Forks.

In Grand Forks, thousands of volunteers worked round-the-clock, **piling** sandbags on **dikes and levees**. The National Weather Service predicts the river will **crest** here at 49 feet sometime in the next few days.

Grand Forks, North Dakota, was the site of severe flood damage.

SUNDAY, APRIL 20, 1997

Grand Forks Flooded and On Fire, Levees Fail, River Keeps Rising

Grand Forks was in the middle of a **vast** lake today, surrounded by the waters of the Red River. The river **surged** to over 52 feet, washing away dikes and levees and flooding over 60 percent of the town. Tens of thousands of people were forced to flee their homes.

Meanwhile, firefighters struggled to stop a blaze in the downtown area. The fire has destroyed at least seven buildings. "With two to three feet of water

Volunteers help to pile sandbags in Grand Forks.

Swollen Made larger
piling putting stacks of
dikes and levees walls, often of dirt, built to keep water from overflowing a river or stream

crest reach its highest point
vast wide and open
surged rose quickly

in the area, it's very difficult," said Captain Wade Davis of the National Guard. Helicopters dropped 2,000-gallon buckets of muddy water on the fires.

TUESDAY, APRIL 22, 1997

President Visits Grand Forks

The President of the United States visited the flooded town of Grand Forks today, taking a helicopter tour of the area and speaking to **evacuees** at a nearby Air Force base. The President offered **words of sympathy** and also promises of federal aid to flooded areas.

"It may be hard to believe now," he told his audience, "but you can rebuild stronger and better than ever."

Grand Forks is nearly **deserted**. The water supply, gas, and electricity have been cut off to most of the city. Almost all of the people have fled.

"You can't believe the emotion that goes through your mind and your heart," said one resident. "Please help these people."

----

words of sympathy words to show that he understood and was sad about their problem

deserted empty of people

POINT-BY-POINT

HOW COMMUNITIES RESPOND TO DISASTERS

Before a Flood:
- Volunteers pile sandbags to hold back water.
- People are evacuated from the flood zone.

After a Flood:
- The government sets up shelters for people left homeless.
- The government provides aid to help people rebuild and recover.

BEFORE YOU MOVE ON...

1. **Cause and Effect** What caused the Red River to rise?
2. **Details** How did people try to stop the flood damage?

ABOUT THE AUTHOR

Richie Chevat lives with his wife and two daughters in New Jersey. Earthquakes and hurricanes are very rare in New Jersey. Richie is glad that he has never been the victim of a flood or any other natural disaster. He hopes that these articles will get people thinking about how they can help when disaster strikes.

Respond to the Articles
Check Your Understanding

SUM IT UP

Read for Information Fill in the chart with information from the articles. Use the photos, captions, maps, and diagram to help you.

Details	Earthquake	Hurricane	Flood
Date			
Location			
Damage			
Rescuer Work			
What Survivors Do			

Make Comparisons Write a paragraph. Tell how two disasters are the same and different.

- Write a **topic sentence** to tell the main idea.
- Add **details** to support the main idea.
- Use **comparison words** like these:

same	**different**
both	unlike
alike	but

Example:
   A hurricane and an earthquake are the **same** in some ways, but **different** in others. They **both** cause a lot of damage and wreckage. A hurricane brings rain, **but** an earthquake does not.

THINK IT OVER

Discuss Talk about these questions with a partner.

1. **Personal Experience** What natural disasters happen where you live? What do people do when they happen?

2. **Inference** What lessons can we learn about helping others from these articles?

3. **Opinion** Which disaster would frighten you the most? Why?

4. **Conclusions** How can communities prepare for natural disasters?

EXPRESS YOURSELF
▶ ASK AND ANSWER QUESTIONS, ELABORATE

Play a quiz game about natural disasters.

1. Join one of these groups: A, B, or C.
   - A will study the Taiwan earthquake.
   - B will study the Caribbean hurricane.
   - C will study the Grand Forks flood.

2. Write questions about the disaster your group is studying. Write the answers.

3. Take turns asking the other groups questions about your disaster. Ask them to elaborate on their ideas.

4. The team with the most correct answers wins.

Language Arts and Literature

GRAMMAR IN CONTEXT

USE HELPING VERBS

Learn About Helping Verbs The words **is** and **are** are **helping verbs**. Use them with verbs that end in **–ing** to show that an action is still happening.

- Use **is** when the subject is one person or thing.

    An earthquake **is** rocking the island.

- Use **are** when the subject is more than one person or thing.

    Buildings **are** crashing to the ground.

Find Verbs Make a list of the helping verbs and main verbs in this paragraph. Then use them in a new sentence:

> Everywhere, rescuers are working. Cranes and bulldozers are digging. A neighbor is removing the rubble. The workers are looking for survivors.

Practice Copy the paragraph. Add the helping verb *is* or *are* to complete each sentence.

> Hurricane Georges _____ hitting Puerto Rico. Trees _____ flying through the air. Airplanes _____ flipping over like toys. Mud _____ pouring down the hillsides. Homes _____ washing away in the storm.

LITERARY ANALYSIS
WRITING

LEARN ABOUT NEWS STORIES

A **news story** gives facts about an event. News stories have these parts:

- The **headline** is the title of the article.

- The **lead paragraph** gives a summary of the article. In the article called "President Visits Grand Forks," the lead paragraph tells:

    Who: President of the U.S.

    What: visited the flooded town

    When: April 22, 1997

    Where: Grand Forks

    Why: to offer words of sympathy

- The **body** gives more details and facts about the event.

Write a News Story Tell about news in your school or community. Put the news stories together to make a class newspaper.

Learn how to improve your writing in the **writer's craft.** See Handbook pages 390–401.

Respond to the Articles, continued
Language Arts and Content Area Connections

▶ VOCABULARY

CLASSIFY SCIENCE WORDS

Learn to Classify Words When you **classify** words, you put them into groups. The words in the group all have something in common.

These words all tell about weather:

    wind   rain   snow   sunshine

Classify Disaster Words Put these words where they belong on a chart like the one below.

aftershocks, blasts, crest, mudslides, Richter scale, rocked, sandbags, swollen, winds

Earthquake	Hurricane	Flood
aftershocks		

Use Your New Vocabulary Copy the paragraph. Use words from the chart to fill in the missing words.

    Rescue workers are very important during natural disasters. They pile ____(1)____ on dikes to prevent floods. They look for survivors in the rubble caused by an earthquake and its ____(2)____. Some workers help evacuees get out of the way of winds and fast-moving ____(3)____ caused by hurricanes.

▶ VOCABULARY

USE PREFIXES AND SUFFIXES

Learn About Prefixes and Suffixes A prefix is a word part that comes at the beginning of a word.

The prefix **re-** means "again."

    People had to **rebuild** their homes.
    People had to **build their home again**.

A **suffix** is a word part that comes at the end of the word.

The suffix **-less** means "without."

    100,000 people are **homeless**.
    100,000 people are **without homes**.

The suffix **-ous** means "full of."

    The work is **dangerous**.
    The work is **full of danger**.

Adding prefixes and suffixes changes the meaning of the word.

Practice Copy the sentences. Add the prefix **re-** or the suffix **-ous** or **-less** to make new words. Use a dictionary to check your work.

1. I was speech_____ when I saw the damage from the earthquake.

2. The woman gave a joy_____ shout when she saw that her cat was safe.

3. It will take years to _____construct the area.

SOCIAL STUDIES
TECHNOLOGY/MEDIA

EXPLORE GEOGRAPHY

Make a Disaster Map Show where major earthquakes, hurricanes, and floods happened in the past. Use almanacs or try the Web sites below, but remember that new sites appear every day! Use the disasters as key words to begin your search.

INTERNET

INFORMATION ON-LINE

➤ **On-line Almanacs**
  • kids.infoplease.com/world.html
  • www.yahooligans.com/content/ka/index.html

Study the Data Look for patterns about where disasters happen. Share your ideas and map with your class.

Learn how to use the **Internet**.
See Handbook pages 364–365.

SOCIAL STUDIES

CREATE A PUBLIC SERVICE POSTER

Public service posters help people prepare for disasters. Work with a group to make a poster about earthquakes, hurricanes, or floods.

Research a Disaster Find information from the library, public services like the fire department or the American Red Cross, or on the Internet.

Make the Poster Include these things:

• what people should have ready
• what people should and shouldn't do
• emergency phone numbers.

Display the Poster Maybe your poster will help someone prepare for a disaster!

Writing That Persuades

Persuasive writing presents an opinion and tries to get the reader to agree with the opinion. Some persuasive writing describes a problem and persuades people to help solve it.

WRITING MODELS

Read the following sentences from the essay "Common Ground," by Molly Bang. What problem does she see? What is her opinion? What action does she want you to take? Why?

from "Common Ground"

> Today each lumber company wants to cut down as many trees as it can, to sell for wood, paper, and fuel. The more trees the lumber company cuts down, the more money it makes— in the short run. But after cutting down so many trees, there are fewer and fewer forests. This is not good for the trees, or for the forest creatures, or the forest soil.

In "Evergreen, Everblue," Raffi tries to persuade us. What action does he want us to take?

from "Evergreen, Everblue"

> Right now is when we're needed.
> We can all do something.
> The young, the old together.
> The more we get together,
> The more we help this planet Earth.

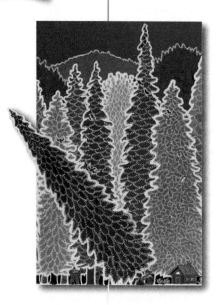

Write Together

WRITING PROMPT

First write a class essay about a problem in your community. Persuade your readers to do something about it.

1 Brainstorm Topics What problem does your class want to solve? What is your opinion about it? Brainstorm a list and choose a topic for the class essay.

2 Plan the Essay Your essay will have three paragraphs. Make an outline to plan it:

I. State the problem and tell your opinion about it.

II. Tell why there is a problem.

III. Summarize your opinion and tell your readers what you want them to do.

Sample Outline

I. Kids are getting hurt on school buses. We need to make the buses safer.

II. Buses are dangerous because they are too crowded.

III. We need to get more buses.

3 Write the Essay Follow your outline to write the class essay.

STUDENT WRITING MODEL

School Bus Problem

Riding the bus can be a disaster. A lot of kids are getting hurt. We need to make the buses safer to ride.

The buses are just too crowded. There are not enough seats. Kids have to stand. Then they start fighting and won't listen to the driver.

We must all help solve the bus problem. The school should get enough buses for all the students to have seats. Students need to follow the rules and show respect.

Use **persuasive words** to persuade your readers to take action.

Writing That Persuades, continued

Write on Your Own

WRITING PROMPT

Now write your own opinion essay about a problem in your school. Persuade your classmates to agree with your opinion.

PREWRITE

1 **Choose a Problem to Write About** Think about problems in your school. Choose a problem that you think can be solved. This is your **topic**. Fill out an **FATP** chart to guide your writing.

2 **Get Organized** Complete an outline. Name the topic in your title.

Title: Stop School Damage

I. Kids should not damage school property.

II. Students cause damage in two ways.

   A. They write graffiti on the walls.

   B. They destroy books.

III. Students need to take care of school property.

   A. Make them clean off the walls.

   B. Have them pay for the books.

FATP Chart

HOW TO UNLOCK A PROMPT
Form: _opinion essay_
Audience: _students who don't take care of school property_
Topic: _damage to school property_
Purpose: _to persuade students to take care of school property_

Think About Your Writing

- Do you care a lot about your topic? If not, choose one you do care about.

- Do you have enough good ideas for solutions?

DRAFT

1 **Write Your Essay** Follow your outline to write your essay.

2 **Consider Your Audience** Think about who will read your essay. Start out with a statement of your opinion. Try different ways to get your reader's attention.

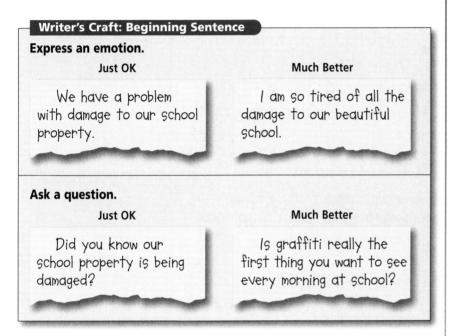

Writer's Craft: Beginning Sentence

Express an emotion.

Just OK	Much Better
We have a problem with damage to our school property.	I am so tired of all the damage to our beautiful school.

Ask a question.

Just OK	Much Better
Did you know our school property is being damaged?	Is graffiti really the first thing you want to see every morning at school?

End your essay with a strong sentence. It should encourage your reader to take action.

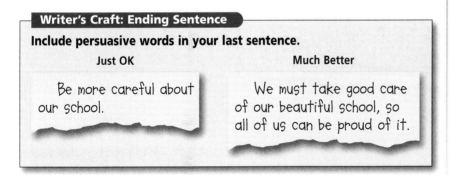

Writer's Craft: Ending Sentence

Include persuasive words in your last sentence.

Just OK	Much Better
Be more careful about our school.	We must take good care of our beautiful school, so all of us can be proud of it.

Writing is a way of cutting away at the surface of things, of exploring, of understanding.

— Robert Duncan

Think About Your Writing

• Read your draft. Have you stated your opinion clearly?

• Does your draft have good beginning and ending sentences?

• Does your draft include enough persuasive words?

• Will it persuade your readers?

Writing That Persuades, continued

REVISE

1 **Read Your Essay** Does your essay persuade your reader to take action? Do you have strong beginning and ending sentences?

2 **Share Your Essay** Work in a group of four students. Read each essay. First tell what you like about it. Then ask questions and make suggestions:

- To tell what you like, start with:
  I really like the part where . . .
  It's great how you . . .
  The best thing about your essay is . . .

- To suggest changes, start with:
  You could add . . .
  This would be clearer if . . .
  What do you mean when you say . . .?

3 **Make Your Changes** Think about your group's comments and questions. Then make changes to improve your essay. Use the marks for revising your writing.

I am so tired of all the damage to our beautiful
                    mean things about people
school. Students write on the walls. They ought to
          how this makes ∧ feel
think about ∧ other students.
            ∧

   They should also think about how damage makes

our school look ~~sometimes~~. I think you will agree

that we want to be proud of our building (always).

Revising Marks

∧	Add.
↶	Move to here.
⋏	Replace with this.
⌣	Take out.

Think About Your Writing

- Do you like your first and last sentence?

- Did you persuade your readers to help with the problem?

- Do you like the way your essay sounds now?

> **GRAMMAR IN CONTEXT**

VERB TENSE

The tense of a verb shows when an action happens.

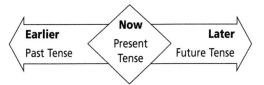

- The **present tense** of a verb tells about an action that is happening now.

    Example: Leon **cleans** the wall.

  A present tense verb can also tell about something that happens all the time.

    Example: Leon **goes** to our middle school.

- The **past tense** of a verb tells about an action that happened earlier, or in the past.

    Examples: Some kids **painted** pictures on the wall.
    They **wrote** on it, too.

- The **future tense** of a verb tells about an action that will happen later, or in the future.

    Examples: We **will help** Leon.
    All of us **are going to clean** the wall.

- The word **won't** also shows future tense. **Won't** is a contraction of the words **will** and **not.**

    Example: We **won't** finish today.

Practice Write each sentence. Choose the correct verb.

1. Ms. Vega ___works / worked___ in the school library every day.
2. Last week she ___will see / saw___ many damaged books.
3. Tomorrow, she ___will speak / spoke___ to us about the books.
4. She ___asked / is going to ask___ us to help.
5. Bill ___will tape / taped___ the torn pages.
6. I ___am going to fix / fix___ the backs of the books.
7. Last year, I also ___will help / helped___ in the school library.
8. It ___felt / won't feel___ good to do something for my school.

Writing That Persuades, continued

EDIT AND PROOFREAD

1 **Proofread Your Essay** When you find a mistake in capitalization, punctuation, or spelling, correct it. See pages 431–439 of the Handbook for help. Use the Proofreading Marks.

2 **Check Verb Tenses** Did you use present, past, and future tenses correctly?

3 **Make a Final Copy** If you are working on a computer, print out a final copy of your work. If not, rewrite it and make the corrections you marked.

PUBLISH

Choose one of these ideas for sharing your essay.

- Tape your essay to a poster. Draw pictures around it.

- Make a video presentation. Videotape students cleaning up graffiti, for example. Edit the tape. Read your essay like a news reporter and show your video.

Proofreading Marks

∧	Add.
⩍	Add a comma.
⊙	Add a period.
≡	Capitalize.
/	Make lowercase.
⌣	Take out.
¶	Indent.

Think About Your Writing

- Do you think your essay is effective?
  - ☑ Did you state the problem and your opinion about it?
  - ☑ Did you tell why there is a problem?
  - ☑ Did you tell what action your readers should take?
  - ☑ Did you use persuasive words?
- Will this essay go in your portfolio? Why or why not?

Communities Count

1 Look Back at the Unit

Rank Communities In this unit, you read about many communities.

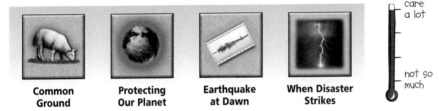

Common Ground	Protecting Our Planet	Earthquake at Dawn	When Disaster Strikes

care a lot

not so much

Work with a partner. Draw a large thermometer. Mark a place for each selection. If the selection made you think or care more about your own community, mark it near the top. If the selection did not make you think about your community, put it near the bottom.

2 Show What You Know

Sum It All Up Add new ideas to your mind map about community. Tell a partner about the community that is the most important to you.

Geographical

Community

Organizations

Special interests

Reflect and Evaluate Finish this sentence:
• The most important community is _____.

Add the sentence to your portfolio. Choose work from the unit that shows what you learned.

3 Make Connections

To Your Community Host a science assembly at your school. Invite scientists to talk about natural disasters or the environment. Give reports and make displays. Invite other classes and people in your community to attend.

Ulysses and the Sirens, 4th century CE, mosaic tile.

STORIES TO TELL

THIS ART FROM ANCIENT GREECE SHOWS A SCENE FROM
A STORY. WHAT DO YOU THINK THE STORY IS ABOUT?
HOW CAN YOU TELL THAT THE STORY IS VERY OLD?
WORK WITH A PARTNER OR SMALL GROUP TO MAKE
UP THE STORY. WHAT DID YOU LEARN ABOUT STORIES
AND STORYTELLING?

Ad Marginem, Paul Klee, oil on canvas, 1930.

In the Beginning

- Why did ancient peoples use stories to explain how things happen?

- What makes the stories of one culture different from the stories of another culture?

- What do stories tell you about the traditions and beliefs of a culture?

THEME-RELATED BOOKS

Coyote: a Trickster Tale from the American Southwest
by Gerald McDermott

An amusing tale that tells why Coyote is the color of dust and has a burnt tip on his tail.

Why Rat Comes First
by Clara Yen

The story of how Rat wins a contest and becomes the first of 12 animals in the Chinese calendar.

ANTHOLOGY

Creation: Read-Aloud Stories from Many Lands
retold by Ann Pilling

Stories from around the world explain the wonders of Earth and its creatures.

Build Language and Vocabulary

DESCRIBE

Listen to this rap about the gods and goddesses of ancient Greece.

ZEUS AND HERA

ATHENA

ARES

APHRODITE

GAIA

THE MOUNT OLYMPUS RAP

In the beginning there was one great abyss,
    and Chaos formed the earth and heaven out of this.
Then Earth Mother Gaia had her babies like mad.
    The twelve giant Titans were the children she had.
One Titan named Cronus was the father of Zeus.
    His five other children were soon on the loose.
Mount Olympus was home to the family of gods.
    They sometimes got along, but were often at odds.
After Zeus married Hera, life was never a bore.
    She had a son, Ares, the god of war.
Wise Athena was also a charmer.
    She protected Greek cities and wore a suit of armor.
Aphrodite was the goddess of love and flowers.
    The countryside bloomed because of her powers.
Today, we tell stories of these gods from the past.
    As long as we remember them, they'll last and last.

—Anne Miranda

CHAOS

CRONUS

MAKE A CHARACTER CHART

Work with the group to list all the characters in the poem on a chart. Also record what each character did. Follow this model:

Name	What Character Did	
Chaos	formed earth and heaven	
Gaia	had the 12 Titans	

Word Bank

BUILD YOUR VOCABULARY

Describing Words Look at the pictures of the gods and goddesses on page 266. Think of a word to describe each one, or choose one from the **Word Bank**. Add a third column to your chart. In it, write a word to describe each character:

Name	What Character Did	What Character Was Like
Chaos	formed earth and heaven	powerful
Gaia	had the 12 Titans	strong

Word Bank

beautiful
big
dark
fierce
powerful
strong
tall
ugly

USE LANGUAGE STRUCTURES ▶ COMPLETE SENTENCES

Writing: Describe Greek Gods Choose a Greek god or goddess. Use the information from the character chart to write two complete sentences. Tell what the god or goddess did, and what he or she was like. Be sure each sentence includes a subject and a predicate.

Example:
Athena protected Greek cities. She was powerful.

Greek myth retold
by Antonia Barber

Prepare to Read

THINK ABOUT WHAT YOU KNOW

Quickwrite Choose something in nature, such as thunder, fire, or the ocean. Write why or how you think it came to be. Give a real or imaginary explanation. Share your ideas with the class.

adorable Something is **adorable** when it is pretty and delightful.

attendant An **attendant** is someone who serves another person.

disrespectful You are **disrespectful** when you are rude or impolite.

echo You hear an **echo** when you hear the same sound repeated many times in a row.

pine When you **pine** for something, you feel sad and sick because you want it.

repeat When you **repeat** something, you say it again.

took pity If you **took pity** on someone, you felt sorry for that person.

wept When you **weep**, you cry. **Wept** is the past tense of *weep*.

wood nymph In Greek myths, a **wood nymph** is a spirit that lives in the forest and looks like a beautiful young woman.

LEARN KEY VOCABULARY

Relate Words Study the new words. Then work with a partner to connect pairs of words in the list. Explain why they go together.

> **Example:**
>
> ___Echo___ and ___repeat___ go together
>
> because ___an echo repeats a sound___.

LEARN TO MONITOR YOUR READING

When you **monitor your reading**, you make sure that you understand the selection as you read.

> **READING STRATEGY**
> **How to Monitor Your Reading**
> 1. **Preview** the selection. Ask yourself: What will the selection be about?
> 2. **Visualize** the events as you read. Ask yourself: What pictures does the story make me see?
> 3. **Clarify** the meaning of words. Ask yourself: What words go together? How are the words used in a sentence?
> 4. **Paraphrase** the selection. Ask yourself: How can I retell the selection in my own words?

Monitor your reading as you read "Echo and Narcissus" and the article on ancient Greece.

Echo & Narcissus

a Greek myth retold by Antonia Barber

Long ago people made up stories to explain things they did not understand. This story tells how the narcissus flower came to be—and why we hear echoes.

ECHO IS PUNISHED

The queen of the gods gets angry with Echo for talking too much. To punish her, the queen allows Echo to only repeat other people's words.

*H*era was the queen of the gods. Among her many **attendants** was a **lovely wood nymph** named **Echo**. Hera **was very fond of her**. But the little nymph talked too much, and Hera grew tired of the sound of her voice. What was worse, Echo always tried to **have the last word**. That was **disrespectful** to the queen of the gods. It was also very **irritating**.

One day, Hera **could bear it no longer**. "You shall have the last word," she told Echo angrily. "But you shall have no other. And the last word you have shall not be your own." From that moment, Echo was unable to speak unless she **repeated** words already spoken.

The poor nymph **pined** until she became a thin shadow. She left her companions and **roamed** the lonely valleys, where her **faint** voice could sometimes be heard repeating the calls of happier mortals.

---

lovely beautiful, pretty
was very fond of her liked her a lot
have the last word be the person who said the last thing in a conversation, have a clever answer
irritating annoying, bothersome

could bear it no longer was very upset, lost her patience
roamed walked around
faint weak, quiet

BEFORE YOU MOVE ON...

1. **Main Idea and Details** This story explains how two things came to be. What are these two things?

2. **Character** Echo thought Narcissus was cruel and heartless. How would you describe him? Explain your answer.

3. **Comparisons** How is the goddess Hera different from the wood nymph Echo? Explain your answer.

And poor Echo replied, "My love! . . . my love!"

Narcissus died beside the pool, but Aphrodite, goddess of love and of flowers, **took pity** on the lovely boy. Where he **had lain**, a new flower sprang up, a flower with white and golden petals, which to this day we call the narcissus.

....

had lain had put his body on the ground

ABOUT THE AUTHOR

Antonia Barber is the author of more than 25 books for readers of all ages. *Apollo and Daphne* is her sixteenth book. She believes that young people need to know about myths because they are part of our cultural heritage. People who are not aware of these stories will not understand many things in art and literature. Myths are the author's favorite stories. For her, the characters are not separate from ordinary life because their stories are about things that we all experience. Antonia Barber lives in Kent, England.

LIFE IN ANCIENT GREECE

an article by Shirleyann Costigan

THE GREEK CITY-STATES

Ancient Greece was not a country. It was a group of many **territories** separated by sea and mountains. These territories were called city-states. The people in each city-state **formed** their own government. They lived off their own land. They sometimes fought with other city-states. Even so, all the people of these city-states were Greeks. They **shared** the same language. They believed in many of the same gods. They held a deep love for beauty. Most of all, they firmly believed in **personal liberty** and **public laws**.

territories areas of land, each with its own government

formed created, made

shared all used

personal liberty each person's rights and freedoms

public laws the laws that people in the land must follow

In the 5th Century BCE, one Greek city-state rose above the others. It was Athens (far left), a beautiful city named for Athena, the Goddess of Wisdom (left).

THE GREEK SYSTEM OF JUSTICE

The Greeks believed that gods and goddesses lived **atop** Mount Olympus in Northern Greece. In Greek myths, these powerful gods controlled the lives of people. Sometimes, the gods even punished humans, as Hera punished Narcissus. The punishment of the gods was often **harsh and unpredictable**.

In reality, the ancient Greeks believed in order and fairness. They had laws for all people to follow. They had courts to punish people who broke the laws. They even created a system that allowed people to choose their leaders by voting. This system of government was called *demokratia*, meaning "the rule of the people." The first democratic system of government began in Athens around 500 BCE. The United States' democratic system of government is **based on** ancient Greek democracy.

GREEK LAW

- was based on what the people decided
- could be changed only by the people's vote
- protected the life and **property** of all citizens.

"Our constitution is called a democracy because power is in the hands of the whole people...everyone is equal before the law."

—Pericles, statesman, 5th Century, BCE

Bust of Pericles

....

atop on top of
harsh and unpredictable hard and always changing
In reality In everyday life
based on created from
property belongings

BEFORE YOU MOVE ON...

1. **Generalization** What were the gods and goddesses of ancient Greece like?
2. **Comparisons** How are the governments of Greece and the United States alike?
3. **Inference** What does *democracy* mean?

Respond to the Myth and Article
Check Your Understanding

SUM IT UP

Identify Important Information What are the main events of the myth? What did you learn about ancient Greece? Make and complete a chart like this:

Visualize	The selections made me see pictures of:
Clarify	I learned these important words:
Paraphrase	The selections were mostly about:

Make Judgments Write statements from the selections. Then write whether you agree or disagree and why.

Example:

"Echo always tried to have the last word. That was disrespectful to the queen of the gods."

I don't think Echo was disrespectful. She just liked to talk too much.

THINK IT OVER

Discuss Talk about these questions with a partner.

1. **Comparisons** How is Echo's love for Narcissus like Narcissus' love for himself?

2. **Opinion** Which character do you like the most in the story? Explain your answer.

3. **Inference** Pericles said, "Everyone is equal before the law." What did he mean?

EXPRESS YOURSELF

▶ EXPRESS OPINIONS; DESCRIBE

Pretend that you are talking to Hera. Do you agree with how she treated Echo and Narcissus? Describe her actions in your own words. Then tell Hera how you feel about her actions. Tell her how you think she should behave in the future. Present your speech to the group.

Language Arts and Content Area Connections

▶ GRAMMAR IN CONTEXT

USE COMPLETE SENTENCES

Learn About Subjects and Predicates Every complete sentence has two main parts, the subject and the predicate.

The **subject** tells whom or what the sentence is about. The `complete subject` includes all the words that tell about the subject.

> `The Ancient Greeks` lived in city-states.

The **predicate** tells what the subject is, has, or does. The `complete predicate` includes all the words in the predicate.

> Citizens `voted for their rulers.`

Create Complete Sentences Make up a sentence. Write the complete subject on one card and the complete predicate on another card. Trade your predicate card with a partner. Write a subject to go with it. Then compare your sentence with your partner's original sentence.

Practice Write each sentence. Add a subject or a predicate to make a complete sentence.

1. Each city-state _____.

2. _____ believed in order and fairness.

3. The Greeks _____.

4. _____ is based on *demokratia*.

▶ WRITING/SPEAKING

WRITE A NEW ENDING FOR A MYTH

Write a different ending for "Echo and Narcissus." Will Hera change her mind? Will Echo and Narcissus ever fall in love? Share your story with the class.

▶ SOCIAL STUDIES

COMPARE GOVERNMENTS

Copy and complete the chart. Use the article to find information about ancient Greece. Do research in the library or on the Internet to find information about the United States.

Democracy in Ancient Greece and in the U.S.A.

Questions	Ancient Greece	United States
When did democracy begin?	Democracy began around 500 BCE.	Democracy began in 1776.
Where do the people live?		
How do they choose leaders?		
How are people punished?		

Learn how to do **research**.
See Handbook pages 366–370.

Build Language and Vocabulary

MAKE COMPARISONS

Listen to this traditional song. How does the Chinese peasant feel?

Peasant's Song

At sunup to work,

Sundown to rest,

Eating off the fields I plow—

The Emperor and his might—what are they to me?

—*traditional Chinese peasant's song*

MAKE A COMPARISON CHART

In traditional China, peasants had a hard life working the land. The Emperor had a much easier life in the palace. Brainstorm differences between the life of the peasants and the Emperor. Record them on a chart like this:

Peasants	Emperor
grew food	in charge of government
did hard work	had servants to do work
had simple clothing	had fancy clothing

BUILD YOUR VOCABULARY

Antonyms Words that have opposite meanings are called *antonyms*. Work with a partner to find pairs of antonyms in the **Word Bank**. Add the words to the comparison chart.

Word Bank

educated
fat
hungry
poor
rich
thin
uneducated
well-fed

USE LANGUAGE STRUCTURES ▶ COMPOUND SENTENCES

Writing: Compare the Peasants and the Emperor Use the information on the comparison chart to make comparisons. Write compound sentences and join your ideas with one of these words: *or*, *and*, or *but*.

> **Example:**
> The peasants were thin, **but** the Emperor was fat.
> The peasants grew the food, **and** the Emperor ate it.
> The peasants worked for the Emperor, **or** the Emperor punished them.

Ox Star

Chinese myth retold
by Lily Toy Hong

Prepare to Read

THINK ABOUT WHAT YOU KNOW

Brainstorm Imagine that you are a farmer. How do you work your fields? How do you harvest your crops? Show your ideas on a mind map.

blessing

crop

harvest time

labor

peasant

plow

sundown

sunup

thick

LEARN KEY VOCABULARY

Locate and Use Definitions Find the definition for each word in the Glossary. Then use the web to write a paragraph about the ox.

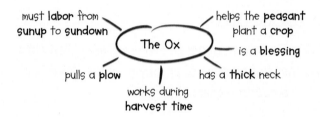

LEARN ABOUT FICTION AND NONFICTION

Fiction and nonfiction are kinds of literature. In **fiction**, the events are from the author's imagination. In **nonfiction**, the events are from real life.

READING STRATEGY
How to Recognize Fiction and Nonfiction

1. To identify fiction, look for imaginary characters and events. There is a sequence from beginning to end.
2. To identify nonfiction, look for facts about real people or events.
3. Preview the selection to see if it is fiction or nonfiction. Fiction is for entertainment. You can read it quickly. Nonfiction is for information. You should read it slowly and carefully.

Read "How the Ox Star Fell from Heaven" and the article. Look for clues to help you recognize if the selections are fiction or nonfiction.

How the Ox Star Fell from Heaven

by Lily Toy Hong

This ancient Chinese story tells about a message that gets mixed up. It also explains why people use oxen to help grow crops for food.

LIFE ABOVE AND BELOW

Long ago, the Emperor had an easy life up in the heavens. Down on Earth, the life of the peasants was hard.

In the beginning, oxen did not live on Earth. They could only be found in **the heavens**, among the stars. They lived with the Emperor of All the Heavens in his Imperial Palace.

Clothed in robes of the finest **silk**, they **reclined** on **billowy** clouds. They never had to work, and their lives were easy.

Life on Earth was hard, especially hard since oxen did not live here. Farmers had no **beast of burden** to help with the planting of vegetables and rice in the spring, or with the gathering of **crops** at **harvest time**.

People were always tired and hungry. They **labored** from **sunup** to **sundown**, yet they could never finish all their work.

Because there was so little food, they sometimes went three, four, even five days without **one single meal**.

....

the heavens the sky
silk soft, shiny cloth
reclined leaned back, rested
billowy soft and fluffy
beast of burden animal used for heavy work
one single meal one meal to eat, anything to eat

BEFORE YOU MOVE ON...

1. **Details** What made life on Earth difficult for the farmers?

2. **Comparisons** How were the lives of the oxen and the humans different?

3. **Prediction** This story describes what life was like "in the beginning." How do you think the story may change by the end?

2

A MESSAGE FROM THE EMPEROR

The Emperor decides to make life a little easier for the peasants, but his messenger, Ox Star, mixes up an important message.

The Emperor of All the Heavens had not forgotten the Earth, however. He knew that the poor **peasants** worked long and hard, and he believed that they should be able to eat every third day. With this in mind, he **issued a decree**: "The people of Earth shall eat at least once every three days!"

He called upon his most **trusted** messenger, the Ox Star, to **deliver the message**. Dressed in a magnificent silk robe and a golden crown, the Ox Star **set off on** the long and lonely journey down to Earth.

When he arrived, all the peasants hurried out to meet him. "I come with a message from the Emperor of All the Heavens," he bellowed. But the Ox Star, while strong, was not very smart. He **twisted** the Emperor's words: "The Emperor has **declared** that you shall eat three times a day, every day!" The peasants cheered and cheered.

---

issued a decree announced a new law
trusted honest and dependable
deliver the message tell them about the law, take the message to the peasants
set off on began
twisted mixed up
declared said, announced

BEFORE YOU MOVE ON...

1. **Details** What was the Ox Star's job in the heavens?

2. **Judgment** Do you think the Emperor's new law was a good law? Why or why not?

3. **Cause and Effect** How did the Ox Star change the Emperor's message? What did this change mean for the peasants?

A HELPFUL MISTAKE

The Emperor punishes Ox Star for his mistake. The Ox's life becomes
harder, but the life of the peasants becomes a little easier.

The Emperor of All the Heavens
heard his messenger's **mistake** and was
angry. When the Ox Star arrived back at
the Imperial Palace, he found the gates
were locked. His princely robe and royal
crown **vanished**. "Since you have

betrayed my trust," the Emperor
roared, "you shall never again be
allowed in the heavens." The sky filled
with lightning and thunder, and the
Ox Star wept.

Suddenly everything turned dark. In
a **whirlwind**, the Ox Star was hurried
through the stormy sky. Down, down,
down to Earth he fell.

From that day, the Ox Star became a
beast of burden, helping farmers. Around
his **thick** neck he wore a heavy yoke,
and through his nose he wore a ring.

The other oxen were sent to Earth,
too. They labored day after day in the
fields, pulling **plows** through the ground
at planting time and helping to gather the
crops at harvest time.

---

mistake error, (something that is wrong or incorrect)
vanished went away, disappeared
betrayed my trust shown me that I cannot count
on you

roared yelled
whirlwind strong wind, a spinning wind

Today, because of the Ox Star's **ill fortune** and his **careless mistake**, a bit of heaven **remains** on Earth. For those who have an ox, good soil, and enough rain, life is not as hard as it once was. Best of all, they can eat warm rice, **tender** vegetables, and Chinese sweet cakes three times a day, every day!

Now when you look up at the night sky, so beautiful and bright, think of the Ox Star, who fell from the heavens, and of his **blunder**, which became a **blessing**.

BEFORE YOU MOVE ON...

1. **Comparisons** What were the Ox Star's clothes like when he lived in the heavens? How did they change when he fell to Earth?
2. **Cause and Effect** In your own words, explain what caused the Ox Star to fall from the heavens to Earth.
3. **Summary** How did the Ox Star's blunder become a blessing for the peasants?

ill fortune bad luck
careless mistake error caused by not being careful
remains stays
tender soft, not tough or hard
blunder mistake

ABOUT THE AUTHOR

Lily Toy Hong grew up as one of nine children. From the time she was a child, she wanted to write books for young people. Here is her message to her readers: "I was delighted when I found the myth about how oxen came to Earth. It was a joy for me to turn it into a book for young readers. My parents are from China, but I was born in America. This story helps me to better understand my family roots. It also explains why I love to eat rice three times a day!"

Ancient China during the Zhou
Dynasty, 1050 BCE–256 CE

A Peasant's Life in
ANCIENT CHINA

an article by Shirleyann Costigan

Life was never easy for the peasant farmers of ancient China. They worked the earth, planted, and **harvested** the crops by hand. It was slow, **backbreaking** work. Around 700 BCE, many farmers began to use oxen or water buffalo to pull the plows and seed the fields. **Food production increased**. Everyone ate better. Life got a little easier, but not by much.

Most peasants lived in small villages near the **manor houses** of their **lords**. Their small huts were made of **packed earth** with dirt floors. Peasants rented the land they lived and worked on. They gave a large part of every crop to **their landlord**. They paid taxes to the Emperor. For the most part, they lived simply, died quietly, and in time were forgotten.

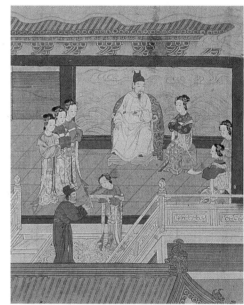

In ancient China, the lords and scholars lived in big houses and dressed in silks. They depended on the peasant farmers for all their needs, but they did not do much to make the peasants' lives easier.

harvested collected, gathered
backbreaking physically hard
Food production increased. They grew more crops.
manor houses large houses for the rich, mansions

lords rulers
packed earth dirt that is pressed together to make solid walls
their landlord the person who owned the land

Emperor
the Son of Heaven

Lords & Scholars
rulers of the land

Knights
protectors of the land

Peasants
workers of the land

CLASSES OF SOCIETY IN ANCIENT CHINA, 700 BCE

There were three classes of people under the Emperor of ancient China. The people of each class had a place to fill in the Chinese order of life. The order rarely changed.

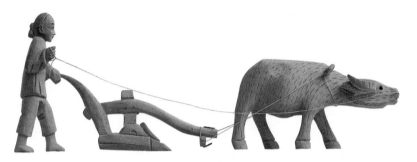

Peasant farmers worked from sunup to sundown all year long. They also had to work on roads and canals that ran through the countryside.

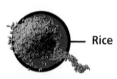
Rice

Peasants grew their own food, as well as food for the ruling classes. Rice, soybeans, and millet were all common crops.

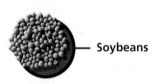
Soybeans

Millet

BEFORE YOU MOVE ON...

1. **Evidence and Conclusion** How did the oxen help the farmers produce more crops?

2. **Comparisons** How were the lives of the peasants and the lords different?

3. **Details** The peasants ate what they grew. What are some examples of this?

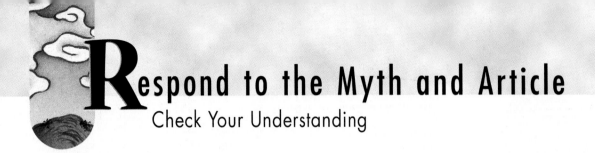

Respond to the Myth and Article
Check Your Understanding

SUM IT UP

Identify a Sequence of Events Make a sequence chart for the myth.

Sequence Chart

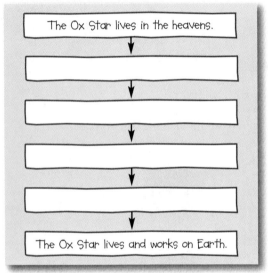

The Ox Star lives in the heavens.

↓

↓

↓

↓

The Ox Star lives and works on Earth.

Compare Literature The myth about the Ox Star is fiction, but some parts of the story are based on facts. Make a list of events in the story that agree with facts from the article.

Oxen still help farmers in Asia work their fields.

THINK IT OVER

Discuss Talk about these questions with a partner.

1. **Character's Motive** Why didn't the Emperor send the Ox Star back with the correct message?

2. **Comparisons** How is the Emperor like Hera in "Echo and Narcissus"?

3. **Opinion** Would you want to live in ancient China? Explain why or why not.

4. **Personal Experience** Think about a time that you made a mistake. Were the results good or bad?

EXPRESS YOURSELF ▶ NEGOTIATE

Work with a partner. Role-play a conversation between the Ox Star and the Emperor. The Ox Star can:

- try to show the Emperor another way to fix his mistake
- suggest a better punishment or solution
- explain how he feels about living on Earth.

Language Arts and Literature

▶ GRAMMAR IN CONTEXT

USE COMPLETE SENTENCES

Learn About Subjects and Predicates Every complete sentence has two main parts, the subject and the predicate.

The **simple subject** is the most important word in the **complete subject**. It tells whom or what the sentence is about.

> The poor **peasants** labored all day.

The **simple predicate** is the most important word in the **complete predicate**. It is the verb.

> The rulers **lived** in big houses.

Identify Simple Subjects and Predicates

Write a sentence about ancient China. Trade your work with a partner. Circle the simple subject. Underline the verb. Compare your sentences.

Practice Write each sentence. Add a simple subject on each green line. Add a verb on each blue line.

1. Most _____ slept in small huts.

2. They _____ hard in the fields.

3. Farmers _____ taxes to the Emperor.

4. The _____ in ancient China lived quietly.

▶ LITERARY ANALYSIS

▶ WRITING

COMPARE MYTHS IN AN ESSAY

Write an essay to compare the two myths in this unit. Follow these steps.

① **Prewrite** Make a T-chart like this:

Similarities	Differences
Both myths tell how something in nature came to be.	"Echo" happens in ancient Greece, but "Ox Star" happens in ancient China.

② **Write a Draft** Include these paragraphs:

- Write an **introduction** to tell what your essay is about.

- Write a paragraph to show how the two myths are alike.

- Write a paragraph to show how the two myths are different.

- Write a **conclusion** to sum up your essay.

③ **Revise Your Work** Think of ways to improve your essay. Ask a classmate or a teacher for ideas. Then write a better, final draft.

Learn how to improve your writing in the **writer's craft**. See Handbook pages 390–401.

Respond to the Myth and Article, continued

Language Arts and Literature, continued

USE COMPOUND SENTENCES

Learn About Clauses A clause is a group of words with a subject and a verb. An **independent clause** tells a complete thought. It can stand alone as a sentence.

Independent Clauses:
The Emperor lived in the Heavens
The peasants lived on Earth

Learn About Compound Sentences
A **compound sentence** is made up of two independent clauses. To join the clauses, use a comma and the word **and**, **but**, or **or**.

Compound Sentence:
The Emperor lived in the Heavens, **and** the peasants lived on Earth.

Make up Compound Sentences Work with a partner. Join each pair of independent clauses to make a compound sentence.

- I am a farmer. I push a plow.

- I worked alone. Now I have an ox.

Practice Write compound sentences. Put **and**, **but**, or **or** on the red line. Finish the sentence by adding an independent clause on the black line.

1. The Ox Star was happy, _____ _____ .

2. He had a message, _____ _____ .

3. The Ox Star worked, _____ _____ .

COMPARE FICTION AND NONFICTION

Work with a group to copy and complete a comparison chart. Use "Echo and Narcissus" and "How the Ox Star Fell From Heaven" to fill in the fiction section. Use information from the articles on ancient Greece and ancient China to fill in the nonfiction section.

Story Elements	In Fiction	In Nonfiction
Characters	imaginary people, gods, and animals	
Setting		real place in the real world
Events	did not really happen	
Sequence		events are not in sequence
Author's Purpose	to entertain	

Content Area Connections

STUDY MODERN CHINA

What is life like in China today? Work in a group. Choose a topic like:

farming	culture	languages
geography	holidays	people

1 **Gather Information** Use encyclopedias, maps, and almanacs. Talk to someone who has lived in China. Take notes. Here are some key words and Web sites that may help you get started, but remember that new sites appear every day.

INTERNET

INFORMATION ON-LINE

Key Words:
China
"People's Republic of China"

Web Sites:
➤ **China**
  • www.geographia.com
  • kids.infoplease.com

2 **Prepare a Multimedia Presentation** Work with a team. Think of ways to share what you learned. Think of pictures you found in your research. Think of diagrams, charts, or maps you could show. You may want to download photos for a poster.

Modern and traditional styles are used in the buildings around Hong Kong harbor.

3 **Have a Chinese Celebration** Plan a special day with your class. Decorate the room with Chinese art. Bring food to share. Then watch each group's presentation.

Learn how to make a **multimedia presentation**. See Handbook pages 362–363.

Storyteller statue from Jemez Pueblo, New Mexico, © 1997 Helen Sands.

Telling the Tale

- How has storytelling changed over time? How has it remained the same?

- How do storytellers pass along the history of a culture?

- What techniques can storytellers use to make their tales come alive?

THEME-RELATED BOOKS

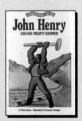

John Henry and His Mighty Hammer
by Patsy Jensen

The story of an American folk hero who splits rock faster than a machine.

Gilgamesh the King
by Ludmila Zeman

In one of the world's oldest stories, Enkidu teaches the evil Gilgamesh how to become a good king.

The Singing Man
by Angela Shelf Medearis

Long ago in West Africa, a young man leaves home to become a musician. He returns years later as the king's singing storyteller.

293

Build Language and Vocabulary

RETELL A STORY

Listen to this story from the Jewish tradition. It has been told for hundreds of years. Here a student, Sarah Ross, tells the story as she learned it from her mother, a professional storyteller.

Sarah Ross tells "King Solomon and the Smell of Bread."

COMPLETE A STORY MAP

Work with the group to complete a story map like this one for "King Solomon and the Smell of Bread." Listen to the story again if you need to.

Story Map

Title: King Solomon and the Smell of Bread

Setting: Ancient Jerusalem

Characters: Baker, poor woman, King Solomon

Problem: Poor woman smells baker's bread. Baker wants to be paid.

Event 1 _____

Event 2 _____

Event 3 _____

Event 4 _____

Solution: _____

BUILD YOUR VOCABULARY

Time Order and Cause Words A signal gives you a clue about something. Some words signal special information in a sentence.

Time order words, such as *after* or *while,* signal when something happens.

Cause words, such as *because* or *since,* signal the reason for something. When you speak or write, you can use words like these to show how ideas go together.

> **Example:**
> The poor woman smelled the bread **because** she could not buy it.
> King Solomon made a decision **after** he talked to the baker and the woman.

In these complex sentences, the words *because* and *after* are **conjunctions**.

Word Bank

Time Order Words

after
before
when
while

Cause Words

because
since

USE LANGUAGE STRUCTURES ▶ COMPLEX SENTENCES

Speaking: Retell a Story Practice telling "King Solomon and the Smell of Bread" with a partner. Use ideas from the story map. Tell your story to the group.

> **Example:**
> The baker was upset **when** the woman smelled the bread.
> The baker took her to court **because** he wanted to get paid.

THE TALL TALE

article and tall tale retold
by Chuck Larkin

Prepare to Read

THINK ABOUT WHAT YOU KNOW

Play "Stretch the Truth" Work with a group to make exaggerated sentences. *The baby was bigger than a bear. No, it was bigger than _____. No, it was bigger than _____.* Play as long as you can.

absolute truth When something is completely true, it is the **absolute truth**.

audience An **audience** is a group of people who watch and listen to a performance.

believable A **believable** event could really happen.

cause A **cause** is something that makes something else happen.

effect An **effect** is something that happens because of something that happened earlier.

exaggerated Something is **exaggerated** when it is bigger and wilder than the truth.

humor When something makes you laugh, it has **humor**.

insist When you **insist** on something, you will not change your mind.

logic When something has **logic**, it makes sense.

outlandish Something is **outlandish** if it is very strange or odd.

LEARN KEY VOCABULARY

Relate Words Study the new words. Then write sentences by combining a beginning from column 1 with an ending from column 2.

Beginning	Ending
1. A **exaggerated** event is	A. and that it is the **absolute truth**.
2. You **insist** that you are not lying	B. the storyteller's **humor**.
3. A rainstorm was the **cause** and	C. funny, but not **believable**.
4. The **audience** laughed at	D. has its own funny **logic**.
5. An **outlandish** tale	E. a flood was the **effect**.

LEARN TO USE GRAPHIC ORGANIZERS

A **graphic organizer** helps you "see" information quickly. Word webs, mind maps, time lines, and charts are graphic organizers.

> ### READING STRATEGY
> #### How to Make a Time Line
> 1. Think of the main events in a story.
> 2. Write the events in order. Use words like *first, after,* and *finally* to help you.
> 3. Draw a line and divide it into parts to show time.
> 4. Write the events in order along the time line.

As you read "Pecos Bill," write the important events. After reading, you can put the events in order to make a time line.

The Art of The Tall Tale

by **Chuck Larkin**

- **Chuck Larkin Talks About His Art**
- **Chuck Larkin Tells the Tale of** *Pecos Bill*

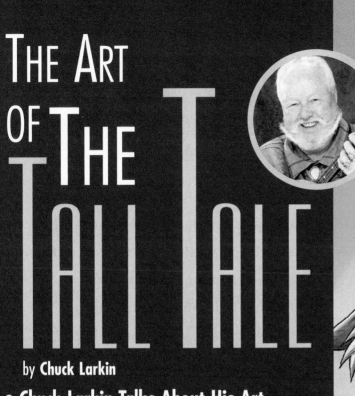

Chuck Larkin Talks About His Art

ABOUT THE AUTHOR

Chuck Larkin loves to tell tall tales. Here's what he has to say about himself: "I was raised in the small town of Pocomoke. Pocomoke is so small that its zip code is a **fraction**. In Pocomoke, the winters were so cold that the **flames** in the fireplace would freeze up **solid**! Momma would **grind up** that frozen fire and we'd **sprinkle** it on our food for red pepper. That's a fact. I was there." Chuck Larkin makes up his own tall tales and also retells classics like "Pecos Bill."

Tall tales are funny stories. They are made up of **exaggerated** events. The events describe a **cause** and an **effect**. The cause is a **believable** event—something that could be true in real life: *Pocomoke was a small town.* But it's followed by an **outlandish** effect: *The zip code is a fraction.* You know that it can't be true, but there is a strange **logic** to it that makes you laugh. Of course, the storyteller **insists** that the story is the **absolute truth**. That just adds to the **humor**.

I always tell about **my personal experiences**. As I always say to my **audience**: "I was there, and I'd walk on my lips before I would tell a lie."

------

fraction number that is less than 1 ($\frac{1}{2}, \frac{1}{4}$, etc.)
flames the burning part of a fire
solid strong and hard
grind up crush, break into small pieces
sprinkle drop a small amount of
my personal experiences things that have happened to me

I have one tale about a giant peach. Storytellers around the country have used it. You can use it, too, to make your own tall tale.

Imagine you had a giant peach. What would you do with it? I decided to take my peach to a festival. I pulled it along the road with 16 mules. When I got to the festival, I stuck a faucet into the side of the peach, turned it on, and sold 1,300 gallons of peach juice! That's a fact. I was there.

Now, read the tall tale of . . .

PECOS BILL

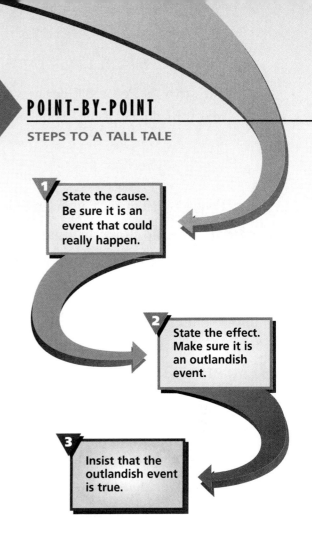

POINT-BY-POINT
STEPS TO A TALL TALE

1 State the cause. Be sure it is an event that could really happen.

2 State the effect. Make sure it is an outlandish event.

3 Insist that the outlandish event is true.

BEFORE YOU MOVE ON...

1. **Author's Purpose** Why does Chuck Larkin say: "Pocomoke is so small that its zip code is a fraction."?

2. **Summary** Describe how to create a tall tale.

3. **Personal Experience** Think of a true event that you could turn into a tall tale. Share your idea with a partner.

THE EARLY LIFE OF PECOS BILL

The story of Pecos Bill begins when he is born in New England during a wild tornado. His family soon moves West, near the Pecos River in Texas.

I'm Pecos Bill. I'm part man and part **coyote**. I've slid down lightning bolts holding wildcats under both arms and never been scratched. I was raised in Texas along the Pecos River, but my life began in New England. I was born while my Ma was **taming a tornado**. Pa had caught the tornado **tearing up** our farm.

After the tornado, we needed a new farm. **My folks** decided to move West. They **hitched up** their wagon to Tillie—that's what Pa named that tornado. Finally, we got to the Pecos River and **settled down**. I was five years old.

My, how I loved that Pecos River! One day I **rigged up** a fishing line and hooked a baby fish that measured about six feet from eye to eye. I held that fishing pole and stepped into the water. That little fish pulled me barefoot down

the river! That's how water skiing got started. I **wound up** so far away from home that I decided to just keep on going.

BEFORE YOU MOVE ON...

1. **Cause and Effect** Why did Bill's family decide to move West?
2. **Character** What were Bill's parents like?
3. **Details** Describe some of the events of Bill's childhood.

---

coyote wild animal, like a dog or wolf
taming a tornado making a wild storm calm and peaceful
tearing up destroying, ruining
my folks my parents

hitched up tied
settled down made our home there
rigged up made, set up
wound up ended up

PECOS BILL GROWS UP

Pecos Bill grows up in the wild with a family of coyotes. One day, he meets Cactus Joe and learns to get honey from bees.

For a while I **lived off the land**, eating rattlesnakes and horned toads. Then I joined a **clan** of coyotes. They **raised me**. Pretty soon, I thought I *was* a coyote.

One day, it was so hot that the shade and I moved under a bush to keep cool. A beekeeper came walking by. He said, "Howdy there. My name's Cactus Joe. What are you doing in the bushes? Where are your clothes?"

I said, "I've been living with the coyotes for years. I outgrew all my clothing." Cactus Joe laughed **mighty** hard at that, and he gave me a blanket to wear 'til I could get some clothes.

After that, I worked with Cactus Joe as a beekeeper. We **herded** honey bees out of their **hives**. We sang beekeeper songs as the bees gathered **nectar**.

BEFORE YOU MOVE ON...

1. **Setting/Vocabulary** Study the text and pictures. Then list things Bill could find to eat in the desert.
2. **Comparisons** How did Bill's life change after he met Cactus Joe?
3. **Author's Style** How does the author use exaggeration to describe a hot day?

---

lived off the land found all my food around the land nearby

clan family with many members and generations

raised me took care of me and helped me grow up

mighty very

herded led, gathered

hives homes made by or for bees

nectar the sweet liquid produced by plants and used by bees to make honey

PECOS BILL BECOMES A COWBOY

Cactus Joe and Pecos Bill become cowboys. They herd cows instead of bees, and begin the first cattle drives in the West.

One day, Cactus Joe found out that **folks** in Kansas wanted their own big Texas cows.

I said, "Let's get ourselves a couple of **cougars** to ride. We can **round up** a bunch of cows and herd them north to Kansas. It can't be much different from herding bees."

So that's what we did. Let me tell you, the horns on those Texas longhorn cows are good for **picking your teeth**! Just make sure you don't use a horn that's **attached to** a cow. Those Texas longhorns have a mighty kick!

After that first cattle drive, other Texas boys decided to herd cattle, too, but they had to ride horses. Horses were easier to **come by** than cougars. Together, we chased those cows from Texas to Kansas and back. And that's how the great **cattle drives** began.

> **BEFORE YOU MOVE ON...**
>
> 1. **Cause and Effect** Why did Bill think that herding cows would be easy?
> 2. **Comparisons** What was one difference between Bill and the other cowboys who herded cows?
> 3. **Character** What are some words you could use to describe Bill?

---

folks people
cougars mountain lions
round up gather
picking your teeth cleaning food from between your teeth

attached to connected to, part of
come by get
cattle drives travels over land with cowboys taking cows from one place to another

Respond to the Tall Tale

Check Your Understanding

SUM IT UP

Identify Sequence Copy and complete this time line to show the events in Pecos Bill's life.

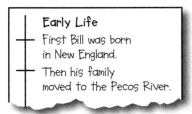

Time Line

Early Life
Ⱶ First Bill was born in New England.
Ⱶ Then his family moved to the Pecos River.

Retell a Story and Synthesize Information

Tell Pecos Bill's story to a partner. Also tell it to your family. Ask them what they thought about the story. Then write sentences that **synthesize**— or put together— your family's ideas.

Example:

My family liked the humor in Pecos Bill's story.

THINK IT OVER

Discuss Talk about these questions with a partner.

1. **Author's Style** What does Chuck Larkin say at the end of his tales? Why does he say that?

2. **Figurative Language** Bill says that the baby fish was "about six feet from eye to eye." What does he mean? How else could you describe a huge fish?

3. **Comparisons** How is a tall tale different from other kinds of stories?

4. **Judgments** Do you like the tall tale style? Explain.

EXPRESS YOURSELF ▶ELABORATE

When you **elaborate**, you add new ideas and details. With a group, change an event in "Pecos Bill" to make it even more unbelievable! Then share your stories with other groups. Think of an outlandish prize for the best story.

Respond to the Tall Tale, continued
Language Arts and Literature

GRAMMAR IN CONTEXT

USE COMPLEX SENTENCES

Learn About Clauses A **clause** is a group of words that has a subject and a verb.

An **independent clause** is a complete sentence.

> Chuck Larkin uses exaggerated events

A **dependent clause** is not a complete sentence.

> when he tells tall tales

Learn About Complex Sentences To make a **complex sentence**, join an independent clause and a dependent clause. Words like **when**, **because**, and **since** signal the dependent clause.

> Chuck exaggerates **because** it adds humor.
> _____   _____
> independent clause   dependent clause

Make Up Complex Sentences Choose one independent clause and one dependent clause to make a complex sentence.

Independent Clauses	Dependent Clauses
Cattle drives began	because he lived alone
Bill was wild	when Bill went to Kansas

Practice Write complex sentences. Put **when**, **because**, or **since** on the red line, then finish the sentence.

1. Bill left his family _____ _____ .

2. Bill ate toads _____ _____ .

3. Bill got a cougar _____ _____ .

WRITING/SPEAKING

WRITE A NEW EPISODE

Add to the tall tale about Pecos Bill.

1 Make a Story Chart Copy and complete the chart with your ideas.

Cause (a realistic event)	Effect (an outlandish event)	Insist that the story is true
Pecos Bill caught a big fish.	The fish pulled him many miles down the river.	That's a fact. I saw it with my own eyes.
Pecos Bill saw an eagle fly by.		
	Pecos Bill made a lasso out of a rattlesnake.	

2 Write Your Episode Include exaggeration, or **hyperbole**, in your writing.

Examples:
The eagle was as big as an airplane.
The rattlesnake was a block long.

3 Share Your Episode Tell the tale with expression. Use a different voice for each character.

Content Area Connections

EXPLORE GEOGRAPHY

Make a Tall Tale Map Start with a map of the United States. Mark the places described in the story. Then label the events that happened to Bill in each place. Look for other tall tales in books at the library or on the Internet.

Find characters like:

- Paul Bunyan
- Annie Christmas
- John Henry
- Mike Fink

On your map, find and label the places where these new stories happen.

SCIENCE

TECHNOLOGY/MEDIA

STUDY WILD ANIMALS

Research an animal of the Wild West:

| rattlesnake | coyote | cougar |
| mustang | buffalo | horned toad |

Find Information Use books or the Internet. Use the animal's name as a key word for your search. Try these Web sites, but remember that new sites appear every day!

INTERNET

INFORMATION ON-LINE

Web Sites:
➤ **Animals**
  - www.AllAboutNature.com/coloring
  - www.desertusa.com

Take notes about where the animal lives, what it eats, and other interesting facts.

Write a Report Describe your animal. Add photos, illustrations, and other art.

 Learn how to write a **research report**. See Handbook pages 366–372.

Build Language and Vocabulary

TELL AN ORIGINAL STORY

View the pictures and listen to the beginning of a story.

DISCUSS STORY EPISODES

Who else did the boy talk to? What else did he get? Look at the pictures on page 306 and share your ideas with a partner.

BUILD YOUR VOCABULARY

Story Words Every story happens in a time and a place. That is called the **setting**. The people or animals in a story are called the **characters**. The **goal** is what the character is trying to get or do. The **outcome** is what happens at the end of the story. It tells you if the goal was met. Fill in information about "The Boy Who Looked for the Wind" on a chart like this. Add your own ideas for the outcome of this story.

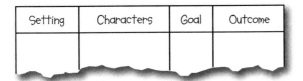

Setting	Characters	Goal	Outcome

USE LANGUAGE STRUCTURES ▶ PRESENT PERFECT TENSE

Speaking: Tell a Story Use the information on your chart to tell your version of "The Boy Who Looked for the Wind." Practice with a partner, then tell your story to the group.

Example:
    Once upon a time, a boy who lived in the country went looking for the wind. "Have you seen the wind?" he asked everyone he met.

Magic Thread

article and Haitian folk tale
retold by Diane Wolkstein

Prepare to Read

THINK ABOUT WHAT YOU KNOW

Make a Storytelling Web Storytellers use techniques like elaboration, sequence, and hyperbole. Write more storytelling techniques on a word web.

expression Your **expression** is the way you make your face look. Smiling is an **expression** that shows happiness.

familiar Things you know well are **familiar**.

full attention You give your **full attention** when you watch and listen carefully.

gesture A **gesture** is a movement you make with your hands and arms.

inventiveness The ability to think up new things is called **inventiveness**.

present **Present** means at this time.

respond When you answer back, you **respond**.

talent When you have a **talent** for something, you do it well.

LEARN KEY VOCABULARY

Relate Words Study the new words. With a group, use vocabulary words to complete this sentence: *Talented storytellers can . . .* Make a new sentence for each vocabulary word.

> **Example:**
> Talented storytellers can show **inventiveness**.

LEARN TO RELATE GOALS AND OUTCOMES

In many stories, the character's **goal** is to have or do something. The **outcome** tells if the goal is reached. When you relate the goals and outcomes in a story, you will know the most important ideas.

> ### READING STRATEGY
> **How to Relate Goals and Outcomes**
> 1. Read the beginning of the story.
> 2. Think about what the character wants to do or have.
> 3. Ask yourself: What does the character need to do to reach the goal?
> 4. Read the rest of the story to find the outcome.

As you read "Owl," find goals and outcomes for the characters.

UNWINDING the MAGIC THREAD

STORYTELLING IN HAITI

by Diane Wolkstein

- Diane Wolkstein Talks About Haitian Storytelling
- Diane Wolkstein Tells the Tale of *Owl*

DIANE WOLKSTEIN TELLS ABOUT THE MAGIC THREAD

"*Cric?*" the Haitian storyteller calls out. "*Crac!*" the audience answers if they want the storyteller to begin. If they do not **respond** with *crac*, the storyteller cannot begin.

"*Cric?*" another storyteller calls out, hoping for the **welcoming** "*crac!*" If the listeners cry *crac!*, they **are expected to** give their **full attention** to the storyteller. They will listen to hear that the story is told correctly. They will **comment on** the events and characters of the stories. They will comment on the storyteller's **talents**. As soon as a song within a story begins, the listeners will join in. I have heard groups **joyously** sing the **chorus** of a song ten or twenty times.

Storytelling in Haiti takes place in the plains, mountains, and countryside. When the adults are not too tired, and especially when the moon is full, families gather on their steps to talk and **gossip**. Soon someone may think of a story. *Cric?*

In moments, others may join the family: friends, neighbors, teenagers, children, and toddlers. Many are ready to tell a story, so the storytellers must

---

welcoming encouraging, friendly
are expected to must, are supposed to
comment on talk about
joyously happily

chorus repeating part
gossip tell about what's happening in the lives of other people

compete for a chance. A storyteller will call out *cric?* But perhaps someone else has already called out *cric?* Then the audience must decide who will be the next one to **unwind the magic thread of the story**.

Most of the stories are well-known. Each story has its own **familiar** set of **gestures** and **expressions**. What is most exciting to see is the **inventiveness** of the storyteller. Everyone may know the tale, but they are **eager** to see what the storyteller will give to it this time.

It is my hope that you, my reader, will turn the page and **bite into the strange fruit of the Haitian night**; that your **present** world will **dissolve**; that you will **be possessed by** the mysterious world of the story.

Let's begin the story of

Cric?

Crac!

BEFORE YOU MOVE ON...

1. **Steps in a Process** In your own words, describe the steps for telling a story in Haiti.

2. **Comparisons** How is Haitian storytelling different from reading a book aloud?

3. **Evidence and Conclusion** In Haiti, the audience is as important as the storyteller. What are some ways that the audience becomes a part of the storytelling?

---

compete for try to win
unwind the magic thread of the story tell a story
eager wanting very much

bite into the strange fruit of the Haitian night enjoy an unusual story told at night in Haiti
dissolve melt away, disappear
be possessed by become a part of

OWL FALLS IN LOVE

Owl and a young woman fall in love. Owl is afraid to visit during the day.
He believes the woman will think he's ugly if she sees his face in the daylight.

Owl thought he was **very ugly**. One evening he met a girl and talked with her and she liked him. "If it had been day," Owl thought, "and she had seen my face, she never would have liked me." Still, she had liked him.

So Owl went to her house the next night. And the next. And the night after that. Every evening he would **arrive at** the girl's house at seven, and they would sit outside on the porch steps, talking together **politely**.

Then one evening after Owl had left, the girl's mother said to her, "Why doesn't **your fiancé** come and visit you during the day?"

"But Mama, he's explained that to me. He works during the day. Then he must go home and **change** and he cannot get here before seven."

"Still, I would like to see his face before the marriage," the mother said. "Let's invite him to our house for a dance this Sunday afternoon. Surely he doesn't work on Sunday."

---

very ugly not very good-looking
arrive at come to
politely nicely, in a respectful or courteous way
your fiancé the man you are engaged to marry
change put on clean clothing

Owl was very pleased with the invitation: a dance **in his honor**. He was also very **frightened**. He told his cousin, Rooster, about the girl and asked him to **accompany** him to the dance. That Sunday afternoon, as Owl and Rooster were riding on their horses to the dance, Owl **glanced** over at Rooster. Rooster **held himself with such assurance**, he was so elegantly and fashionably dressed, that Owl imagined the girl seeing the two of them and **was filled with shame**.

"I can't go on," he choked. "You go and tell them I've had an accident and will be there later."

Rooster rode to the dance. "Tsk tsk, poor Owl," he explained. "He has had an accident, and he has asked me to let you know that he will be here later."

---

in his honor especially for him

frightened afraid, scared

accompany go with

glanced looked quickly

held himself with such assurance felt so comfortable about himself

was filled with shame became embarrassed, felt badly about himself

---

BEFORE YOU MOVE ON...

1. **Character's Motive** Why didn't Owl want to visit the girl during the day?
2. **Prediction** What do you think the girl will do if she sees what Owl looks like? Why?
3. **Inference** How did Owl feel about going to the dance? Why?

OWL GOES TO THE PARTY

Owl arrives at the party, hiding his head under a hat. Owl's fiancée is pleased to see how well he dances, but Owl is worried that people will see his face.

When it was quite dark, Owl tied his horse **a good distance** from the dance and **stumbled** up to the porch steps. "Pssst," he whispered to a young man sitting on the steps. "Is Rooster here?"

"Well now, I don't know."

"Go and look. Tell him a friend is waiting for him by **the mapou tree**."

Rooster came out. "OWL!"

"Shhhhhh—"

"Owl!"

"Shhh—"

"Owl, what are you wearing over your head—I mean your face?"

"It's a hat. Haven't you ever seen a hat before? Look, tell them anything. Tell them I **scratched** my eyes on a branch as I was riding here and the light—even the light from a lamp—hurts them. And you must be certain to watch for the day for me, and to **crow** as soon as you see the light, so we can leave."

"Yes, yes," Rooster said. "Come in and I shall **introduce you to** the girl's relatives."

---

a good distance far away
stumbled walked while tripping or dragging his feet
the mapou tree a type of tree that grows in Haiti

scratched hurt, cut
crow make the sound of a rooster
introduce you to take you to meet

Rooster introduced Owl to everyone, explaining Owl's **predicament**. Owl went around shaking hands, his hat hung down almost completely covering his face. Owl then tried to **retreat into** a corner, but the girl came over.

"Come into the yard and let's dance," she said.

Dong ga da, Dong ga da, Dong ga da, Dong. Dong ga da, Dong. Eh-ee-oh.

Owl danced. And Owl could dance well. The girl was proud of Owl. Even if he wore his hat strangely and had **sensitive** eyes, he could dance.

Dong ga da, Dong ga da, Dong ga da, Dong. Dong ga da, Dong. Eh-ee-oh.

Rooster was dancing, too. When Owl noticed that Rooster was dancing, instead of watching for the day, Owl was afraid that Rooster would forget to warn him, and he **excused himself** to the girl. He ran out of the yard, past the houses to a **clearing** where he could see the **horizon**. No, it was still night. Owl came back.

Dong ga da, Dong ga da, Dong ga da, Dong. Dong ga da, Dong. Eh-ee-oh.

Owl motioned to Rooster, but Rooster was lost in the dance. Owl excused himself again to the girl, ran to the clearing; no, it was still night. Owl returned.

Dong ga da, Dong ga da, Dong ga da, Dong. Dong ga da, Dong. Eh-ee-oh.

Owl tried to excuse himself again, but the girl held on to him. "Yes, stay with me," she said. And so they danced and danced and danced.

Dong ga da, Dong ga da, Dong ga da, Dong. Dong ga da, Dong. Eh-ee-oh.

BEFORE YOU MOVE ON...

1. **Details** How did Owl try to hide his face?
2. **Cause and Effect** Why did Owl want Rooster to crow when the new day began?
3. **Character's Motive** Why did Owl keep leaving the party?

---

predicament problem
retreat into get away to, hide in
sensitive easily hurt

excused himself said he had to leave for a moment
clearing place with no trees, open place
horizon place where the sun comes up

3
OWL RUNS AWAY

When Owl's fiancée sees his face, he becomes embarrassed
and runs away forever.

The sun moved up in the sky, higher and higher, until it filled the house and the yard with light.

"Now—let us see your fiancé's face!" the mother said.

"Kokioko!" Rooster crowed.

And before Owl could hide, she reached out and pulled the hat from his face.

"MY EYES!" Owl cried, and covering his face with his hands, he ran for his horse.

"Wait, Owl!" the girl called.

"Kokioko!" Rooster crowed.

"Wait, Owl, wait."

And as Owl put his hands down to **untie** his horse, the girl saw his face.

---

untie take the knot out of the rope that held

It was **striking** and **fierce**, and the girl thought it was the most **handsome** face she had ever seen.

"Owl—"

But Owl was already on his horse, riding away, farther and farther away.

Owl never came back.

The girl waited. Then she married Rooster. She was happy, except sometimes in the morning when Rooster would crow "kokioko-o-o." Then she would think about Owl and wonder where he was.

....

striking unusual and good-looking
fierce strong and wild
handsome good-looking, attractive

BEFORE YOU MOVE ON...

1. **Vocabulary** The author uses the words *striking*, *fierce*, and *handsome* to describe Owl's face. What words would you use to describe Owl's personality?
2. **Opinion** Did the story have a happy ending for everyone? Explain.
3. **Theme** What do you think is the moral, or lesson, of this story?

ABOUT THE AUTHOR

Diane Wolkstein is a storyteller who has visited Haiti many times. She began writing down Haitian folk tales after she saw a talented storyteller sing and dance the story of "Owl." "I will write the stories, write about the storytellers, and write about the storytelling experience that creates community," she decided. She put 27 of her stories into a collection called *The Magic Orange Tree and Other Haitian Folktales*. Today, more than 20 years later, the stories are still being told around the world. "Now when I tell these stories," she says, "I am exploring, like the Haitians. Both the audience and I know the beginning and the ending, but we don't know until we come to the heart of the story what we will discover."

Respond to the Folk Tale
Check Your Understanding

SUM IT UP

Make a Goal and Outcome Chart Show the goals, actions, and outcomes for each character in "Owl."

Goal and Outcome Chart for the Girl

Goal	Actions	Outcome	Goal Met?
She wanted to marry Owl.	She invited Owl to meet her family.	She married Rooster after Owl ran away.	No

Generate Ideas Work with a group. Think of actions the characters should have taken to meet their goals.

THINK IT OVER

Discuss Talk about these questions with a partner.

1. **Opinion** Why did the girl marry Rooster? Do you think she made the right decision?

2. **Prediction** What do you think happened to Owl after he ran away?

3. **Generalization** Owl believed his fiancée thought he was ugly. Is it a good idea to guess what others think without asking? Explain.

4. **Personal Experience** Who are you more like, Owl or Rooster? Explain.

EXPRESS YOURSELF

▶ TELL AN ORIGINAL STORY;
  LISTEN ACTIVELY

Work with a group to make up your own folk tale. Tell your story to another group as they listen carefully. A member of the other group will retell your story. Then listen to their folk tale. Choose someone from your group to retell their story.

Language Arts and Literature

USE PRESENT PERFECT TENSE

Learn About Tense A verb in the **present perfect tense** can tell about an action that began in the past and may still be going on.

Storytellers **have told** tales for many years. Some actions happened in the past, but you don't know when. Use a verb in the present perfect tense to tell about these actions, too.

My friend **has heard** "Owl" three times. To form the present perfect tense, use the helping verb `have` or `has` plus the **past participle** of the main verb.

- Use `have` with *I*, *you*, *we*, or *they*.
  I `have` told the tale often.
- Use `has` with *he*, *she*, or *it*.
  It `has` **become** famous.

Write in the Present Perfect Tense Write a sentence for each of these verbs. Then read your sentences aloud.

| has said | have talked |
| has danced | have played |

Practice Write the sentences. Add *has* or *have* to complete each sentence.

1. Haitians _____ told stories for centuries.

2. My father _____ told many stories.

3. I _____ always loved Papa's stories.

4. My aunt _____ started tape-recording them.

WRITE A CHARACTER STUDY

Study the characters in "Owl," then write about how each character's traits affect the story.

Make a Character Chart Copy and complete this chart. Show what each character is like. Tell how the character's traits affect the story.

	Girl	Owl	Rooster
Character Traits	generous kind loving		
Example from the Story	She loved Owl before she saw his face.		
Outcome of the Story	She still cared about Owl after he left.		

Write Your Ideas Use your chart to write about what each character is like. Then tell how the characters' traits affect the story.

Example:

The girl in the story is generous, kind, and loving.

She loved Owl even before she saw his face. She still cared about Owl after he ran away.

Respond to the Folk Tale, continued
Language Arts and Content Area Connections

▶ **WRITING**

WRITE A FRIENDLY LETTER

Imagine you are a character in "Owl." Write a letter to tell how you feel. Here are some ideas:

- Owl explains why he left.
- The girl tries to get Owl to come back.
- Rooster explains why he married the girl.

Use this model to write your friendly letter.

Heading—| June 3, 2004
Greeting—| Dear Owl,
_____
_____
Body——— _____
_____
_____
Closing——| Your friend,
Signature—| Rooster

▶ **SOCIAL STUDIES**

▶ **TECHNOLOGY/MEDIA**

MAKE A TRAVEL GUIDE

Travel guides give information about places you can visit. Make a travel guide about a country you want to visit.

1 **Gather Information** Use the Internet, an encyclopedia, or library books to research facts about the country. Take notes.

2 **Organize Your Information** Make a chart.

Haiti

location	
climate	
foods	
places to see	
things to do	

3 **Make a Travel Guide** Write your information in a way that encourages people to visit your country. You can use a word-processing program on a computer to make a travel guide look professional.

4 **Take a World Tour** Display your travel guide. Then look at your classmates' travel guides. Find new places you want to visit.

 Learn how use a **word-processing program**. See Handbook pages 354–361.

When I Taste Salt

never-ending poem
by Carmen Agra Deedy

Prepare to Read Poetry

THINK ABOUT WHAT YOU KNOW

Share Memories Have you ever felt sad and happy at the same time? Talk about a time that you felt this way.

dance 1. *noun* A **dance** is a party where people move to music. 2. *verb* When you **dance**, you move to a rhythm.

salt 1. *noun* **Salt** is a natural product that adds flavor to food. 2. *verb* You can **salt** food to add flavor.

skirt 1. *noun* A **skirt** is a piece of women's clothing that hangs from the waist. 2. *verb* When you **skirt** something, you go along its edge.

taste 1. *noun* A **taste** of something is a small amount of it. 2. *verb* You **taste** something when you put it in your mouth.

water 1. *noun* Living things need **water**. 2. *verb* You **water** plants to help them grow.

wave 1. *noun* In the ocean, water comes to the shore in a **wave**. 2. *verb* You **wave** when you move your hand back and forth.

LEARN KEY VOCABULARY

Use Context Clues to Meaning Study the new words. They are **multiple-meaning words**, or words that can mean more than one thing. Read the paragraph. Find the correct meaning of each underlined word.

When I sit on the wall that <u>skirts</u> the ocean, memories <u>dance</u> in my mind. I swam in the <u>water</u> when I was young. I moved back and forth with the <u>waves</u>. My memories are so strong that I can <u>taste</u> the <u>salt</u> of the sea.

LEARN TO INTERPRET FIGURATIVE LANGUAGE

Some writers use **figurative language** when they put words together in creative ways to make comparisons. Understanding figurative language can help you get a clear picture of people, places, and events in a selection.

READING STRATEGY
How to Interpret Figurative Language

1. As you read, make a picture in your mind of the people, places, and events.
2. Think about comparisons that the poet makes. How are the two people or two things alike?
3. Ask yourself: What does the poet really mean? Then explain the meaning in your own words.

As you read "When I Taste Salt," look for examples of figurative language. Try to figure out what the poet means.

When I Taste Salt

When I taste salt,
I think of Cuban waters.
I hear my sister shriek
As she tries to outrun the waves
That break over *el Malecón*,
The sea-wall
That skirts Havana harbor.

I watch my sister dance with the sea.
She is a hero
            and a goddess
                    and a mermaid
With laughing coffee-colored eyes.
She turns wet arms to me.
I shake my dry head
At the invitation.
I am too timid.
I am the little sister.

Our mother returns with melting
Snow cones and fire on her lips.
She scolds and sighs as she wrings the salt
From my sister's hair.

In silence, then, we three
Walk home at dusk.
But our mother is in a mood
For remembering,
And, as the breeze makes my sister shiver,
Mother tells how she, too,
Once raced the waves.

This memory always makes me cry,
And when I cry, I taste salt . . .

—*Carmen Agra Deedy*

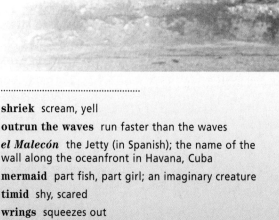

shriek scream, yell

outrun the waves run faster than the waves

el Malecón the Jetty (in Spanish); the name of the
wall along the oceanfront in Havana, Cuba

mermaid part fish, part girl; an imaginary creature

timid shy, scared

wrings squeezes out

ABOUT THE POET

Carmen Agra Deedy was born in Havana, Cuba. She and her family immigrated to the United States after the Cuban Revolution. They settled in Decatur, Georgia. Her combined Latin American and Southern heritage has had a rich influence on her work. Carmen is a professional storyteller. She has delighted audiences across the nation with her tales. She is also the author of several award-winning books for children.

Respond to the Poem
Check Your Understanding

SUM IT UP

Paraphrase Make a chart to help you paraphrase "When I Taste Salt."

What the Poem Says	What the Poem Means
I watch my sister dance with the sea.	I see her run in and out of the waves.
She is a hero . . .	
. . . and a goddess . . .	
. . . and a mermaid	
Our mother returns with . . . fire on her lips.	

Draw Conclusions When you **draw a conclusion**, you combine what you have read with what you know and make an opinion about it. Draw conclusions about the poet or the poem.

Examples:
The poet thinks her sister is special.
The poet has good memories of her childhood.

THINK IT OVER

Discuss Talk about these questions with a partner.

1. **Inference** Why does the poet "taste salt" when she thinks of this memory?

2. **Author's Style** What does the poet do to make this a never-ending poem?

3. **Opinion** Do you think that this is a happy or sad poem? Explain.

4. **Personal Experience** What older person do you admire? Why?

EXPRESS YOURSELF ▶ CLARIFY

Work with a group. Talk about memories you each have.

Example:
When I ___smell roses___,
I think of ___playing in my aunt's garden___.

When you **clarify** something, you make it clearer. Help to clarify each other's memories. Take turns asking questions like these:

• Where did your memory take place?

• Is there a smell, taste, sound, or color that comes with this memory?

• What does this memory mean to you?

Language Arts and Literature

LITERARY ANALYSIS

LEARN ABOUT ALLITERATION

Learn About Alliteration Look at these lines from "When I Taste Salt."

> The sea-wall
> That skirts Havana harbor.

Sea-wall and *skirts* have the same beginning sounds. So do *Havana* and *harbor*. The repetition of beginning sounds is called **alliteration**. Poets often choose to use words with alliteration because they sound good together.

Find Examples of Alliteration Find the words in the sentence that begin with the same sound.

> She scolds and sighs as she wrings the salt
> From my sister's hair.

Practice Use the words in parentheses to rewrite this poem using alliteration.

In the hot summer days	(sunny)
My brother and I used to	(big)
Walk by a river	(Run)
Where we caught fish and	(found)
Gathered pebbles.	(Picked up)
Then we sat on rocks and	(rested)
Listened to the water.	(Watched)

VOCABULARY
WRITING

USE SENSORY WORDS

Learn About Sensory Words Writers use **sensory words** to tell how things look, sound, smell, taste, and feel. Use sensory words to write about a memory.

1 Find Sensory Words Copy the chart below. Then add words from the poem.

See	Hear	Smell	Taste	Touch

2 Think About a Memory Think of a special place or event from your childhood. What sensory words can you use to describe the memory? Add them to the chart.

3 Write About Your Memory Write a story or a poem about your memory. Try to help your reader see, hear, smell, taste, and feel the place or event.

Learn how to improve your writing in the **writer's craft**. See Handbook pages 390–401.

Writing That Tells a Story

Narrative writing tells a story. The plot tells what the story is about. The characters are the people or animals in the story. The setting is where and when the story takes place.

WRITING MODELS

Read these sentences from "Pecos Bill." How does the writer describe the main character? What kind of setting do you see?

from "Pecos Bill"

I'm Pecos Bill. I'm part man and part coyote. I've slid down lightning bolts holding wildcats under both arms and never been scratched. I was raised in Texas along the Pecos River, but my life began in New England. I was born while my Ma was taming a tornado. Pa had caught the tornado tearing up our farm.

The plot of a story has a beginning, a middle, and an end. Read these paragraphs from the beginning of "Owl." They introduce the characters and tell about a problem. What events happened in the middle of the story? How did they lead up to the end?

from "Owl"

Owl thought he was very ugly. One evening he met a girl and talked with her and she liked him. "If it had been day," Owl thought, "and she had seen my face, she never would have liked me." Still, she had liked him.

So Owl went to her house. Every evening he would arrive at the girl's house at seven, and they would sit outside on the porch steps, talking together politely.

Then one evening after Owl had left, the girl's mother said to her, "Why doesn't your fiancé come and visit you during the day?"

Write Together

WRITING PROMPT

Write a class story for a younger class, for another class, or for your families and friends to read.

1 Plan the Story Your story will need two or more characters. It also will need a setting and a plot. Here is a map to help you plan your story. Study the example.

Characters: Who is the story about?
Setting: Where and when does the story take place?

Plot:

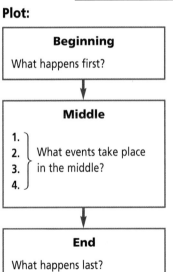

Beginning
What happens first?

↓

Middle
1. 2. What events take place 3. in the middle? 4.

↓

End
What happens last?

Characters: Ant, Grasshopper, Shrimp
Setting: a field, "once upon a time"

Plot:

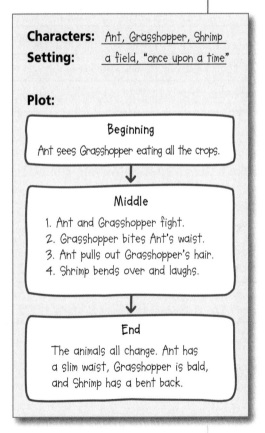

Beginning
Ant sees Grasshopper eating all the crops.

↓

Middle
1. Ant and Grasshopper fight. 2. Grasshopper bites Ant's waist. 3. Ant pulls out Grasshopper's hair. 4. Shrimp bends over and laughs.

↓

End
The animals all change. Ant has a slim waist, Grasshopper is bald, and Shrimp has a bent back.

2 Write the Story Use the story map to write a class story. Or, make a map for a new story and write it.

Writing That Tells a Story, continued

Write on Your Own

> **WRITING PROMPT**
>
> Now write your own story for classmates to read. Tell an adventure story. Make it exciting!

PREWRITE

1 **Choose a Story Idea** What adventure would you like to write about? Record your ideas in a chart.

Characters	Setting	Plot Idea
space aliens	Earth, 2110	They come here to try to make friends.
two hikers	mountain, today	They get caught in a terrible storm.

Choose one of your story ideas. Fill in an **FATP** chart.

2 **Get Organized** Make a story map to show your characters, setting, and plot.

Story Map

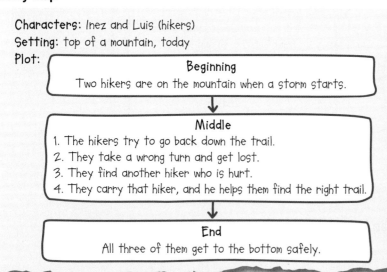

FATP Chart

> **HOW TO UNLOCK A PROMPT**
>
> **Form:** _story_
>
> **Audience:** _classmates_
>
> **Topic:** _surviving a thunderstorm on a mountaintop_
>
> **Purpose:** _to tell an exciting story about hikers caught in the storm_

```
Think About Your Writing
```

- Are you happy with your story idea?
- Do you have enough details to show what the characters and setting are like?
- Will the events make an interesting plot?

DRAFT

1 **Write Your Story** Use your story map to write your story.

2 **Use Dialogue and Descriptive Details** Study these examples.

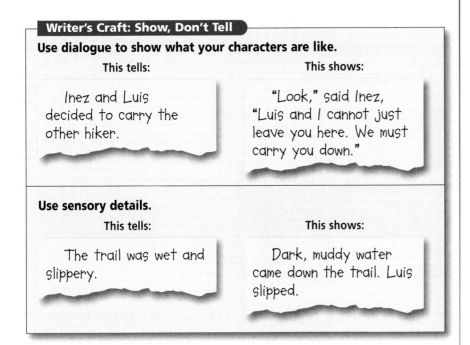

Writer's Craft: Show, Don't Tell

Use dialogue to show what your characters are like.

This tells:

Inez and Luis decided to carry the other hiker.

This shows:

"Look," said Inez, "Luis and I cannot just leave you here. We must carry you down."

Use sensory details.

This tells:

The trail was wet and slippery.

This shows:

Dark, muddy water came down the trail. Luis slipped.

Study these examples of sensory details. What sensory details would go with your topic?

Sight
bare branches
darkening sky
sharp rocks

Sound
branches snapping
cries of "help!"
rumbling thunder

Touch
wet clothes
frozen fingers
a hot meal

Taste
salty tears
sweet cocoa
bitter greens

Smell
a burning fire
sweet pine trees
baking bread

Key In TO Technology

Your word-processing software probably has a feature that allows you to check your spelling. Click on Spelling in your Tools window. A screen will then show each misspelled word and how to correct it.

Think About Your Writing

- Read your draft. Do you like what you wrote?
- Will the dialogue help your readers understand the characters?
- Did you include sensory details?

Writing That Tells a Story, continued

REVISE

1 **Read Your Story** Does it have a beginning, a middle, and an end?

2 **Share Your Story** Have your teacher or a friend read your story. Ask:

- Does the dialogue help you understand the characters?
- Do I have a variety of long and short sentences?
- Do my sentences begin in different ways?

3 **Make Your Changes** If you are using a computer, make the changes like this:

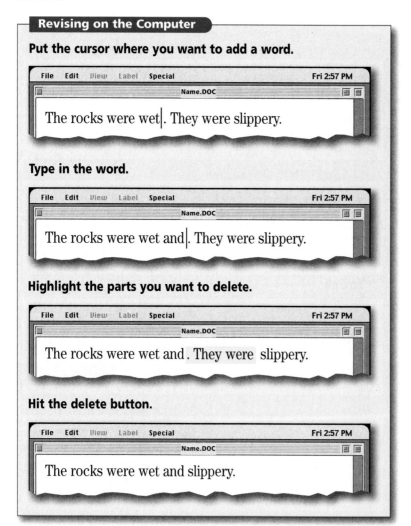

Revising on the Computer

Put the cursor where you want to add a word.

| File | Edit | View | Label | Special | | Fri 2:57 PM |

Name.DOC

The rocks were wet|. They were slippery.

Type in the word.

| File | Edit | View | Label | Special | | Fri 2:57 PM |

Name.DOC

The rocks were wet and|. They were slippery.

Highlight the parts you want to delete.

| File | Edit | View | Label | Special | | Fri 2:57 PM |

Name.DOC

The rocks were wet and. They were slippery.

Hit the delete button.

| File | Edit | View | Label | Special | | Fri 2:57 PM |

Name.DOC

The rocks were wet and slippery.

Think About Your Writing

- Does your dialogue sound like real conversation?
- Does your plot have a beginning, a middle, and an end?
- Did you vary your sentences?

> **GRAMMAR IN CONTEXT**

COMPLETE SENTENCES

A complete sentence has two main parts—the subject and the predicate.
Together, they tell a complete thought.

- The **subject** tells whom or what the sentence is about. It usually comes at the beginning of the sentence.

- The **predicate** tells what the subject is, does, or has. The most important word in the predicate is the **verb**.

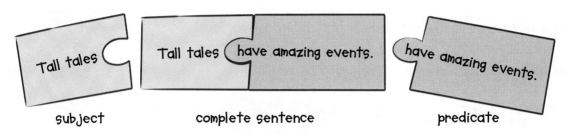

subject   complete sentence   predicate

Study these examples:

Subject	Predicate
We	**love** to read tall tales!
Characters in tall tales	**do** impossible things.
The story of Pecos Bill	**is** a tall tale.
Bill's mother	once **tamed** a tornado.
The family	**moved** west.

Practice Look at the words in the box. Use each as a subject to complete the sentences below.

1. _____ decided to race against each other.
2. _____ came to watch.
3. _____ hopped ahead very quickly.
4. _____ took a nap because he was so far ahead.
5. _____ crawled past the sleeping rabbit and won the race!

Word Box

Turtle

Rabbit

Turtle and Rabbit

All the other animals

He

Writing That Tells a Story, continued

EDIT AND PROOFREAD

1 **Proofread Your Story** When you find a mistake in capitalization, punctuation, or spelling, correct it. See pages 431–439 in the Handbook for help. Use the Proofreading Marks.

2 **Check Your Sentences** Did you use complete sentences? Did you begin your sentences in different ways?

3 **Make a Final Copy** If you are working on the computer, print out the corrected work. If not, rewrite it. Make the corrections you marked.

PUBLISH

Here are some ways to share your writing.

- Write your story and print it from your computer. Add a picture. Combine all the class stories into a book.

Mountain Adventure

by Anne Narkpraset

"We're almost there, Luis!" Inez shouted happily. "I can see the top of the mountain."

The two friends were excited. They had hiked all morning and now they were almost at the top of the trail.

Suddenly, there was a loud crash. "That was lightning," Luis said.

"It's raining!" Inez cried. Large raindrops fell in every direction. "We have to go back!"

- Read your story aloud to a friend. When you are done, ask your friend to describe the main characters and the setting.
- If your family or school has a Home Page on the Web, include a copy of your story to share with others. Invite readers to e-mail their comments.

Proofreading Marks

∧	Add.
⩘	Add a comma.
⊙	Add a period.
≡	Capitalize.
╱	Make lowercase.
⌣	Take out.
¶	Indent.

Think About Your Writing

- Are you pleased with your story?
  - ☑ Does it have a beginning, a middle, and an end?
  - ☑ Does it include dialogue that shows what the characters are like?
- What do you like best about your story?
- Will this story go in your portfolio? Why or why not?

STORIES
TO TELL

1 ▸ Look Back at the Unit

Rate Stories In this unit, you read about many stories and storytellers.

Echo and Narcissus

How the Ox Star Fell From Heaven

The Art of the Tall Tale

Unwinding the Magic Thread

Work with a partner. Talk about the four selections. Organize them on one side of a pyramid. Put the selection you liked the best at the top. Put others in order below. On the opposite side of the pyramid, tell what you liked best about each story.

2 ▸ Show What You Know

Sum It All Up Add new ideas to your mind map about traditions. Tell a partner something you learned about storytelling.

People who tell stories

How people tell stories

Storytelling

What people tell stories about

Why people tell stories

Reflect and Evaluate Finish this sentence:
• Good storytellers can _____.
Add the sentence to your portfolio. Choose work from the unit that shows what you learned.

3 ▸ Make Connections

To Your School and Community Plan a storytelling day for your class or school. Invite storytellers from your community. Then visit other classes. Share the stories you've heard with younger students.

HIGH POINT
Handbook

PART ▶1 Language and Learning

- Technology in Pictures
- How to Send E-mail
- How to Use a Word-Processing Program
- How to Create a Multimedia Presentation
- How to Use the Internet

PART ▶2 Writing

- How to Use the Writing Process
- How to Evaluate Your Writing

PART ▶3 Grammar, Usage, Mechanics, and Spelling

Strategies for Learning Language

These strategies can help you learn to use and understand the English language.

1 Listen actively and try out language.

WHAT TO DO	EXAMPLES
Repeat what you hear.	**You hear:** Way to go, Joe! Fantastic catch! **You say:** Way to go, Joe! Fantastic catch!
Recite songs and poems.	**When the Ground Shakes** When the ground shakes along the street, There's something happening beneath your feet. Earth layers are shifting, Slipping, Sliding, Bumping together. Shock waves are rising! *When the ground shakes along the street,...*
Listen to others and use their language.	**You hear:** "When did you know that something was missing?" **You say:** "I knew that something was missing when I got to class."
Add new words and phrases to your speech.	**You hear:** "You can send the invitation by e-mail or snail mail." **You think:** Snails move very slowly, and e-mail is much faster than regular mail. Snail mail must be regular mail. **You say:** I'll send it by snail mail. There's plenty of time, and I can write it on special paper.
Practice the language you use for adults and the language you use for friends.	**Formal:** "Hello, Ms. Taylor. How are you?" "Fine, thank you. And how are you today?" **Informal:** "Hey, Paco. How's it going?" "Okay. And you?"

WHAT TO DO	EXAMPLES
Use the language you learn in school. You can use the same words and phrases at home or in other places.	You read this in Social Studies: The Voting Rights Act of 1965 guaranteed all U.S. citizens the right to vote. You write this in your reading journal: *I wonder if The Secret of Gumbo Grove has something to do with the right to vote.* At home, you might say: Mom, did you vote? You're guaranteed the right to vote.
Find different ways to say things.	These all mean the same thing: My teacher helps me push my thinking. My teacher makes me think before I make up my mind. My teacher helps me stretch my mind to see different viewpoints. Before I make a decision, my teacher suggests I role-play different choices in my mind.

2 Ask for help and feedback.

WHAT TO DO	EXAMPLES
Interrupt politely.	Excuse me. Please explain what the word "habitat" means. Other options: "Pardon me, but could you say that again?" "Could you help me? I don't understand the phrase 'how precious life is.'"
Ask questions about how to use language.	Did I say that right? Did I use that word in the right way? Which is correct, "bringed" or "brought"?
Use your native language or English to make sure that you understand.	You say: "Wait! Could you go over that point again, a little more slowly, please?" Other options: "Does 'have a heart' mean to be kind?" "Is 'enormous' another way to say 'big'?"

Strategies for Learning Language, continued

3 **Use nonverbal clues.**

WHAT TO DO	EXAMPLES
Use gestures and movements to help others understand your idea.	I will hold up five fingers to show that I need five more minutes.
Look for clues from people's movements and expressions. They can help you understand the meaning.	María wants me to go to the Subhumans' concert, but I think their music is awful—and insulting. I'm not sure what she said about the Subhumans' music, but I can tell she doesn't like it. Just look at her!
Watch people as they speak. The way they move can help you understand the meaning of their words.	Let's give him a hand. Everyone is clapping. "Give him a hand" must mean to clap for him.

4 **Verify how language works.**

WHAT TO DO	EXAMPLES
Test your ideas about language.	**You try out what you learned:** I can add *-ation* to the verb *observe* to get the noun *observation*. So maybe I can make a noun by adding *-ation* to all verbs that end in *-e*. Let's see. *Prepare* and *preparation*. Yes, that works! *Preserve* and *preservation*. That works, too. *Compare* and *comparation*. That doesn't sound right. I will see what the dictionary says... Now I see — it's *comparison*.

4 Verify how language works, continued

WHAT TO DO	EXAMPLES
Use spell-checkers, glossaries, and dictionaries.	You just finished your draft of a story, so you think: *Now I'll run the spell-check to see what words I need to fix.*
Decide if you should use formal or informal language.	**Formal:** "Thank you, Mr. Giacometti, for helping me enter the science fair." **Informal:** "Mom, thanks for getting the jars for my science fair exhibit." "Hey, Roberto, it was cool of you to help me set up."

5 Monitor and evaluate your learning.

WHAT TO DO	EXAMPLES
Ask yourself: Are my language skills getting better? How can I improve?	*Did I use the right words? Was it correct to use "they" when I talked about my grandparents?* *Were my words all in the correct order?* *Was I polite?*
Keep notes about what you've learned. Use your notes to practice using English.	**How to Ask Questions** • I can turn a statement around to make a question: It is a nice day. Is it a nice day? • I can put the question at the end of a statement: It is a nice day, isn't it? • If I want more than a "yes" or "no" answer, I should use "who," "what," "where," "when," "how," or "why" at the beginning of my question: What will the weather be like today?

Graphic Organizers

Graphic organizers help you picture information. Use them to take notes, to organize your ideas, or to present information to others.

CLUSTERS

Clusters show how words or ideas are connected. You can use a cluster to show:

▶ **How Words or Ideas are Related**

▶ **Details of an Event**

CHARTS

Charts have rows, columns, and labels to show information. Use a chart to:

▶ **Picture Information**

Intelligence Types in Room 21	
Word	9
Musical	5
Math	7
Artistic	3

▶ **Relate Ideas**

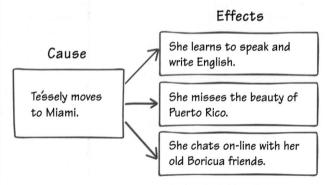

Make Comparisons

Name	Birth Information	Current Home	Job
Nancy Hom	1949 Toisan, China	San Francisco, California	Artist
George Littlechild	1958 Alberta, Canada	Vancouver, British Columbia	Artist

Show the Steps in a Process

How to Make an Adobe

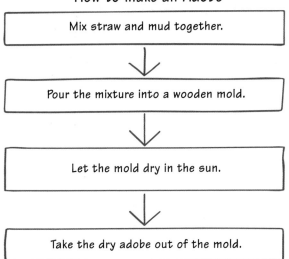

Mix straw and mud together.

↓

Pour the mixture into a wooden mold.

↓

Let the mold dry in the sun.

↓

Take the dry adobe out of the mold.

Show What You Know, What You Want to Learn, and What You Learned

Topic: Kinds of Intelligence		
K **What I Know**	**W** **What I Want to Learn**	**L** **What I Learned**
Everyone has intelligence. There are many kinds of intelligence.	How many intelligences are there? What are my intelligences? Can intelligence get stronger?	**Fill in this column after you read.**

Classify or Organize

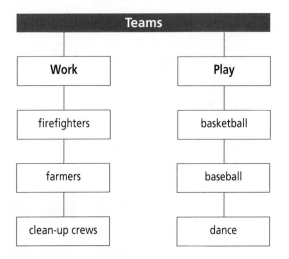

Teams

Work	Play
firefighters	basketball
farmers	baseball
clean-up crews	dance

Graphic Organizers, continued

GRAPHS

Graphs use words, numbers, lines, and shapes to show information. Graphs can show:

▶ **Parts of a Whole**

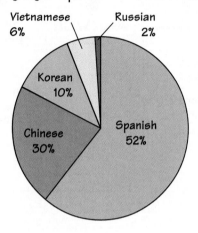

Languages Spoken in Mr. Villa's Class

Vietnamese 6%
Russian 2%
Korean 10%
Chinese 30%
Spanish 52%

▶ **How Something Changes Over Time**

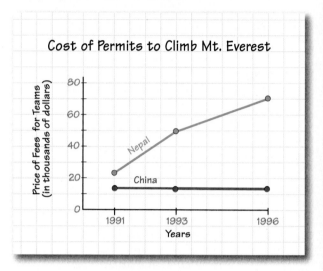

Cost of Permits to Climb Mt. Everest

▶ **Comparisons**

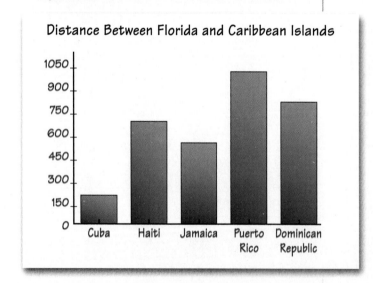

Distance Between Florida and Caribbean Islands

DIAGRAMS

Diagrams use drawings and text to show how events or ideas are related. Use a diagram to:

▶ **Show When Events Happen**

The Early Life of Helen Keller

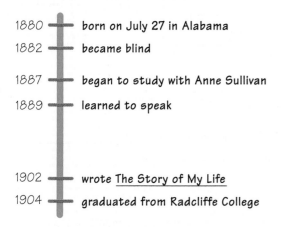

1880 — born on July 27 in Alabama
1882 — became blind
1887 — began to study with Anne Sullivan
1889 — learned to speak

1902 — wrote <u>The Story of My Life</u>
1904 — graduated from Radcliffe College

▶ **Show Parts of Something**

The Parts of a Volcano

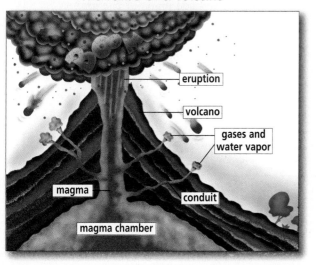

eruption
volcano
gases and water vapor
magma
conduit
magma chamber

▶ **Explore the Meanings of Words**

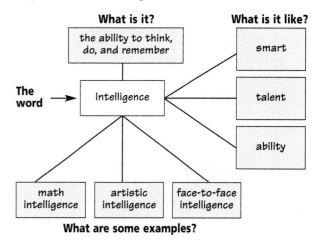

What is it?
the ability to think, do, and remember

What is it like?
smart
talent
ability

The word → Intelligence

math intelligence
artistic intelligence
face-to-face intelligence

What are some examples?

▶ **Show Main Idea and Details**

Main Idea	Details
	He is positive.
John has merits and shortcomings.	He is optimistic.
	He is lazy.
	He is irresponsible.

Graphic Organizers, continued

Show Similarities and Differences

STORY MAPS

Story maps show how a story is organized.

Sequence of Events

Narrow or Develop a Topic

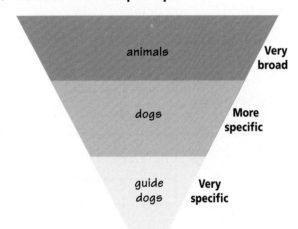

Beginning, Middle, and End

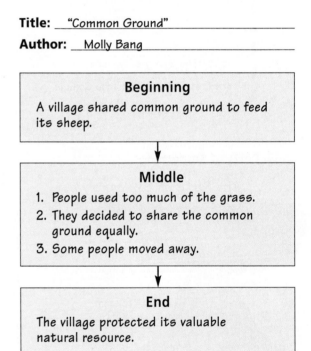

Title: "Common Ground"

Author: Molly Bang

Beginning
A village shared common ground to feed its sheep.

Middle
1. People used too much of the grass.
2. They decided to share the common ground equally.
3. Some people moved away.

End
The village protected its valuable natural resource.

▶ Goal and Outcome

Title: "The Monkey and the Camel"

Author: Aesop

Goal
Camel wants attention from the animals.

Event 1	Event 2	Event 3	Event 4
Monkey dances for the animals.	Everyone likes Monkey.	Camel tries to dance like Monkey.	Everyone laughs at Camel.

Outcome
Camel learns a lesson about friendship.

▶ Problem and Solution

Title: "A Dog You Can Count On"

Setting: The Guide Dog Training Center

Characters: Moe, Aria, Stacy

Problem: Moe is blind. He needs help every day.

↓

Event 1: Moe gets a guide dog named Aria.

Event 2: Stacy gives them special training.

Event 3: Moe and Aria go home.

↓

Solution: Moe and Aria help each other.

Graphic Organizers, continued

▶ **Story Staircase**

"Earthquake at Dawn"
a historical play
by Kristiana Gregory

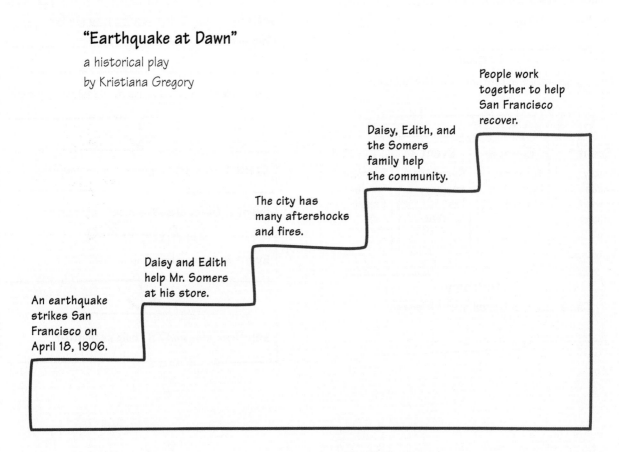

People work
together to help
San Francisco
recover.

Daisy, Edith, and
the Somers
family help
the community.

The city has
many aftershocks
and fires.

Daisy and Edith
help Mr. Somers
at his store.

An earthquake
strikes San
Francisco on
April 18, 1906.

▶ Rising and Falling Action

"A Mountain Rescue"

by James Ramsey Ullman

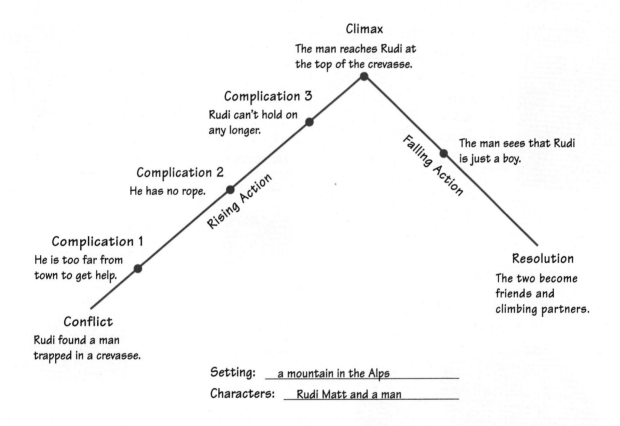

Climax
The man reaches Rudi at the top of the crevasse.

Complication 3
Rudi can't hold on any longer.

Complication 2
He has no rope.

Rising Action

Falling Action

The man sees that Rudi is just a boy.

Complication 1
He is too far from town to get help.

Resolution
The two become friends and climbing partners.

Conflict
Rudi found a man trapped in a crevasse.

Setting: a mountain in the Alps

Characters: Rudi Matt and a man

Technology and Media
Technology in Pictures

Technology is used every day in schools, offices, and homes. This section will help you recognize and use machines and electronic tools.

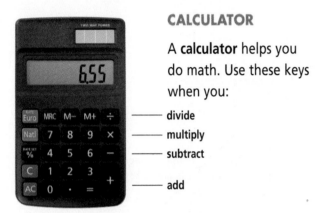

CALCULATOR

A **calculator** helps you do math. Use these keys when you:

—— divide

—— multiply

—— subtract

—— add

COMPACT DISC PLAYER

A **compact disc (CD) player** plays compact discs with music or other sounds.

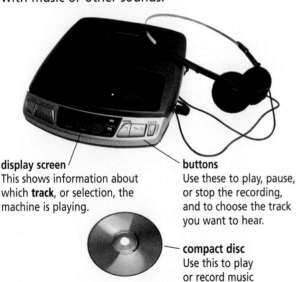

display screen
This shows information about which **track**, or selection, the machine is playing.

buttons
Use these to play, pause, or stop the recording, and to choose the track you want to hear.

compact disc
Use this to play or record music or other sounds.

CASSETTE PLAYERS

A **cassette player** records and plays audiocassettes.

headphones
Use these to listen alone.

audiocassette tape
Use this to play or record sound.

buttons
Use these to play, stop, and move the tape forward or back.

microphone
Use this to record sound. Some players have built-in microphones.

CAMCORDER

A **camcorder** is a hand-held video camera. It records pictures and sounds on videotape. You can watch the videotape on a television.

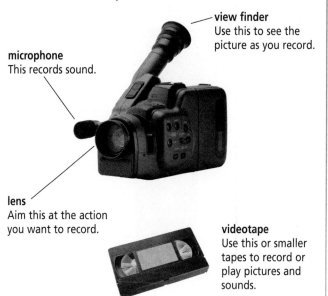

view finder
Use this to see the picture as you record.

microphone
This records sound.

lens
Aim this at the action you want to record.

videotape
Use this or smaller tapes to record or play pictures and sounds.

VIDEOCASSETTE RECORDER

A **videocassette recorder (VCR)** records and plays videotapes through a television. You can record television programs or watch videos that you make, buy, rent, or check out from the library.

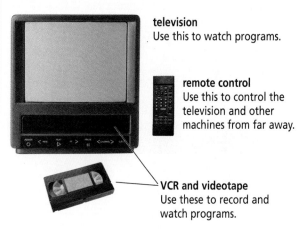

television
Use this to watch programs.

remote control
Use this to control the television and other machines from far away.

VCR and videotape
Use these to record and watch programs.

DIGITAL VIDEODISC PLAYER

A **digital videodisc (DVD) player** plays discs that have very clear pictures and sounds. You can watch movies by connecting a DVD player to a television or a computer.

digital videodisc
This holds recordings of programs.

Technology in Pictures, continued

FAX MACHINE

A **fax machine** uses phone lines to send or receive a copy of pages with pictures or words.

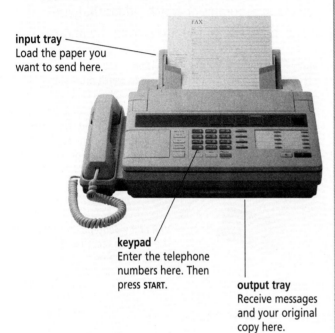

input tray
Load the paper you want to send here.

keypad
Enter the telephone numbers here. Then press START.

output tray
Receive messages and your original copy here.

WIRELESS TELEPHONE

A **wireless telephone** lets you talk to people wherever you are.

power key
Use this to turn the phone on and off.

talk key
Press TALK or SEND to dial the phone number you set.

number keys
Enter the phone number with these keys.

end key
Press this when your call is finished.

THE COMPUTER

A **computer** is an electronic tool that helps you create, save, and use information.

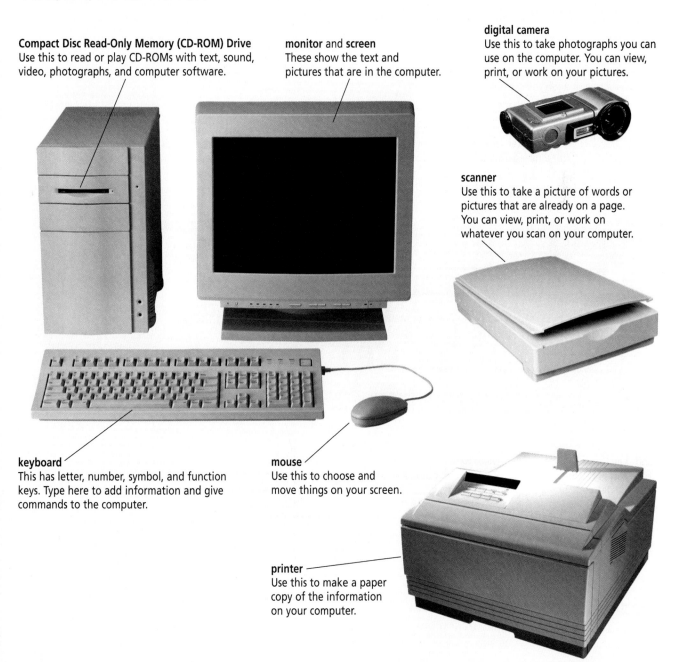

Compact Disc Read-Only Memory (CD-ROM) Drive
Use this to read or play CD-ROMs with text, sound, video, photographs, and computer software.

monitor and **screen**
These show the text and pictures that are in the computer.

digital camera
Use this to take photographs you can use on the computer. You can view, print, or work on your pictures.

scanner
Use this to take a picture of words or pictures that are already on a page. You can view, print, or work on whatever you scan on your computer.

keyboard
This has letter, number, symbol, and function keys. Type here to add information and give commands to the computer.

mouse
Use this to choose and move things on your screen.

printer
Use this to make a paper copy of the information on your computer.

Technology and Media, continued

Technology in Pictures, continued

THE COMPUTER KEYBOARD

Use the **keys** on the **keyboard** to write, do math, or give the computer commands. Keyboards may look different, but they all have keys like these:

escape key
Press here to quit a job you are doing.

tab
Press this key to indent for a new paragraph.

function keys
Press these keys to give the computer commands.

delete or **backspace key**
Press here to erase the character to the left of the flashing cursor. You can also erase text that you highlight.

shift key
Hold this down to make a capital letter or to type the symbol on the top half of a key.

space bar
Press here to put in a space when you type.

return or **enter key**
Press here to tell the computer to do a task or move the cursor down to a new line.

arrow keys
Press these keys to move your cursor on the screen.

How to Send E-mail

E-mail is electronic mail that can be sent on-line from one computer to another. Anyone who has an e-mail address can send and receive messages. E-mail can travel around the classroom or around the world.

You can use e-mail to:

- write messages to one or more friends at a time
- send computer files
- save money on postage and telephone calls
- send and receive messages almost instantly.

To send an e-mail message:

1. Open the e-mail program.

2. Open a new message.

3. Enter this information:

- Type the recipient's e-mail address in the "To" box.
- Type a short title for your e-mail in the "Subject" box.
- Type your message.

4. Send your message.

Each e-mail program is different. Here is one example of a "mailbox":

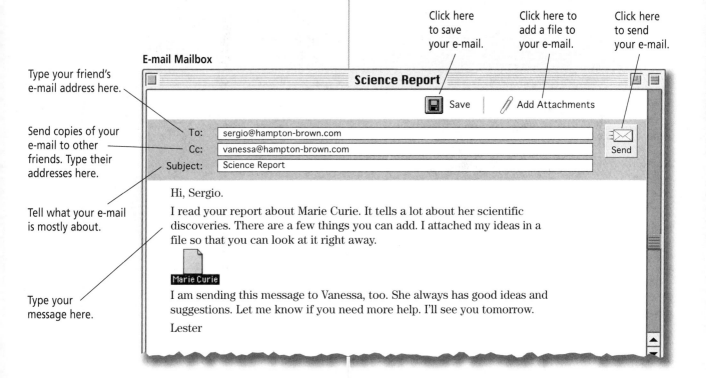

Click here to save your e-mail.

Click here to add a file to your e-mail.

Click here to send your e-mail.

E-mail Mailbox

Type your friend's e-mail address here.

Send copies of your e-mail to other friends. Type their addresses here.

Tell what your e-mail is mostly about.

Type your message here.

Science Report

Save | Add Attachments

Send

To: sergio@hampton-brown.com

Cc: vanessa@hampton-brown.com

Subject: Science Report

Hi, Sergio.

I read your report about Marie Curie. It tells a lot about her scientific discoveries. There are a few things you can add. I attached my ideas in a file so that you can look at it right away.

Marie Curie

I am sending this message to Vanessa, too. She always has good ideas and suggestions. Let me know if you need more help. I'll see you tomorrow.

Lester

Technology and Media, continued
How to Use a Word-Processing Program

A **computer program** is a set of directions that tells a computer what to do. A **word-processing program** helps you create and store written work. You can use it to:

- store ideas, outlines, plans, and papers
- write drafts of your work
- revise, edit, and proofread your writing
- format and publish your work
- make written work look neat and organized.

There are many kinds of word-processing programs. There are also different ways to use the computer to make each job easier. This section of the Handbook will give you some ideas. Ask your teacher or classmates for other ways they have found to use your school's word-processing program.

Working on the computer

My First Day in an American School

by Marco Quezada

My first day of school in the United States was very scary because I didn't speak English. I didn't know how I was going to talk to people. I didn't have any friends. I tried to understand the teacher, but I couldn't. I felt like a chair.

Suddenly, a very loud bell rang. The teacher opened the door, and all the kids jumped up and rushed out the door.

Why was everyone leaving? In Haiti, we stayed in the same classroom all day. I followed the class, and we went into a new room. A stranger gave me a book and some papers. I was really puzzled. Fortunately, the man spoke some Creole and explained that he was my science teacher.

Finally, I understood. In America, there are special teachers for science, music, and gym. Students also move to new classrooms. At first, it was very confusing, but now I like having different teachers for my subjects.

GET STARTED

1 How to Set Up a File Before you start to write, make a **file**—a place to keep your work. Follow these steps:

1. Click **File** to see the **File Menu**. A **menu** gives you a list of choices.

File Menu and New

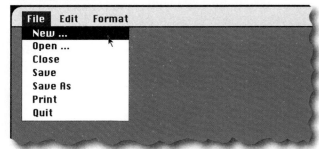

2. Click **New** to create a new document. A blank page will appear.

New Document

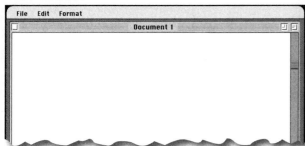

2 How to Save a File To save your new file in a folder, click **Save As** on the **File Menu**.

File Menu and Save As

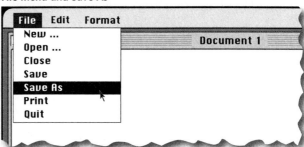

A **dialogue box** will appear to ask for information.

1. Type a short name for your file.

2. Make sure that the file name and folder are correct. If you don't have a folder for your work, ask your teacher for help to start one.

3. Click **Save** to save your file.

Save Dialogue Box

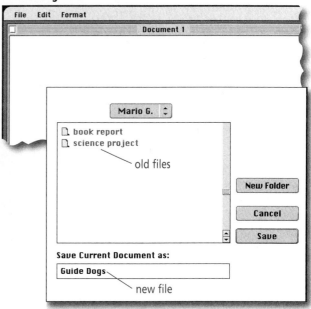

Technology and Media, continued
How to Use a Word-Processing Program, continued

CREATE DOCUMENTS

1 How to Type a Document Now you are ready to type. Your work will appear in front of a flashing cursor. The **cursor** shows where you are working on the page.

Cursor

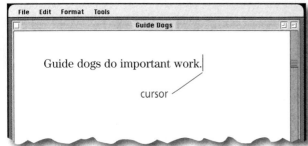

As you type, the **indicator box** shows where you are in the document. You can use the **scroll bar** to move up and down in your file.

- Click and hold the **up arrow** to move toward the top of the screen.
- Click and hold the **down arrow** to move toward the bottom of the screen.

Scrolling

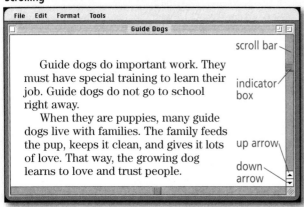

2 How to Save Your Work Remember to save your work as you write. If you do not save, you may lose the work you have done on your file. Remember:

✔ Save your work every 10 minutes!
✔ Save before you leave your computer.
✔ Save before you **Print**.
✔ Save before you **Quit**.
✔ Save, save, save!

To save your work, click **Save** in the **File Menu**.

Save

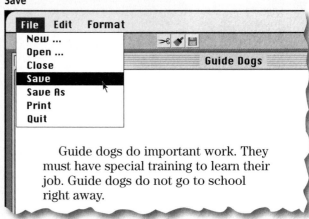

Or, click the **save icon** on the **toolbar**.

Toolbar Icons

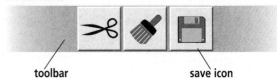

toolbar   save icon

MAKE CHANGES TO YOUR WORK

1 **How to Add Words** It is easy to add words to your work.

1. Use your mouse to move the cursor to the place where you want to add words.

2. Click the mouse once. The cursor will start to flash.

Add Words (before)

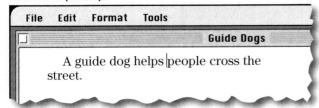

3. Type the new words.

Add Words (after)

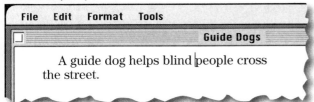

2 **How to Delete Words** When you **delete**, you take words out. Before you delete, you need to highlight the words you want to remove.

1. To remove one word, put the cursor on the word. Click the mouse twice.

Delete Words (before)

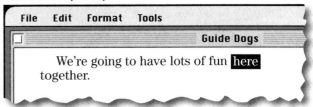

2. You can also **click and drag** to highlight and remove words.

- Click and hold the mouse and slide it over all the words you want to take out. The words will be highlighted.

Delete Words (after)

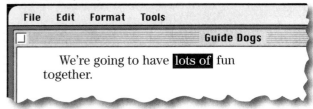

- After the words are highlighted, press the **delete key**. The words will disappear from the screen.

Delete Words (after)

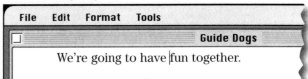

Technology and Media, continued

How to Use a Word-Processing Program, continued

❸ How to Cut and Paste You can **cut and paste** to move sentences or paragraphs to a different place in your paper.

When you **cut** text, the computer takes out the highlighted words. The words are not deleted. They are stored in the computer's memory to be placed somewhere new.

To cut text, click **Cut** from the **Edit Menu**.

Cut (before)

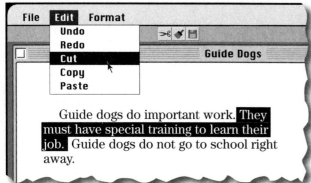

Or, click the **cut icon** on the **toolbar**.

Toolbar Icons

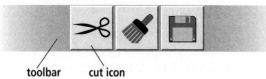

toolbar   cut icon

Your text will look like this:

Cut (after)

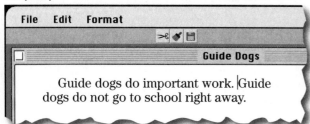

When you **paste** text, the cut words are placed at the flashing cursor. To paste text, move the cursor to where you want the text and click **Paste** from the **Edit Menu**.

Paste (before)

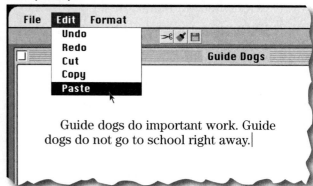

Or, click the **paste icon** on the **toolbar**.

Toolbar Icons

toolbar   paste icon

Your text will look like this:

Paste (after)

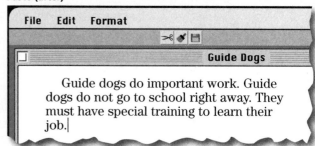

4 How to Check Your Spelling Most word-processing programs have tools to check your spelling. Follow these steps:

1. Open the **Tools Menu** and choose **Spelling**. The computer will show you a highlighted word from your text.
2. Choose the correct spelling from the list of suggestions. If the word is not listed, check a dictionary.

Spell Check

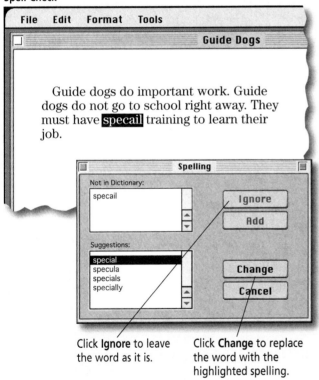

Click **Ignore** to leave the word as it is.

Click **Change** to replace the word with the highlighted spelling.

5 How to Find Synonyms Use the computer's thesaurus to find synonyms for words you use.

1. Highlight the word you want to change. Then open the **Tools Menu** and choose **Thesaurus**.
2. Some words have different meanings. Choose the correct one from the list of meanings.
3. Look at the list of synonyms for that meaning. Highlight the word you want.

Thesaurus

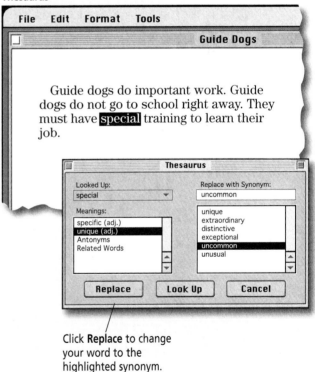

Click **Replace** to change your word to the highlighted synonym.

FORMAT YOUR PAPER

When you **format** your work, you make it look neat and organized. Here are some ways to format, or arrange, your paper.

1 **How to Change the Font, Style, and Size**

A **font** is a unique style for the letters and numbers that you type. Follow these steps:

- Highlight the section you want to change.
- Open the **Format Menu** and choose **Font**, or click the font, style, and size icons on your toolbar.

B	I	U
bold	italic	underline

- Choose the font, word style, and word size you want for your text. Then click **OK**.

You can choose from many fonts. For class work, choose a font that is clear and easy to read. If you are writing to friends, you can choose more fun styles! Here are some examples:

Fonts

good for reports	good for essays
good for a friendly letter	***great for your journal***

Styles

normal	*italic*
bold	underlined

Sizes

12	14	16	18

2 **How to Change Text Alignment** When you set **text alignment**, you choose how words will line up on the page. You may want to put a title in the center of the page, or put your name in the right-hand corner. Follow these steps:

- Highlight the text you want to align.
- Click the icon that shows where you want the text placed. For example:

align left   center   align right   justify

3 **How to Set Spacing** You can choose the **spacing**—how much space comes between each line you type. Follow these steps:

- Open the **Edit Menu** and choose **Select All**.
- Click the correct spacing icon:

single space   1.5 line   double space

Ask your teacher or your friends for more ideas about how to format your work. Soon, your work will have a new style that is unique and attractive.

Sample Letter

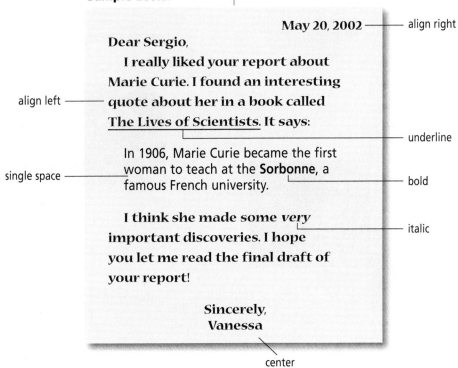

May 20, 2002 — align right

align left — Dear Sergio,
    I really liked your report about Marie Curie. I found an interesting quote about her in a book called **The Lives of Scientists**. It says: — underline

single space — In 1906, Marie Curie became the first woman to teach at the **Sorbonne**, a famous French university. — bold

    I think she made some *very* important discoveries. I hope you let me read the final draft of your report! — italic

    Sincerely,
    Vanessa

center

Technology and Media, continued
How to Create a Multimedia Presentation

A **multimedia presentation** uses technology to present ideas. Your audience can read, see, and hear your work.

LEARN ABOUT MEDIA

There are many ways to share information. Choose media that fit your purpose. Here are some possibilities:

▶ **Visuals**

- Use a computer to create slides of important points, outlines, or quotations.
- Scan tables or diagrams to show information.

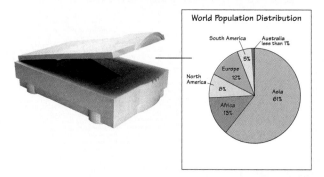

▶ **Photographs**

- Scan photographs.
- Download pictures from the Internet.
- Use pictures from a CD-ROM.

▶ **Video and Animation**

- Use videos from the news.
- Create animation to show how something changes.
- Make a videotape of yourself or others.

▶ **Sounds**

- Play music on a cassette, CD, or CD-ROM.
- Make a recording of yourself or others.
- Download sound files from the Internet.

"I have a dream..."

MAKE A MULTIMEDIA PRESENTATION

Follow these steps to give your own multimedia presentation.

1 **Plan** Think about how you can present your ideas creatively.

- Put your ideas into a logical order.
- Ask yourself: What pictures, videos, and sounds will help the class understand my ideas? What technology can I use?
- Use a **graphic organizer** to put the steps of your presentation in order. Here is one example:

Flow Chart

```
┌─────────────────────────────────┐
│      Show title slide:          │
│  Democracy in Ancient Greece.   │
└─────────────────────────────────┘
                ▼
┌─────────────────────────────────┐
│    Talk about Greek city-states.│
└─────────────────────────────────┘
                ▼
┌─────────────────────────────────┐
│  Show slide of map of ancient   │
│   Greece on the computer.       │
└─────────────────────────────────┘
                ▼
┌─────────────────────────────────┐
│       Play 2-minute video       │
│      of Greek elections.        │
└─────────────────────────────────┘
```

2 **Practice** Rehearse your presentation until you are comfortable with your speech and the technology you will use.

- Practice in front of your family and friends. Ask them for ideas and suggestions.
- Unexpected things can happen when you work with technology. Before your presentation, test your equipment to be sure it works.

3 **Present** Remember that your goal is to give an effective presentation.

- Speak slowly and clearly.
- Give your audience time to understand the ideas you are sharing.
- Have fun!

Technology and Media, continued
How to Use the Internet

The **Internet** connects computers around the world so that they can share information. The **World Wide Web** lets you to find, read, go through, and organize information.

The Internet is a fast way to get the most current information. You can find many resources like encyclopedias and dictionaries on the Internet. You can also find amazing pictures, movies, and sounds.

WHAT YOU WILL NEED

To use the Internet, you need a computer with Internet software. You'll also need a **modem** that connects the computer to a telephone line.

HOW TO GET STARTED

There are many ways to search the Internet. Ask your teacher how to use the Internet at school. Usually you can just double click on the Internet **icon**, or picture.

HOW TO DO THE RESEARCH

Once the search page comes up, you can begin the research process. Just follow these steps.

1 Type Your Subject Type your key words in the search box and click **Search**. You'll see a toolbar at the top of the screen. Click on the **icons** to do things like print the page.

Try different ways to type in your subject. You'll get different results! For example:

- If you type in **Mars**, you'll see all the sites that have the word *Mars* in them. This may give you too many sites.
- If you type in **"Mars exploration,"** you'll see all the sites with the exact phrase, *Mars exploration*.
- If you type in **+Mars +exploration**, you'll see all the sites with the words *Mars* and *exploration* in them.

2 **Read the Search Results** All underlined, colored words are **links** that connect you to other sites. They help you get from page to page quickly.

- Click on a site to go to a Web page.
- Click on a category to see more options.
- Read the descriptions of the sites.

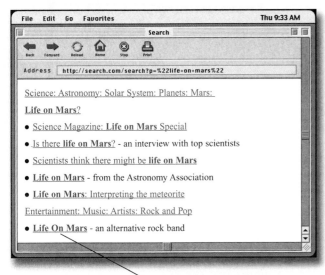

This site could be very interesting, but it probably won't help with a report about life on Mars.

3 **Select a Site and Read** You can pick a new site or start a new search. Click on the **Back** arrow to go back a page to the search results. If you want to go to another Web page, click on a link.

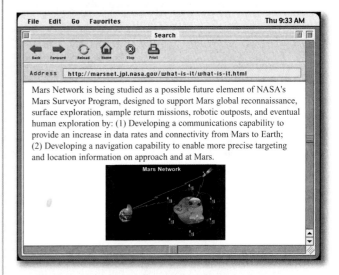

4 **Locate More Resources** The **URL (Uniform Resource Locator)**, is the address of a Web site. If you already know the URL, type it in the address box at the top of the screen.

Remember that information on Web sites changes all the time. Sometimes Web pages are not kept up. If you can't find one Web site, try another one.

The Research Process

When you research, you look up information about a topic. You can use the information you find to write a story, article, book, or research report.

❶ CHOOSE A TOPIC

Think of something you want to learn about. That will be your **research topic**. Pick a specific, or small topic. A smaller topic is easier to research and to write about. Look at these topics:

The Ancient World
This is a big topic! To research and write about each ancient civilization would be too much for one report.

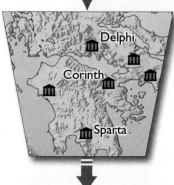

Ancient Greece
This topic is better, but there are a lot of things you could research about Greece. Do you want to know about its government, art, or myths?

Ancient Greek Government
This topic is small enough to study. It could be interesting to find out about the roots of democracy.

❷ DECIDE WHAT TO LOOK UP

What do you want to know about your topic? Write down some questions. Look at the most important words in your questions. Those are **key words** you can look up when you start your research.

> Research Questions
>
> — Who were **leaders** in ancient Greece?
>
> — How did Greek citizens **vote**?
>
> — What was **demokratia**?
>
> — What were Athenian **elections** like?
>
> — Has **democracy** changed?

❸ LOCATE RESOURCES

Now you can use different resources to find out about your topic. Resources can be:

- people like teachers and family members
- magazines and newspapers
- videos and film clips
- the Internet

You also can find lots of information at the library. Look in reference materials like these:

- An **atlas** is a book of maps.
- An **almanac** has many facts about history.
- An **encyclopedia** has articles and pictures about many topics.
- A **dictionary** tells what words mean.

❹ GATHER INFORMATION

When you gather information, you find the best resources for your topic. You look up your key words to find facts about your topic. Then you take notes.

How to Find Information Quickly Use alphabetical order to look up words in a list. In many resources, the words, titles, and subjects are listed in **alphabetical order**.

Look at these words. They are in order by the **first** letter of each word.

> **A**cropolis
> **d**emocracy
> **v**oting

If the word you are looking up has the same first letter as other words in the list, look at the **second** letters.

> **Ac**ropolis
> **Al**exander
> **At**hens

If the word you are looking up has the same first and second letters as others in the list, look at the **third** letters.

> **col**ony
> **Cor**inth
> **cou**ncil

The Research Process, continued

4 GATHER INFORMATION, continued

How to Skim and Scan When you **skim and scan** a text, read it quickly to see if the article has the information you need. If it does, you can take the time to read it more carefully. If it doesn't, go on to another source.

To Skim:

- Read the **title**. Ask yourself: Is this useful for my topic?
- Read the **headings**. Read the **beginning sentences**. Ask yourself: What is the main idea?
- Read the **ending sentence**. Look for a summary of the article. Ask yourself: Can I use this information?

To Scan:

Look for **key words** or **details**. Many authors use dark type or italics to show that a word or idea is important. If the key words match your topic, read the article more carefully. If not, look for another article.

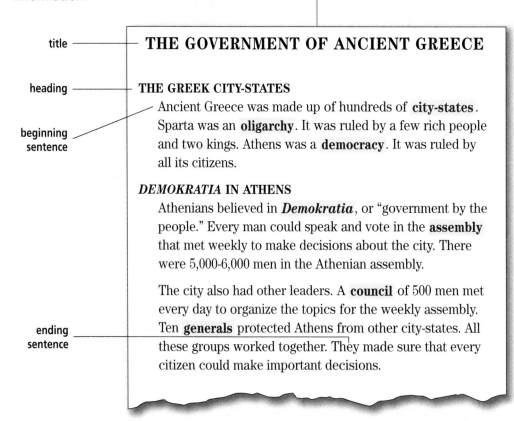

title ——

THE GOVERNMENT OF ANCIENT GREECE

heading ——

THE GREEK CITY-STATES

beginning sentence ——

Ancient Greece was made up of hundreds of **city-states**. Sparta was an **oligarchy**. It was ruled by a few rich people and two kings. Athens was a **democracy**. It was ruled by all its citizens.

DEMOKRATIA IN ATHENS

Athenians believed in ***Demokratia***, or "government by the people." Every man could speak and vote in the **assembly** that met weekly to make decisions about the city. There were 5,000-6,000 men in the Athenian assembly.

ending sentence ——

The city also had other leaders. A **council** of 500 men met every day to organize the topics for the weekly assembly. Ten **generals** protected Athens from other city-states. All these groups worked together. They made sure that every citizen could make important decisions.

How to Take Notes You can write important words, phrases, and ideas as you read and research topics. The notes will help you remember and organize the information.

Follow these steps to set up your notecards:

1. Write your **research question** .

2. Write the **source** where you found your information.
   - **For books:** Write the title, author, and page number.
   - **For magazines and newspapers:** Write the name, date, volume, and issue number of the source. Add the title of the article in quotation marks.

3. List **details and facts** in your own words.

4. Use **quotation marks** when you copy exactly what you read.

Notecard for a Book

Who were leaders in ancient Greece?

Greek History by Ed Melgar, page 45

— 500 men in the Council

— met every day

— worked to **"organize the topics for the weekly assembly."**

Notecard for a Magazine or Newspaper

How did Greek citizens vote?

Civilization Magazine, Feb. 2000

Vol. 18, No. 1 "Athenian Voting"

— generals and council chosen by lottery

— voting by ostraka and bronze discs

— "Ancient Greeks took voting very seriously."

The Research Process, continued

⑤ ORGANIZE INFORMATION

Make an Outline An outline can help you organize your report. Follow these steps to turn your notes into an outline.

1. Put all the notecards with the same research question together.

2. Turn your notes into an outline.

   - First, turn your question into a **main idea.** Each main idea follows a Roman numeral.

   - Next, find details that go with the main idea. Add them to your outline. Each **detail** follows a capital letter. Each **related detail** follows a number.

3. Write a **title** for your outline. The title tells what your outline is all about. You can use it again when you write your report.

Sample Outline

> The Birth of Democracy
> I. Athenian Citizen-Leaders
>   A. The assembly
>   B. The council
>   1. 500 men
>   2. Met every day
>   C. The ten generals
> II. Voting in ancient Greece
>   A. Athenian elections
>   1. Generals chosen by lottery
>   2. Council chosen by lottery
>   B. Voting in courts
>   1. "The ancient Greeks took voting very seriously."
>   2. Ostraka pottery
>   3. Bronze discs

6 WRITE A RESEARCH REPORT

Now use your outline to write a **research report**. Turn the main ideas and details from your outline into sentences and paragraphs.

Write the Title and Introduction Copy the title from your outline, and write an interesting introduction to tell what your report is mostly about.

Outline

The Birth of Democracy

Title and Introduction

The Birth of Democracy

Did you ever wonder where democracy began? You may think that it started with George Washington in 1776, but you would be wrong by almost 3,000 years! It began with the ancient Greeks of Athens and spread around the world.

Write the Body Use your main ideas to write a topic sentence for each paragraph. Then use your details and related details to write sentences about the main idea.

Outline

I. Athenian Citizen-Leaders
   A. The assembly
   B. The council
      1. 500 men
      2. Met every day
   C. The ten generals

Topic Sentence and Details

Democracy began with the ancient Greek government of demokratia. For example, every man in Athens was a **citizen-leader**. He was a member of the **assembly** for his city-state. He could also be part of the **500 man council** that **met every day** to "organize the topics for the weekly assembly." **Ten generals** protected the city-state from wars.

Write a Conclusion Write a sentence for each main idea in the last paragraph of your report.

Outline

I. Athenian Citizen-Leaders

II. Voting in Ancient Greece

Conclusion

Ancient Athens was the birthplace of democracy. There, **citizen-leaders** listened to every man equally. They invented creative ways to **vote** secretly. In the U.S., we have learned a lot from the Athenian example. Maybe people in the future will use our country as a model of democracy, too!

The Birth of Democracy

Did you ever wonder where democracy began? You may think that it started with George Washington in 1776, but you would be wrong by almost 3,000 years! It began with the ancient Greeks of Athens and spread around the world.

Democracy began with the ancient Greek government of demokratia. For example, every man in Athens was a citizen-leader. He was a member of the assembly for his city-state. He could also be part of the 500 man council that met every day to "organize the topics for the weekly assembly." Ten generals protected the city-state from wars.

Athenian citizens "took voting very seriously." They knew that elections could be unfair. Council members and generals were chosen by lottery. In courts, ostraka pottery and bronze voting discs made sure that people voted privately.

Ancient Athens was the birthplace of democracy. There, citizen-leaders listened to every man equally. They invented creative ways to vote secretly. In the U.S., we have learned a lot from the Athenian example. Maybe people in the future will use our country as a model of democracy, too!

INTRODUCTION
The **title** and **introduction** tell what your report is about.

BODY
The **body** of the report tells the facts you found. Each paragraph goes with a main idea from your outline.

CONCLUSION
The **conclusion** is a summary of the topic.

Speaking and Listening

You talk, or speak, to others every day. That's how you express your ideas. You also listen to others to learn about new ideas.

HOW TO BE A GOOD LISTENER

Good listeners listen carefully to what others say.

How to Be a Good Listener

- Pay attention. Open your eyes and ears. Look at the speaker as you listen.
- Be quiet while the speaker talks.
- Only interrupt when you need the speaker to talk louder.
- Save your questions until the speaker is finished.

HOW TO PARTICIPATE IN A DISCUSSION

Sometimes you will discuss ideas as a class, in a group, or with a partner. You may also have a conference with a teacher or a peer to talk about your writing. Discussions are good ways to find information, check your understanding, and share ideas.

How to Participate in a Discussion

- Use good listening skills.
- Give the speaker a chance to finish before you respond.
- Make positive comments about the ideas of others.
- Respect everyone's ideas and feelings.
- Only talk about one topic at a time.
- Ask questions if you need more information.

Share your ideas with a group.

Speaking and Listening, continued

HOW TO LISTEN CAREFULLY

When you listen carefully, you can find out how to do something or learn more about a topic. As you listen:

- Think about what you hear. How does it relate to what you already know?
- Listen for key words and important details. Take notes to help you remember the ideas.

  Example:

  ecosystem: things in nature and how they work together

- Ask yourself: What is the speaker's purpose? Does the speaker want to inform, entertain, or persuade the audience?
- Pay attention to the speaker's voice, gestures, and expressions. What do they tell you about how the speaker feels about the topic?
- Think about the speaker. Ask yourself: What does the speaker know about the topic?
- Summarize what the speaker says in your own mind. Do you agree or disagree? What new information did you learn?

HOW TO GIVE AN ORAL PRESENTATION

There are many kinds of oral presentations. Decide if you want to make a speech, give a report, recite a poem, or give a performance. Follow these steps to prepare your presentation.

1 **Plan Your Presentation** Think about your audience. What ideas do you want to share? What is the best way to share your ideas?

- Organize your information. You can use a graphic organizer to show the details and the order you will use to present ideas.

  Outline

  I. Ecosystem
     A. Is like a community
     B. Includes all living things in nature
  II. Food Chain
     A. Is different in different places
     B. Has a sequence
        1. Microorganisms in soil
        2. Plants grow
        3. Animals eat plants

- Think of a way to interest the audience and introduce your topic. You may want to use a quotation, make a startling statement, or ask a question.
- Write your main ideas on notecards. You can look at them as you speak to help you remember what to say.

Beginning of food chain
—microorganisms in the soil
   create food for plants
—plants grow

- Use visuals and technology to support your ideas. Organize them to match your notes.

Food Chain Poster

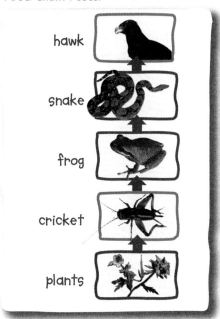

hawk
snake
frog
cricket
plants

- Use your notecards, visuals, and technology to practice your presentation in front of a mirror or your family. You can videotape or tape record your presentation as you practice. This can help you find ideas about how to improve.

Speaking and Listening, continued

HOW TO GIVE AN ORAL PRESENTATION
continued

2 **Choose the Right Language and Tone** Will you speak to your friends, to young kids, or to adults? Think about your topic, audience, and purpose. Then decide the best way to give your presentation.

To give a persuasive speech:
- Use a strong, clear voice. Change your tone to describe important points.
- Use formal language to tell the facts. Use persuasive words to give opinions.

To tell a story:
- Use informal language to make the characters seem real. Change your voice to show when a new character speaks.
- Use expressions, gestures, and other movements to show the characters' feelings and the action.

To give a formal report:
- Use formal language to tell the facts and information.
- Speak slowly and clearly so everyone can understand the information.
- Tell the information in a logical order.
- Use examples and visuals that show your main points.

Use formal language to give a report.

3 **Give Your Presentation** Now you are ready. As you present your ideas:

- Stand up straight.
- Look at everyone in the audience.
- Speak slowly and clearly. Use a loud voice so everyone can hear you.
- Use expressions and movements that go with the information you are presenting.
- Make sure that the audience can see you and your visuals.
- Stay calm and relaxed.
- Thank the audience when you're done. Ask for questions when you are finished.

Viewing and Representing

You can get information from the things you see, or view. You can also use visuals to help you show your ideas.

HOW TO EVALUATE WHAT YOU SEE

There are many things to view—photographs, videos, graphs, charts, and Web sites. You can also watch when people use movements to send messages without words. Try this process with the visual below.

1 **View and Look for Details** Study the visual. Ask yourself:

- Who or what does the image show? Are there other details that tell when, where, why, or how?
- How does the visual make me feel? Do I like looking at it?
- Do I like the colors? How does the size or shape of the visual affect me?

2 **Think About the Purpose and the Message** What you see can change the way you feel about a topic. Ask yourself:

- What message does the visual give?
- Why did the artist create the visual? Does it make me want to do something? Does it give me new information?
- What does the visual tell about the topic?
- How does the artist want me to feel when I look at the visual?

3 **Look for Stereotypes** A stereotype is a general opinion that is not always true. It's like saying that because one dog is mean, all dogs are mean. Try to find any stereotypes in the visual.

Persistent Sea No. 2, by O. Louis Guglielmi, oil on canvas

Viewing and Representing, continued

HOW TO REPRESENT YOUR IDEAS

There are many resources, or **media**, to help you make your point more clearly. Choose media that match your purpose and your topic.

A beautiful **illustration** can add creativity and make a story come alive.

Illustration

A **flow chart** can show steps in a process.

Flow Chart

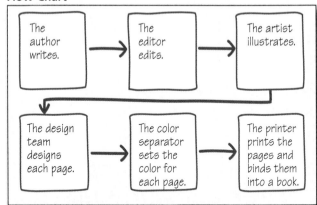

A **chart** or a **graph** can show comparisons. You can find more graphic organizers on pages 340–347.

Chart

Number of Endangered Species in the United States

Classification	Number of Species
Mammals	61
Birds	75
Reptiles	14
Fishes	69
Insects	28

Graph

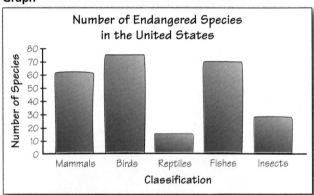

HOW TO MATCH MEDIA TO YOUR MESSAGE

Choose the best media to give your message and help you get your audience's attention. Look at the different media you can use on pages 362–363. Here are a few examples.

1 **To Entertain** Include props, illustrations of the setting, or slides for a backdrop. Create a film strip, animation, or a video.

2 **To Inform** Use maps and charts to show information. You can make a time line to show the order of events or use a transparency to show information on an overhead projector.

Most Giant Pandas originated in China.

3 **To Persuade** Show images that will change people's opinions. You might use slides or photographs to touch people's emotions.

Fewer than 1,000 pandas live in the wild.

Strategies for Taking Tests

These strategies will help you learn how to take tests and show what you know.

MULTIPLE-CHOICE TEST

For a **multiple-choice test**, mark the best answer from a list of choices.

1 Read Test Directions Carefully Directions tell what you need to do. Words like *best*, *always*, *only*, *all*, and *never* will help you find the correct answer.

> **Directions: Read each question. Circle the best answer.**
>
> **4.** Which type of transportation causes the least air pollution?
> | | |
> |---|---|
> | **A** a bus | **C** a bike |
> | **B** a car | **D** a motorcycle |

2 Mark Your Answers You may need to fill in a bubble on an answer sheet, circle an answer, or write your answer on another paper. Be sure to mark your answer in the right place.

> **Read the sentence. Mark the answer that gives the best meaning for the underlined word.**
>
> **5.** People can <u>recycle</u> to help save the Earth.
> **F** use products over again
> **G** go backwards on a bicycle
> **H** throw away all their trash
> **J** keep trash in a special place

> **4.** Ⓐ Ⓑ Ⓒ Ⓓ
> **5.** Ⓕ Ⓖ Ⓗ Ⓙ

3 Plan Your Time Skip hard questions. If you have time, you can go back to them later.

4 Read Items Again If you are not sure about an answer, read the item again. Think about all the answer choices. Which one seems best?

TRUE-FALSE TEST

In a **true-false test**, decide if a statement is true or false.

1 Read Carefully If *any* part of the statement is false, the answer is false. If you're still not sure, make your best guess!

2 Look for Key Words Watch for words like *never*, *always*, *all*, and *no*. Statements with those words are usually false.

> _false_   **1.** Businesses never clean up the dirty air from their factories.

SHORT-ANSWER TEST

In a **short-answer test**, write a word, a phrase, or a sentence to answer a question. Look for key words like *who* or *what* that tell you what to write in the answer.

> **12.** What do farmers use to kill insects?
> __pesticides__

ESSAY TEST

For an **essay test**, write one or more paragraphs to answer a question.

1 **Study the Item and Key Words** Read the question at least two times. Look for key words that tell you exactly what to do. You might see prompts like these:

- Compare the rain forest and the tundra.
- Explain how acid rain is formed.
- Describe how recycling helps the Earth.

2 **Plan Your Answer** Think about the key words and the topic. Write facts or details you know in a web, chart, or another graphic organizer. This can help you organize your writing.

3 **Write the Essay** Use the words in the prompt to write an introduction. Then use your notes and details to write your essay.

- Write a topic sentence for each paragraph.
- Write the important details in the body.
- Sum up your essay with a concluding sentence.
- Read your essay before you turn it in. Be sure that you answered all the questions in the prompt.

Prompt

> **1.** Explain three ways that people can reduce air pollution.

Sample Answer

> People can reduce air pollution in three main ways. One way is to carpool. People can share rides. A second way is to walk or ride a bicycle for short trips. Finally, people can encourage businesses to stop making air pollution. If we do these things today, we'll have cleaner air in the future!

The Writing Process

Writing is a creative way to express yourself. The Writing Process can help you write in a clear and interesting way.

PREWRITE

When you **prewrite**, you plan your work. You can decide what to write about and how to organize your ideas.

1 Collect Ideas Use your experiences or brainstorm ideas with others. Keep a list of writing ideas in a notebook, a journal, or a computer file. Look at the list when you get ready to write.

2 Choose a Topic A **topic** is the main idea you write about. Sometimes you may choose your own topic. Other times, your teacher may give a **prompt**, or writing assignment. Choose a topic that is important or interesting to you.

> I could write about...
>
> a concert my friends and I went to
>
> when my grandparents came to the U.S.
>
> why we need more school dances
>
> why the eagle is a popular symbol

3 Plan Your Writing An **FATP chart** helps you organize your paper before you write.

FATP Chart

HOW TO UNLOCK A PROMPT
Form: _personal narrative_
Audience: _my teacher and classmates_
Topic: _when my grandparents came to the U.S._
Purpose: _to describe a personal experience_

Write this information in an FATP chart:

- The **form** is the type of writing. You can write essays, stories, or other forms.
- The **audience** is your reader or readers. Choose the best way to write for your audience.
- A specific **topic** will help you find the details you need.
- The **purpose** is the reason you write. You can describe, inform, persuade, or express your thoughts or feelings.

For more about writing for a specific audience or purpose, see pages 390–392.

4 Gather Details Use your memories to write about a personal experience. For other writing, you can talk to your classmates or do research to find information.

You can show details in

- charts, lists, or word webs
- diagrams and pictures
- notes on notecards
- story maps or time lines
- gathering grids to write down answers to your questions

Gathering Grid

Topic: Vietnam	Get to Know Vietnam (book)	Internet
What is the population?		
What fuels the economy?		

Show your details in a way that works best for you and for your topic.

5 Get Organized Put the details in order. Organize them as you write, or use numbers to show the order.

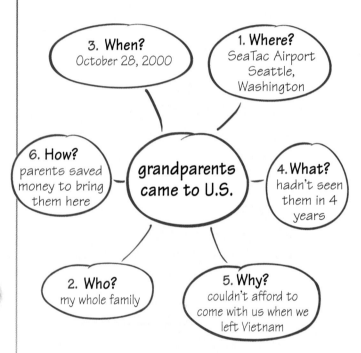

3. **When?** October 28, 2000

1. **Where?** SeaTac Airport Seattle, Washington

6. **How?** parents saved money to bring them here

grandparents came to U.S.

4. **What?** hadn't seen them in 4 years

2. **Who?** my whole family

5. **Why?** couldn't afford to come with us when we left Vietnam

The Writing Process, continued

DRAFT

Now you are ready to write. Write a **first draft** that has all your ideas. Don't worry about mistakes! Use your details to write sentences and paragraphs. As you write, you may think of new ideas and details. Add the new ideas as you think of them.

Trang Bui's Draft

> My family stood by the windows and watched the plane land at SeaTac Airport in Seattle on October 28, 2000. We were so excited to see the plane. The people started coming through the door. We lined up so we could see. I had to lift my little brother up so he could see.
>
> Suddenly everyone was hugging and crying. "I see them," my mother cried. My little brother tried to hide. My brother didn't know my grandparents. He was feeling shy.

REVISE

When you **revise,** you make your draft better.

1 **Read Your Draft** Make sure that your ideas are clear, complete, and written in the best way. Ask yourself questions from the Revision Checklist:

Revision Checklist

- ☑ Did I follow the plan on my FATP chart?
- ☑ Is my writing interesting?
- ☑ Did I use different kinds of sentences?
- ☑ Does my writing have a beginning, a middle, and an ending?
- ☑ Are my ideas clear?
- ☑ Do I need to add more details?
- ☑ Are my details in the best order?
- ☑ Did I use words that say what I mean?

❷ Plan Writing Conferences After you review your work, you can ask others for their opinions.

You may want to ask your teacher for **feedback,** or ideas about how to make your work better. Set up a time to meet with your teacher. Take notes as you talk about ways to improve. Follow your teacher's suggestions. Then meet again to see how the changes look.

You may also have **peer conferences** with your classmates. Sometimes other people have good ideas about how to improve your work. You may also help others find ideas for their papers!

Guidelines for Peer Conferences

When you're the writer:
1. Tell your purpose for writing.
2. Read your writing aloud, or give copies to the readers.
3. Ask for help about specific things.
4. Listen carefully to your reader's comments. Take notes to help you remember.
5. Use the comments that will make your writing better.

When you're the reader:
1. Read each word carefully.
2. Take notes as you read.
3. Look for the best parts of the writing. Explain why those parts are good.
4. If you don't understand something, ask questions.
5. Give specific ideas. Tell how the writer can improve the details, sentences, or organization.

Ask your teacher for feedback.

The Writing Process, continued

REVISE, continued

❸ Mark Your Changes Now you are ready to revise your paper. Think about ways to make your ideas clear and easy to understand. Then use Revising Marks to show corrections to your work.

It may be helpful to use a different color of pencil or pen to mark your changes. A new color will make your notes easier to see and read as you make a new draft.

Use Revising Marks to correct your first draft.

Trang Bui's Revisions

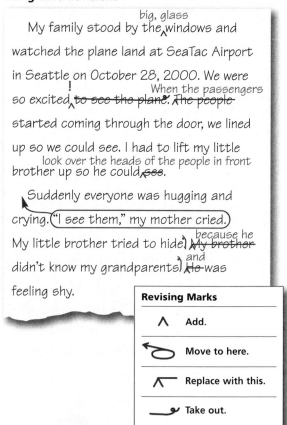

My family stood by the ^big, glass^ windows and watched the plane land at SeaTac Airport in Seattle on October 28, 2000. We were so excited^!^ ~~to see the plane.~~ When the passengers ~~The people~~ started coming through the door, we lined up so we could see. I had to lift my little brother up so he could ~~see.~~ look over the heads of the people in front.

Suddenly everyone was hugging and crying. "I see them," my mother cried. My little brother tried to hide) ~~My brother~~ because he didn't know my grandparents) ~~He was~~ and feeling shy.

Revising Marks

∧	Add.
↶	Move to here.
⌃	Replace with this.
⤸	Take out.

If you are using a computer, look for ways to edit your work on a word-processing program. See pages 357–358 for some ideas about how to add text, cut, and paste.

EDIT AND PROOFREAD

Find and correct any mistakes on your paper.

❶ Check Your Sentences You can **edit** your sentences to make them clear, complete, and correct. Ask yourself:

- Does each sentence have a subject and a predicate?
- Did I break up run-on sentences?
- Can I combine short sentences into longer sentences?

Look for more ideas about how to improve your writing on Handbook pages 390–401.

Check for Mistakes When you proofread,
❷ you look for mistakes in:

- capital letters
- punctuation
- subject–verb agreement
- misspelled words.

❸ Mark Your Corrections Use the Proofreading Marks to show your corrections or make the corrections when you find them in your document on the computer.

Trang Bui's Proofread Draft

¶ When we left Vietnam, my grandparents
had to stay behind. "We are too old to go
someplace new," my grandfather said. My
grandmother cooked a special dinner for us
(an incredible)
before we left, but he could not eat. We
(she)
didnt know how long it would be before we
would see each other again.

Proofreading Marks

∧	Add.
⩓	Add a comma.
⊙	Add a period.
≡	Capitalize.
╱	Make lowercase.
⌿	Take out.
¶	Indent.

❹ Make a Final Draft Rewrite your work neatly. Make the changes you marked. If you are using a computer, print out your new copy. For more ideas about formatting your paper, see Handbook pages 360–361.

PUBLISH

After you correct your work, you can publish, or share it with others. You can:

- E-mail it to friends or family members.
- Make a video or recording of you reading it aloud.
- Display it in your classroom.
- Send it to your favorite magazine. Ask if they will publish it.

The Best Day of My Life
by Trang Bui

My family stood by the big, glass windows and watched the plane land at SeaTac Airport in Seattle on October 28, 2000. We were so excited! When the passengers started coming through the door, we lined up so we could see. I had to lift my little brother up so he could look over the heads of the people in front.

"I see them," my mother cried. Suddenly everyone was hugging and crying. My little brother tried to hide because he didn't know my grandparents and was feeling shy.

When we left Vietnam, my grandparents had to stay behind. "We are too old to go someplace new," my grandfather said. My grandmother cooked an incredible dinner for us before we left, but she could not eat. We didn't know how long it would be before we would see each other again.

My family came to Seattle to start a new life. My parents worked in the donut shop and sent some of the money they earned each month to my grandparents. It took four long years, but my grandparents finally arrived, and we're all together again.

EVALUATE YOUR WRITING

Save examples of your writing in a folder or **portfolio**. Look at your work from time to time to see how you are becoming a better writer.

1 Organize Your Portfolio Put your writing in order by date. Or, make special sections for work with the same purpose, audience, or form.

2 Review Your Portfolio Each time you add work to your portfolio, ask yourself:

- How does this compare to my earlier work?
- How is my writing getting better?
- How can I make my writing better?

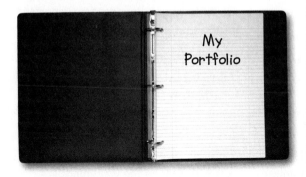

3 Think About How You Write Look at your work. Think about the words you use, the kinds of sentences you write, and the topics you like to write about. These things make up your own style.

You may want to write about the work in your portfolio. Tell why you chose to include each selection. Then write about improvements you have made. A portfolio can be a great way to show others your unique writing style.

The Writer's Craft

Good writers always work to improve their writing. You can use the ideas in this section to make your writing the best it can be.

HOW TO WRITE FOR A SPECIFIC PURPOSE

Good writers change how and why they write to fit their main purpose.
The **purpose** is why you are writing.

PURPOSE	WRITING EXAMPLES
To describe	Use details to help your reader "see" what you are describing. Many weathered pueblos are scattered through the dry, sandy deserts of New Mexico. For a poem, use colorful verbs to describe how something looks. Sky City The rain pounds, The sun bakes, The wind molds, The pueblo stands strong.
To inform or to explain	Give directions to explain how to do something. To make adobe bricks, mix earth, straw, and water. Then pour the mix into wooden molds. Finally, let the bricks dry in the sun. Or, write to give your readers important facts about a topic. The Acoma Pueblo was built around 1075 in central New Mexico. The name Acoma, means "People of the White Rock."
To persuade	Advertisements use persuasive words to convince people to buy or do something. **Are you curious about pueblos? Come to beautiful, mysterious New Mexico to see them for yourself!** **New Mexico!** Editorials give opinions and use persuasive words to change the way things are. The government should do more to protect the pueblos in the United States. They are an important part of our history.

PURPOSE	WRITING EXAMPLES
To express your thoughts and feelings	Write a journal entry to tell about your thoughts and feelings. June 10, 2001 Our class just went to the pueblo exhibit at the museum. I wonder what it was like to live in a pueblo hundreds of years ago.
To entertain	You could use a cartoon to make your readers laugh. What do you call bees that fly around a pueblo? Adobees!
To learn	It helps to write things down as you learn about the topic. That way you can see what you already know—and what you don't know. Pueblos are a fascinating part of North American history. Now I want to know more about the people who lived in pueblos.

The Writer's Craft, continued

HOW TO WRITE FOR A SPECIFIC AUDIENCE

Your **audience** will read what you write. Knowing your audience
will help you decide what words to use and what kinds of details to include.

AUDIENCE	WRITING EXAMPLES
Adults and strangers	Use formal language and details. That will help them understand what they might not know. *I enjoyed the chance to attend the museum's new pueblo exhibit.*
Your friends	Use informal language because they will probably know what you mean. *The pueblo exhibit at the museum was cool! I can't wait to go again!*
People younger than you	Use simple language so that they can understand. *You can learn about the pueblo. Go to a museum. Learn how to make adobes.*

HOW TO CHOOSE THE RIGHT WORDS

When you use the right words, you can help your readers see what you are writing about.

❶ Use Specific Nouns Choose nouns that say exactly what you mean.

Just OK

The boat went across the water.

Much Better

The sailboat sped across the lake.

❷ Use Colorful Verbs Choose verbs that give the best picture of the action.

Just OK

The wave came up on the beach.

Much Better

The wave crashed on the beach.

❸ Add Sensory Words Use words that tell what you see, hear, smell, taste, and touch to help your readers imagine they are there!

Just OK

Mark sat on the beach. He pushed the sand around. The sun was hot.

Much Better

Mark sat on the beach by the crashing waves. He let the soft, white sand fall through his fingers. The hot sun beat down on his parched skin, and he could almost taste the salty air.

❹ Use Words with Just the Right Meaning Some words seem similar in meaning but may give readers a different feeling. Look at the two sentences below. The second sentence tells the same idea in a more positive way.

She looks **skinny** in her red dress.

She looks **slender** in her red dress.

The Writer's Craft, continued

HOW TO CHOOSE THE RIGHT WORDS, continued

5 Use Figurative Language You can use **figurative language** to help your readers "see" ordinary things in new ways.

- Use a **simile** with *like* or *as* to make comparisons:

> The man swims like a dolphin.

- Use a **metaphor** to tell what something is like, without using the words *like* or *as*:

> The man is a playful dolphin.

- Use **personification** to give human qualities to a non-human thing:

> Seagulls laugh overhead.

- Use **hyperbole,** or exaggeration, to add humor to your writing:

> The squawking gulls can be heard around the world.

HOW TO IMPROVE YOUR SENTENCES

1 Combine Sentences Try to combine a lot of short sentences into one longer sentence.

Just OK

> I put on my snowboard.
> I sped down the hill.
> I reached the bottom.

Much Better

> I put on my snowboard and sped down the hill until I reached the bottom.

> I put on my snowboard, sped down the hill, and reached the bottom.

2 Break Up Sentences Long sentences can be hard to understand. Break up run-on sentences to make your meaning clear.

Just OK

> The first time I went snowboarding, I fell a lot, but I watched other snowboarders and I saw that most of them fell, too, then I didn't feel so bad.

Much Better

> The first time I went snowboarding, I fell a lot. I watched other snowboarders and saw that most of them fell, too. Then I didn't feel so bad.

❸ Start Sentences in Different Ways Change the way your sentences begin. It can make your writing more interesting.

Just OK

> Darcy went snowboarding last winter. Darcy started out well. Darcy tried to turn, but she fell. Darcy laughed at herself, brushed off the snow, and got back up. Darcy fell a few more times, but finally made it down the hill!

Much Better

> Last winter, Darcy went snowboarding. She started out well. When she tried to turn, she fell. Darcy brushed off the snow, laughed at herself, and got back up. After a few more falls, Darcy finally made it down the hill!

WHAT IS A PARAGRAPH?

A **paragraph** is a group of sentences that all tell about the same idea. The **topic sentence** tells the main idea. The other sentences give **supporting details** that tell more about the main idea.

A topic sentence can come at the beginning of a paragraph.

> The Pike Place Market in Seattle is a great place to visit. At the market, you can shop for fresh fruits, vegetables, and flowers. You can watch the fish sellers toss fish across the aisles to each other. If you're hungry, you can find just about any kind of food in the many cafes and food stands.

Or, a topic sentence can come at the end of a paragraph.

> At the market, you can shop for fresh fruits, vegetables, and flowers. You can watch the fish sellers toss fish across the aisles to each other. If you're hungry, you can find just about any kind of food in the many cafes and food stands. The Pike Place Market in Seattle is a great place to visit.

The Writer's Craft, continued

HOW TO ORGANIZE PARAGRAPHS

There are many ways to organize your paragraphs.

1 **Sequence Paragraphs** Some paragraphs are organized by time. **Time order words** tell when things happen.

> One day I went fishing with Dad. **First** we woke up at 4 A.M. **Next** we rowed our boat to the middle of the lake. **Then** we waited three hours! We **finally** caught one tiny fish. When Dad goes fishing again, I'm staying home!

2 **Comparison Paragraphs** Some paragraphs tell how things are alike and different. Use **comparison words** to show the similarities and differences.

> **Like** human beings, whales are mammals. **Both** give birth to live babies and feed them milk. **Unlike** most mammals, **however,** whales can stay underwater for a long time.

3 **Paragraphs in Space Order** For a description, use **space order** to tell what you see from left to right, near to far, or top to bottom. **Direction words and phrases** tell where things are.

> An octopus looks strange. Its head and body look like one big bulb. Eight long legs, called tentacles, **come out of** the bulb. Each tentacle has two rows of suckers **along the bottom.** It uses the suckers to hold onto rocks and find food.

4 **Cause-and-Effect Paragraphs** In this kind of paragraph, the topic sentence tells the **cause**, or why something happens. Detail sentences tell the **effects**, or what happens because of the cause.

> Ricky sat on his surfboard. Suddenly, he saw a large, dark object swim toward him. "Could it be a shark?" he thought. His heart pounded. He paddled quickly toward the beach. When he looked back, he saw a huge log on top of the waves!

5 Paragraphs in Logical Order You can change the order you use to present your ideas. You may want to present ideas in order from general to specific or from most important to least important.

> If we do not limit the number of fish we catch, there will not be enough fish in the future. There may be a lot of food at first, but we would run out quickly. Some fish may become extinct. Fish are an important part of the food chain. If we over-fish the ocean, animals like seals and whales could be hurt, too.

6 Opinion Paragraphs In an opinion paragraph, tell your ideas about something. Write your opinion in the **topic sentence.** Give the reasons for your opinion in the detail sentences.

> **I think the octopus is a fascinating sea creature.** It can do many unusual things. An octopus can change its color. It shoots an inky cloud when it senses danger. It can fit into small hiding places. Don't you think the octopus is fascinating, too?

7 Persuasive Paragraphs A persuasive paragraph begins with a **thesis statement** that gives your opinion or tells the main idea. Facts, examples, and other details are called **supporting arguments**.

> **The Eastern North Pacific gray whale should be put back on the endangered species list.** One population of gray whales is already extinct. Another population is endangered. Gray whales stay close to the shore, and can get trapped in fishing nets. Their breeding grounds in Baja, California, are threatened by salt-extraction plants. We should work now to save the Eastern North Pacific gray whale.

The Writer's Craft, continued

HOW TO PUT PARAGRAPHS TOGETHER

If you write more than two paragraphs, organize your writing into three parts: the **introduction,** the **body,** and the **conclusion.**

1 **Write a Strong Introduction** Name the topic and grab your readers' interest.

- **Ask a question.**

> What's so hot about smoking?

- **Express an emotion or an opinion.**

> I think smoking stinks!

- **Describe an action or event.**

> Smoking is one of the biggest killers in the U.S.

- **Make a startling statement, or give an interesting or unusual fact.**

> Cigarettes contain more than fifteen harmful chemicals.

2 **Write the Body** In the **body paragraphs,** write details that support your main idea. The details should give facts and examples.

3 **Write a Conclusion** Tell an emotion or write a thoughtful idea.

> The easiest way to break a bad habit like smoking is never to start it in the first place!

HOW TO MAKE YOUR WRITING FLOW

1 **Use Transition Words** Words or phrases that help connect paragraphs are **transition words.** They help your readers follow your ideas.

Examples:

As a result	Also	Even though
As soon as	In addition	However
Finally	Like	On the other hand
Then	Plus	Yet

2 **Use the Same Point of View** If you are writing how you feel about something, tell about *your* feelings, not someone else's. To write about a character or another person, use details that show how that person thinks or feels.

> I think that smoking is an awful habit. If someone offers
> me
> ~~My friend~~ a cigarette, ~~he~~ always say~~s~~, "No way."

3 **Use the Same Verb Tenses** Keep your verbs all in the same tense so your readers won't get confused about when things happen.

> When someone offers me a cigarette, though, I always
> know
> say, "No way." That's because I ~~know~~ how bad it ~~was~~
> is
> for my lungs.

Smoking: A Bad Habit to Start

What's so hot about smoking? Nothing! Some kids smoke because it makes them feel older. Other kids think it will make them popular. When someone offers me a cigarette, though, I always say "No way." I know how bad it is for my **lungs**.

Did you know that your **lungs** take nearly 26,000 breaths a day? They need clean air and oxygen. Chemicals in cigarette smoke cause emphysema. This disease kills important air sacs in your lungs.

As soon as emphysema starts, it hurts your **lungs**. It becomes hard to breathe. Wouldn't it be smart to protect your lungs?

Plus, if you smoke, you can affect other people's lungs, too. About 3,000 non-smokers die every year from second-hand smoke. Young children can be hurt because their lungs are still growing. Do you really want to harm someone else just to be "cool"?

Sooner or later someone will ask if you want a cigarette. Before you decide, take a deep breath of clean, fresh air. Think about how good you feel now. Then play it safe. Don't smoke!

INTRODUCTION
The introduction gets the readers' interest and tells the writer's opinion.

BODY
The body gives details, facts, and arguments to support the writer's opinion.

This writer connected paragraphs by **repeating a word or phrase** and by using **transition words**.

All the sentences go together to show this writer's point of view. The verbs are all in the present tense.

CONCLUSION
In the last paragraph, the writer tells the readers to do something.

The Writer's Craft, continued

HOW TO MAKE YOUR WRITING BETTER

The words that you choose, the way that you put them together, and the ideas that you present make your writing unique. Try these techniques.

1 Show, Don't Tell You can just tell your readers about an event or a person. To give your readers the best picture, though, show them exactly what you mean!

This tells:

Kevin hated eating in the cafeteria. He was new at school and didn't know anyone. So he sat in a corner by himself. Then one day, a girl in his math class asked him to sit at her table. After that, Kevin felt much better.

This shows:

"I can't wait to finish my lunch and get out of here," thought Kevin. "I don't know anyone, anyway."

Then one day, Kevin heard a cheery voice from behind him. "Hey, do you want to sit with us?" the girl asked. It was Roberta from his math class.

"Sure," said Kevin, grinning. "How's it going?" he asked Roberta.

2 Elaborate *Elaborate* means "Tell me more!" Try these ways to add information to your writing.

- **Tell what came before or after.**

Without Elaboration

The ball dropped into the basket.

With Elaboration

After rolling around on the rim, the ball finally dropped into the basket.

- **Add sensory details.**

Without Details

Their player made an attempt for the basket. The crowd watched as the ball arched across the court and sank into the net without touching the rim.

With Details

Their tallest player made an attempt for the basket. The entire crowd watched silently as the orange ball arched high across the court and sank into the net without touching the skinny metal rim.

- **Add examples, facts, and other details.**

  Without Details

  The fans cheered.

  With Details

  The excited fans jumped up out of their seats, clapped their hands, and stomped their feet.

- **Add quotations or dialogue.**

  Without Dialogue

  The fans shouted.

  With Dialogue

  "Go, Rangers, go! You can do it!" the fans shouted.

③ Develop Your Own Writing Style and Voice

As a writer, you have your own voice, or personality. That means that your writing can show the kinds of words you like, ideas that are important to you, and how you feel about things. Let your readers "see" who you are. It will keep your writing interesting and exciting.

Just OK

I dribbled the ball through the zone. I made a shot for the basket. The ball rolled for a while on the basket rim, then fell in. I made the final shot to win the game.

Much Better

My heart was pounding. I dribbled the ball through the zone and took my best shot. I just stood there with my arms still raised up in the air. Would the ball ever stop rolling on the rim? When it finally dropped into the basket, I couldn't believe it! It was awesome! That basket put us ahead to win the game by one point!

Sentences

A sentence is a group of words that expresses a complete thought.
Every sentence has a subject and a predicate.
Every sentence begins with a capital letter.

SENTENCE TYPES	EXAMPLES
A **declarative sentence** tells something. It ends with a period.	The football game was on Friday. The coach made an important announcement.
An **interrogative sentence** asks a question. It ends with a question mark.	Can you tell me the news?

Kinds of Questions

Questions That Ask for a "Yes" or "No" Answer

	Answers
Is it about the team?	Yes.
Did the team win the game?	Yes.
Has the coach ever made an announcement like this before?	No.
Are the players sad?	No.
Were the fans surprised?	Yes.

Tag Questions

You will tell me the news, **won't you**?	Yes, I will. OR No, I won't.
You didn't forget it, **did you**?	Yes, I did. OR No, I didn't.

Questions That Ask for Specific Information

Who heard the announcement?	The team and the fans heard the announcement.
What did the coach say?	He said the team will play in a special game.
Where will the team play this game?	In Hawaii.
When did the coach find out?	Right before the game.
Why was our team chosen?	Our team was chosen because we won a lot of games.
How many games has the team won this year?	All ten of them.
Which coach made the announcement?	The tall one.

SENTENCE TYPES, continued	EXAMPLES
An **exclamatory sentence** shows surprise or strong emotion. It ends with an exclamation mark.	That's fantastic news! I can't believe it!
An **imperative sentence** gives a command. It usually begins with a verb. It often ends with a period. If an imperative sentence shows strong emotion, it ends with an exclamation mark.	Give the team my congratulations. Don't keep any more secrets from me ever again!

NEGATIVE SENTENCES	EXAMPLES
A **negative sentence** uses a **negative word** to say "no."	The game in Hawaii was **not** boring! **Nobody** in our town missed it on TV. Our team **never** played better.

Negative Words

never	none	nobody
no	no one	nothing
not		nowhere

Use only one negative word in a sentence.	The other team could not do ~~nothing~~ anything right. They never scored ~~no~~ any points.

COMPLETE SENTENCES	EXAMPLES
A **complete sentence** has a **subject** and a **predicate**. A complete sentence expresses a complete thought.	**Our team** **came home on Saturday**.
A **fragment** is not a sentence. It is not a complete thought. You can add information to a fragment to turn it into a complete sentence.	**Fragment:** a great team **Complete sentences:** We have a great team. A great team has great players.

Sentences, continued

SUBJECTS	EXAMPLES
To find the subject in a sentence, ask yourself: **Whom or what is the sentence about?**	
The **complete subject** includes all the words that tell about the subject.	**My favorite parks** are in the West. **People from all over the world** visit them.
The **simple subject** is the most important word in the **complete subject**.	My favorite **parks** are in the West. **People** from all over the world visit them.
Sometimes the subject is a **pronoun**. Be sure to include the pronoun in the sentence. **But:** When you give a command, you do not have to include the subject. The subject **you** is understood in an imperative sentence.	The map shows the campsites. **They** are by the river. Follow the rules of the park. Don't disturb the animals. Never throw trash in the streams.

Subject Pronouns

Singular	Plural
I	we
you	you
he, she, it	they

PREDICATES	EXAMPLES
The predicate of a sentence tells what the subject is, has, or does.	
The **complete predicate** includes all the words in the predicate.	Yosemite **is a beautiful park**. It **has huge waterfalls**. People **hike to the waterfalls**.
The **simple predicate** is the **verb**. It is the most important word in the predicate.	Yosemite **is** a beautiful park. It **has** huge waterfalls. People **hike** to the waterfalls.

Waterfall in Yosemite
National Park

SUBJECT–VERB AGREEMENT	EXAMPLES

The verb must always agree with the subject of the sentence.

A **singular subject** names one person or thing. Use a **singular verb** with a singular subject.

A **plural subject** tells about more than one person or thing. Use a **plural verb** with a plural subject.

Another popular **park** **is** the Grand Canyon.
It **has** a powerful river.

The **cliffs** **are** beautiful.
We **were amazed** by their colors.

> **Singular and Plural Verbs**
>
> | Singular | Plural |
> |---|---|
> | The park **is** big. | The parks **are** big. |
> | The park **was** beautiful. | The parks **were** beautiful. |
> | The park **has** campsites. | The parks **have** campsites. |
> | The park **does** not **open** until spring. | The parks **do** not **open** until spring. |

Study the chart to see how **action verbs** agree with their subjects.

When you tell about one other person or thing, use an action verb that ends in **s**.

> **More Singular and Plural Verbs**
>
> | Singular | Plural |
> |---|---|
> | I **hike** in the park. | We **hike** in the park. |
> | You **hike** in the park. | You **hike** in the park. |
> | He **hikes** in the park. | They **hike** in the park. |
> | She **hikes** in the park. | |
> | The dog **hikes** in the park. | The dogs **hike** in the park. |

The **subject** and **verb** must agree even if the subject comes after the verb.

There **are** other amazing **parks** in Arizona.
Here **is** a **list** of them.

In some questions, look for the **subject** between the **helping and main verbs**. The helping verb must agree with the subject.

Has your **friend** **visited** the parks?
Have your **friends** **visited** the parks?

Sentences, continued

PHRASES	EXAMPLES
A **phrase** is a group of related words that does not have a subject and a predicate.	**during the gold rush** **before the discovery of gold**
A **phrase** can be part of a complete sentence.	Many people came to California **during the gold rush**. **Before the discovery of gold**, about 15,000 people lived there.

CLAUSES	EXAMPLES
A **clause** is a group of words that has a **subject** and a **verb**. Some clauses are complete sentences.	The **population** of California **increased** to about 100,000 by 1849.
Some clauses are not.	because **miners came** to California
An **independent clause** expresses a complete thought and can stand alone as a sentence.	The miners were called "forty-niners."
A **dependent clause** does not express a complete thought. It is not a sentence.	because so many arrived in 1849

Words That Can Signal a Dependent Clause

Cause Words	Time Words		Words that Express Conditions	Relative Pronouns	
because	after	whenever	although	that	who
since	as	while	as long as	which	whom
	before	until	if		whose
	when		unless		

A **dependent clause** can be combined with an **independent clause** to form a sentence.	The miners were called "forty-niners" because so many arrived in 1849. <u>independent clause</u> <u>dependent clause</u> When they found gold, the miners got rich. <u>dependent clause</u> <u>independent clause</u>

SIMPLE SENTENCES	EXAMPLES
A **simple sentence** is one independent clause. It has a **subject** and a **predicate**.	The miners needed goods and services.

COMPOUND SENTENCES	EXAMPLES
When you join two independent clauses, you make a **compound sentence**. Use a **conjunction** to join the clauses.	Some people opened food markets. The miners bought food. ▼ **Some people opened food markets, and the miners bought food.** Other people opened stores. It was still hard to get supplies. ▼ **Other people opened stores, but it was still hard to get supplies.**

Conjunctions

and   but   or

Put a **comma** before the **conjunction**.	The miners used gold to buy things, **and** the shopkeepers ended up with the gold.

COMPLEX SENTENCES	EXAMPLES
To make a **complex sentence**, join an independent clause with one or more dependent clauses. If the dependent clause comes first, put a **comma** after it.	Many writers visited the camps where the miners worked. <u>independent clause</u> <u>dependent clause</u> While they were there, the writers wrote stories about the miners. <u>dependent clause</u> <u>independent clause</u> If people visit the camps today, they won't find any gold. <u>dependent clause</u> <u>independent clause</u>

Prospectors panned for gold in rivers and streams.

Parts of Speech

All the words in the English language can be categorized into eight groups. These groups are the eight parts of speech. Words are grouped into the parts of speech by the way they are used in a sentence.

THE EIGHT PARTS OF SPEECH	EXAMPLES
A **noun** names a person, place, thing, or idea.	**Samantha** lives in **Minnesota**. She skates on the **ice** every **day** to build her **skill**.
A **pronoun** takes the place of a noun.	**She** practices a dance routine for a show.
An **adjective** describes a noun or a pronoun.	She is a **powerful** skater. She is **graceful**, too.
A **verb** can tell what the subject of a sentence does or has. A **verb** can also link a word in the predicate to the subject.	Samantha **twists**, **turns**, and **jumps**. She **has** talent! Like many skaters, Samantha **is** a competitor. But, unlike most skaters, Samantha **is** deaf.
An **adverb** describes a verb, an adjective, or another adverb.	The music plays **loudly**, but she cannot hear it. Still, Samantha has become a **very** good skater. How can she perform **so** well?
A **preposition** shows how two things or ideas are related. It introduces a prepositional phrase.	A skating coach helps Samantha skate **on** the ice. He gives her signals as she moves **around** the rink. **During** the show, the people **in** the stands cheer **for** the skater.
A **conjunction** connects words or groups of words.	Samantha can't hear the people cheer, **but** she sees their smiles. Samantha smiles **and** waves back to the crowd.
An **interjection** expresses strong feeling.	Some people shout, "**Hooray!**" Others say, "**Wow!** What a talented skater!"

Nouns

A noun names a person, place, thing, or idea.
There are many different kinds of nouns.

COMMON AND PROPER NOUNS	EXAMPLES
A **common noun** names any person, place, thing, or idea.	A **teenager** sat by the **ocean** and read a **book**. It was about **ecology**.
A **proper noun** names one particular person, place, thing, or idea. The important words in a proper noun start with a <u>capital letter</u>.	**Daniel** sat by the **Atlantic Ocean** and read *Save the Manatee.*

A manatee

COMPOUND NOUNS	EXAMPLES
A **compound noun** is two or more words that express one idea. A compound noun can be: • two words • two words joined into one word • a hyphenated word	Some people call manatees **sea cows**. Manatees live in shallow waters where there is plenty of **sunlight**. In his book, Daniel saw a picture of a manatee baby and a **grown-up**.

COLLECTIVE NOUNS	EXAMPLES
A **collective noun** names a group of people, animals, places, or things.	Daniel took pictures of manatees on a trip to Florida with his **family**.

Some Collective Nouns

Groups of People	Groups of Animals	Groups of Places	Groups of Things
band	flock	Hawaiian Islands	mail
class	herd		money
family	litter	United States	set
team	pack		trash

A collective noun can be the **subject** of a sentence. It usually needs a **singular verb** because the group is seen as one unit.	Our **class** **hopes** to see Daniel's pictures. His **club** **has** already **seen** them.

Nouns, continued

SINGULAR AND PLURAL NOUNS	EXAMPLES

**The singular form of a count noun names one thing.
The plural form names more than one thing.**

Count nouns are nouns that you can count. Follow these rules to make a count noun plural:

- Add **-s** to most count nouns.

desk	book	teacher	apple	line
desk**s**	book**s**	teacher**s**	apple**s**	line**s**

- If the noun ends in **x**, **ch**, **sh**, **s**, or **z**, add **-es**.

box	lunch	dish	glass	waltz
box**es**	lunch**es**	dish**es**	glass**es**	waltz**es**

- For nouns that end in a consonant plus **y**, change the **y** to **i** and add **-es**.

story	sky	city	penny	army
stor**ies**	sk**ies**	cit**ies**	penn**ies**	arm**ies**

- For nouns that end in a vowel plus **y**, just add **-s**.

boy	toy	day	monkey	valley
boy**s**	toy**s**	day**s**	monkey**s**	valley**s**

- For most nouns that end in **f** or **fe**, change the **f** to **v** and add **-es**. For some nouns that end in **f**, just add **-s**.

leaf	knife	half	roof	chief
lea**ves**	kni**ves**	hal**ves**	roof**s**	chief**s**

- If the noun ends in a vowel plus **o**, add **-s**. For some nouns that end in a consonant plus **o**, add **-s**. For others, add **-es**.

radio	kangaroo	banjo	potato	tomato
radio**s**	kangaroo**s**	banjo**s**	potato**es**	tomato**es**

- A few count nouns have irregular plural forms.

child	foot	person	man	woman
children	**feet**	**people**	**men**	**women**

- For a few count nouns, the singular and plural forms are the same.

deer	fish	salmon	sheep	trout
deer	**fish**	**salmon**	**sheep**	**trout**

SINGULAR AND PLURAL NOUNS	EXAMPLES
Noncount nouns are nouns that you cannot count. A noncount noun does not have a plural form.	My favorite museum has **furniture** and **art**. Sometimes I wonder how much **money** each item is worth.

Types of Noncount Nouns

Activities and Sports

				Examples
baseball	camping	dancing	fishing	I love to play **soccer**.
golf	singing	soccer	swimming	

Category Nouns

clothing	equipment	furniture	hardware	jewelry	My **equipment** is in the car.
machinery	mail	money	time	weather	

Food

bread	cereal	cheese	corn	flour	I'll drink some **water** on my way
lettuce	meat	milk	rice	salt	to the game.
soup	sugar	tea	water		

You can count some food items by using a measurement word like **cup**, **slice**, **glass**, or **head** plus the word **of**. To show the plural form, just make the measurement word plural.

I'll drink **two glasses of water** on my way to the game.

Ideas and Feelings

democracy	enthusiasm	freedom	fun	health	I'll also listen to the radio for
honesty	information	knowledge	luck	work	**information** about the weather.

Materials

air	fuel	gasoline	gold	The radio says the **air** is heavy.
metal	paper	water	wood	What does that mean?

Weather

fog	hail	heat	ice	lightning	Uh-oh! First came the **lightning**
rain	smog	snow	sunshine	thunder	and the **thunder**. I want
					sunshine for my next
					soccer game!

Some words have more than one meaning. Add **-s** for the plural only if the noun means something you can count.	Throw me those **baseballs**. I want to learn to play **baseball**.

Nouns, continued

ARTICLES	EXAMPLES
An **article** is a word that helps identify a noun. An article often comes before a count noun.	After **the** game, we found **a** coat and **an** umbrella on **the** field.
Use **a** or **an** before **nouns** that are not specific. Use **the** before **nouns** that are specific.	**A boy** walked around the field. **The coach's son** walked around the field.
Use **a** before a word that starts with a consonant sound. Use **an** before a word that starts with a vowel sound.	a **b**all a **g**ate a **p**layer a **o**ne-way street (o is pronounced like w) a **c**ap a **k**ick a **n**et a **u**niform (u is pronounced like y) **a** **e** **i** **o** **u** **silent h** an **a**nt an **e**lbow an **i**nch an **o**live an **u**mbrella an **h**our an **a**pron an **ee**l an **i**dea an **o**cean an **a**mount an **e**lection an **ow**l an **ar**tist an **or**ange
Do not use **a** or **an** before a noncount noun.	The soccer ball was made of ~~a~~ leather.
Do not use **the** before the name of: • a city or state • most countries • a language • a day, a month, or most holidays • a sport or activity • most businesses • a person.	Our next game will be in **Dallas**. Games in **Texas** are always exciting. We will play a team from **Mexico**. People will be cheering in **Spanish** and **English**. The game will take place on **Monday**. Is that in **February**? Yes, on **President's Day**. That will be a good day to play **soccer**. The fans will have hot dogs to eat from **Sal's Market**. You may even see **Sal** himself.

POSSESSIVE NOUNS	EXAMPLES
A **possessive noun** is the name of an owner. All possessive nouns include an **apostrophe** .	Several bands performed in our **town's** parade. Everyone liked the **musicians'** costumes.
Follow these rules to make a noun possessive:	
• If there is one owner, add **'s** to the owner's name.	Some kids played the trumpet. One **boy's** trumpet was very loud. **Marsha's** baton went high in the air.
But: If the owner's name ends in **s**, you can add **'s** or just the apostrophe. Either is correct.	**Louis's** hat fell off. **Louis'** hat fell off.
• A noun that names two or more owners is plural and often ends in **s**. If so, just add **'**.	The **girls'** section sang loud songs. I could barely hear my **brothers'** tubas.
But: If the plural noun that names the owners does not end in **s**, add **'s**.	The **men's** cooking club marched with the band. The **children's** band rode on tricycles.

A parade

Pronouns

A pronoun takes the place of a noun or refers to a noun.

PRONOUN AGREEMENT	EXAMPLES
Use a **pronoun** to tell about the right person or thing. • For yourself, use **I** and **me**. • When you speak to another person, use **you**. • For a boy or man, use **he** or **him**. • For a girl or woman, use **she** or **her**. • For a thing, use **it**.	**I** want to find out about careers. What career will be good for **me**? What career are **you** interested in? Scott likes art. **He** wants to be a photographer. It will be a good career for **him**. Janet likes animals. **She** wants to be a veterinarian. That career will give **her** a chance to take care of animals. What about music? Is **it** a good career?
Use a **pronoun** to tell about the right number of people or things. **Singular pronouns** refer to one person. **Plural pronouns** refer to more than one person. Here are some examples: • These pronouns tell about one person or thing. • This pronoun is used to speak to one or more than one person. • Use these pronouns to speak about yourself and another person. • These pronouns are used to speak about other people or things.	**Some Singular and Plural Pronouns** Singular Pronouns Plural Pronouns I, me, my, mine we, us, our, ours you, your, yours you, your, yours he, him, his she, her, hers — they, them, their, theirs it, its **I** am thinking about lots of careers. Ted says **he** is, too. Are **you** set on a career? Ted and I are doing interviews on careers. **We** talked to **our** friends. They talked to **us**. **They** told us about careers in the computer industry. We told **them** about careers in health care.

SUBJECT PRONOUNS	EXAMPLES
Use a **subject pronoun** as the **subject** of a sentence.	Janet likes animals. **She** works at a pet shop.

Subject Pronouns

Singular	Plural
I	we
you	you
he, she, it	they

The pronoun **it** can be used as a **subject** to refer to a noun. *But:* The pronoun **it** can be the **subject** without referring to a specific noun.	Janet lives near the **shop**. **It** is on First Street. **It** is interesting to work in the shop. **It** is fun to play with the animals. **It** is important to take care of them, too.

REFLEXIVE PRONOUNS	EXAMPLES
Sometimes you talk about a person twice in a sentence. Use a **reflexive pronoun** to refer to the **subject**.	**Janet** taught **herself** about the life cycle of parrots. The **shop owners themselves** learned some things from Janet.

Subject and Reflexive Pronouns

Singular		Plural	
I	myself	we	ourselves
you	yourself	you	yourselves
he	himself		
she	herself	they	themselves
it	itself		

OBJECT PRONOUNS	EXAMPLES
You can use an **object pronoun** after an **action verb**. You can also use an **object pronoun** after a **preposition**.	The parrots get hungry at 5 o'clock. Janet **feeds them** every day. The parrots squawk **at her** to say "thank you."

Object Pronouns

Singular	Plural
me	us
you	you
him, her, it	them

Pronouns, continued

POSSESSIVE PRONOUNS

A **possessive pronoun** tells who or what owns something.

A **possessive pronoun** can refer to the name of an owner. It is sometimes called a **possessive adjective**.

A **possessive pronoun** can take the place of a **person's name and what the person owns**.

EXAMPLES

Janet's posters are about pet care.
Her posters show what dogs need.

Which one is **Janet's poster**?
The big one is **hers**.

Possessive Pronouns

Use these pronouns to refer to the name of an owner. These pronouns always come before a noun and act as adjectives.

Singular	Plural
my	our
your	your
his, her, its	their

Use these pronouns to replace a person's name and what the person owns. These pronouns are always used alone.

Singular	Plural
mine	ours
yours	yours
his, hers, its	theirs

DEMONSTRATIVE PRONOUNS

A **demonstrative pronoun** points out a specific noun without naming it.

EXAMPLES

Look at the puppies.
That is a cute puppy.
Those are sleeping.

Demonstrative Pronouns

	Singular	Plural
Nearby	this	these
Far Away	that	those

INDEFINITE PRONOUNS

When you are not talking about a specific person or thing, use an **indefinite pronoun**.

EXAMPLES

Everybody loves to visit the pet shop.
Something is happening in the pet shop today.
Several of the puppies are getting a bath!

Some Indefinite Pronouns

Singular				Plural	
each	everyone	no one	someone	both	many
everybody	everything	nothing	something	few	several

djectives

An adjective describes or modifies a noun or pronoun.
It can tell what kind, which one, how many, or how much.

DESCRIPTIVE ADJECTIVES	EXAMPLES
An **adjective** can tell what something is like. It can tell the color, size, or shape. It can describe a feeling. An adjective can tell how something sounds, feels, looks, tastes, or smells.  An egret	Where can you find **brown** rabbits and **white** egrets? A swamp has **large** and **small** animals like these. The egret has **round** eyes and a **pointed** beak. I feel **happy** when I spend a day in the swamp. I like the **noisy** birds. The egrets are **beautiful**. **Adjectives That Appeal to the Senses** | Hearing	Touch	Sight	Taste	Smell
---	---	---	---	---
crunchy	hard	beautiful	bitter	fishy
noisy	rough	dark	salty	fragrant
quiet	smooth	huge	sour	fresh
soft	wet	shiny	sweet	rotten	
Usually, an **adjective** comes before the noun it describes. *But:* A **predicate adjective** appears in the predicate and still describes the noun or pronoun in the **subject**.	An **old alligator** hides in the **dark mud**. The **alligator** is **powerful**. **It** is **dangerous**, too.  An alligator
Sometimes two or more **adjectives** come before a **noun**. Use a comma (**,**) between the adjectives if they both describe the noun.	Alligators walk on **short, strong** legs.
An **adjective** is never plural, even if the **noun** it describes is plural.	Many **hungry birds** look for food near the water. Their **eyes** are **good**, but they don't see the alligator. Soon the **tasty birds** are the alligator's dinner!

Adjectives, continued

DEMONSTRATIVE ADJECTIVES	EXAMPLES
A **demonstrative adjective** points out the noun that follows it. It answers the question "Which one?"	**These** otters are by my boat. **That** otter over there belongs to one of them.

Demonstrative Adjectives

	Singular	Plural
Nearby	this	these
Far Away	that	those

NUMBER WORDS	EXAMPLES
Number words are often used as **adjectives**. Sometimes the number word tells the **order** that things are in.	Today in the swamp I saw **one** snake, **two** alligators, and **six** turtles. The **first** day I saw many kinds of birds. The **second** day I saw a lot of alligators. What will I see on the **third** day?

INDEFINITE ADJECTIVES	EXAMPLES
Use an **indefinite adjective** when you are not sure of the exact number. Some indefinite adjectives tell **how many** things there are. Use these adjectives before nouns you can count. Some indefinite adjectives tell **how much** there is of something. Use these adjectives before nouns you cannot count.	I didn't see **much** wildlife on the third day. All I saw were **a few** frogs.

Some Indefinite Adjectives

To Tell How Many	To Tell How Much
many insects	**much** sunshine
a few insects	**a little** sunshine
some insects	**some** sunshine
several insects	**not much** sunshine
no insects	**no** sunshine

In a negative sentence, use **any** instead of **some**.	I saw some turtles, too. However, I didn't see ~~some~~ _{any} insects.

PROPER ADJECTIVES	EXAMPLES
A **proper adjective** is formed from a proper noun. It always begins with a capital letter.	There are many swamps in America. The <u>**American**</u> alligator is found in the southeastern United States.

ADJECTIVES THAT COMPARE	EXAMPLES

Adjectives can help you show how things are alike or different.

Use a **comparative adjective** to show how **two** things are alike or different. Add **-er** to most adjectives. Also use **than**. Use **more. . .than** if the adjective has three or more syllables.	Deserts may be small or large. The Sechura Desert in South America is **smaller than** the Sahara Desert in Africa.  Sahara Desert Is the Sechura Desert **more interesting than** the Sahara Desert?
You can use either **-er** or **more** to make a comparison with some two-syllable adjectives. **Be sure not to use both**.	Most desert animals are ~~more~~ livelier at night than during the day. Desert flowers are ~~more~~ prettier than swamp grasses.
Use a **superlative adjective** to compare **three or more** things. Add **-est** to most adjectives. Use **the** before the adjective. Use **the most** with the adjective if it has three or more syllables.	The Sahara Desert is **the largest** desert in the world. The Libyan Desert has **the** world's **highest** record temperature. Both habitats have some of **the most interesting** animals in the world.
Some **adjectives** have **special forms** for comparing things: good bad some little better worse more less best worst most least	Today's weather in the desert is **bad**. Tomorrow's weather will be **worse**. Next week's weather is expected to be **the worst** of the summer.
Use **less** or **the least** to compare things you cannot count. Use **fewer** or **the fewest** to compare things you can count.	Deserts have **less** rainfall than swamps. Deserts have **the least** rainfall of any habitat. Some deserts have **fewer** days of rain than others. Which desert had **the fewest** number of visitors last year?

Verbs

Every sentence is divided into two parts: a subject and a predicate. The verb is the key word in the predicate. A verb tells what a subject does or links words in a sentence.

ACTION VERBS	EXAMPLES
An **action verb** tells what the subject does. Most verbs are action verbs.	The dancers **leap** across the stage. The spotlight **shines** on the lead dancers. Each dancer **twirls** around and around.
Some **action verbs** tell about an action that you cannot see.	The audience **enjoys** the lively music.

Ballet dancer

LINKING VERBS	EXAMPLES
A **linking verb** connects, or links, the subject of a sentence to a word in the predicate.	The dancers **look** powerful.
The word in the predicate can describe the subject.	Their costumes **are** colorful.
Or, the word in the predicate can be another way to name the subject.	These dancers **are** ballerinas.

Linking Verbs

Forms of the Verb *be*

am	was
is	were
are	

Other Linking Verbs

appear	seem	become
feel	smell	taste
look		

HELPING VERBS	EXAMPLES
Some verbs are made up of more than one word. The last word is called the **main verb**. It shows the action. The verb that comes before is the **helping verb** .	Ballet dancers **are regarded** as athletes and storytellers. They **can jump** high into the air. They **might leap** several feet across the stage. They **are building** up muscle strength.

HELPING VERBS, continued	EXAMPLES
The **helping verb** agrees with the subject.	The dancers **have practiced** for hours. The exercise **has made** them strong.
The word <u>not</u> always comes between the **helping verb** and the main verb.	The dancers **do** <u>not</u> **tell** a story in the usual way.
Other <u>adverbs</u> can come between a **helping verb** and the **main verb,** or appear in other places in the sentence.	They **will** <u>never</u> **use** their voices to tell a story. The story **is** <u>always</u> **told** through their graceful movements. <u>Often</u> slow movements **will show** an emotion like sadness. Happiness **is shown** <u>best</u> by quick, springy movements.
In questions, the <u>subject</u> comes between the **helping verb** and the **main verb**.	**Have** <u>you</u> **seen** a performance? **Does** <u>your family</u> **enjoy** ballet?

Helping Verbs

Forms of the Verb *be*

am	was
is	were
are	

Forms of the Verb *do*

do	did
does	

Forms of the Verb *have*

have	had
has	

Other Helping Verbs

To express ability:
  I **can** dance.
  I **could** do the jump.

To express possibility:
  I **may** dance tonight.
  I **might** dance tonight.
  Perhaps I **could** do the dance.

To express a need or want:
  I **must** dance more often.
  I **would** like to dance more often.

To express an intent:
  I **will** dance more often.

To express something you ought to do:
  I **should** practice more often.
  I **ought** to practice more often.

Verbs, continued

PRESENT TENSE VERBS	EXAMPLES
The tense of a verb shows when an action happens.	
The **present tense** of a verb tells about an action that is happening now.	My mom **looks** at her charts. She **checks** her computer screen.
The **present tense** of a verb can also tell about an action that happens regularly or all the time.	My mom **works** for the local TV station. She **is** a weather forecaster. She **reports** the weather every night at 5 p.m.
The **present progressive** form of a verb tells about an action as it is happening. It uses the helping verb **am**, **is**, or **are** and a main verb. The main verb ends in **-ing**.	Right now, she **is getting** ready for the show. "I can't believe it!" she says. "I **am looking** at the biggest storm of the century!" "**Are** those high winds **travelling** toward the coast?" asks her boss.

PAST TENSE VERBS	EXAMPLES
The **past tense** of a verb tells about an action that happened earlier, or in the past.	Yesterday, my mom **warned** everyone about the hurricane. The storm **moved** over the ocean toward land. We **did** not **know** exactly when it would hit.
The past tense form of a **regular verb** ends with **-ed**. See page 439 for spelling rules.	The shop owners in our town **covered** their windows with wood. We **closed** our shutters and **stayed** inside.
Irregular verbs have special forms to show the past tense. See the chart on pages 424–425.	The storm **hit** land. The sky **grew** very dark. It **began** to rain.

Some Irregular Verbs

Present Tense	Past Tense
begin	began
do	did
grow	grew
hit	hit

PAST TENSE VERBS, continued	EXAMPLES
The **past progressive** form of a verb tells about an action that was happening over a period of time in the past. It uses the helping verb **was** or **were** and a main verb. The main verb ends in **-ing**.	The wind **was blowing** at high speeds. Our shutters **were** really **shaking** during the storm. **Were** the trees **falling** down?  Wind damage from Hurricane Floyd, 1999

FUTURE TENSE VERBS	EXAMPLES
The **future tense** of a verb tells about an action that will happen later, or in the future. To show future tense, use one of the following: • the helping verb **will** plus a main verb • the phrase **am going to**, **is going to**, or **are going to** plus a verb.	After the storm, everyone **will come** out of their houses. They **will inspect** the damage. I **am going to take** the tree branches out of my yard. The city **is** not **going to clean** every street. We **are** all **going to help** each other.

PRESENT PERFECT TENSE VERBS	EXAMPLES
Use the **present perfect tense** of a verb when you want to tell about: • an action that happened in the past, but you are not sure of the exact time. • an action that began in the past and may still be going on. To form the present perfect tense, use the helping verbs **has** or **have** and the **past participle** of the main verb.	The people in our neighborhood **have helped** each other during other disasters. Our neighborhood **has** even **received** awards for teamwork. The newspaper **has written** stories about our neighborhood for three days now.

Verbs, continued

FORMS OF IRREGULAR VERBS

Irregular Verb	Past Tense	Past Participle	Irregular Verb	Past Tense	Past Participle
be: am, is	was	been	eat	ate	eaten
are	were	been	fall	fell	fallen
beat	beat	beaten	feed	fed	fed
become	became	become	feel	felt	felt
begin	began	begun	fight	fought	fought
bend	bent	bent	find	found	found
bind	bound	bound	fly	flew	flown
bite	bit	bitten	forget	forgot	forgotten
blow	blew	blown	freeze	froze	frozen
break	broke	broken	get	got	got
bring	brought	brought			gotten
build	built	built	give	gave	given
burst	burst	burst	go	went	gone
buy	bought	bought	grow	grew	grown
catch	caught	caught	have	had	had
choose	chose	chosen	hear	heard	heard
come	came	come	hide	hid	hidden
cost	cost	cost	hit	hit	hit
creep	crept	crept	hold	held	held
cut	cut	cut	hurt	hurt	hurt
dig	dug	dug	keep	kept	kept
do	did	done	know	knew	known
draw	drew	drawn	lay	laid	laid
dream	dreamed, dreamt	dreamed, dreamt	lead	led	led
			leave	left	left
drink	drank	drunk	lend	lent	lent
drive	drove	driven	let	let	let

Irregular Verb	Past Tense	Past Participle	Irregular Verb	Past Tense	Past Participle
lie	lay	lain	sink	sank	sunk
light	lit	lit	sit	sat	sat
lose	lost	lost	sleep	slept	slept
make	made	made	slide	slid	slid
mean	meant	meant	speak	spoke	spoken
meet	met	met	spend	spent	spent
pay	paid	paid	stand	stood	stood
prove	proved	proved, proven	steal	stole	stolen
			stick	stuck	stuck
put	put	put	sting	stung	stung
quit	quit	quit	strike	struck	struck
read	read	read	swear	swore	sworn
ride	rode	ridden	swim	swam	swum
ring	rang	rung	swing	swung	swung
rise	rose	risen	take	took	taken
run	ran	run	teach	taught	taught
say	said	said	tear	tore	torn
see	saw	seen	tell	told	told
seek	sought	sought	think	thought	thought
sell	sold	sold	throw	threw	thrown
send	sent	sent	understand	understood	understood
set	set	set	wake	woke, waked	woken, waked
shake	shook	shaken			
show	showed	shown	wear	wore	worn
shrink	shrank	shrunk	weep	wept	wept
shut	shut	shut	win	won	won
sing	sang	sung	write	wrote	written

Verbs, continued

<table>
<tr><td colspan="2">TWO-WORD VERBS</td><td>EXAMPLES</td></tr>
<tr><td colspan="2">A two-word verb is a verb followed by a preposition.

The meaning of the two-word verb is different from the meaning of the verb by itself.</td><td>I like to call you, but you never answer me.
The coach calls off the game because of the rain.
The workers call for higher pay.</td></tr>
</table>

Some Two-Word Verbs

Verb	Meaning	Example
break	to split into pieces	I didn't **break** the window with the ball.
break down	to stop working	Did the car **break down** again?
break up	to end	The party will **break up** before midnight.
	to come apart	The ice on the lake will **break up** in spring.
bring	to carry something with you	**Bring** your book to class.
bring up	to suggest	She **brings up** good ideas at every meeting.
	to raise children	**Bring up** your children to be good citizens.
check	to make sure you are right	We can **check** our answers at the back of the book.
check in	to stay in touch with someone	I **check in** with my mom at work.
check up	to see if everything is okay	The nurse **checks up** on the patient every hour.
check off	to mark off a list	Look at your list and **check off** the girls' names.
check out	to look at something carefully	Hey, Marisa, **check out** my new bike!
fill	to put as much as possible into a container or space.	**Fill** the pail with water.
fill in	to color or shade in a space	Please **fill in** the circle.
fill out	to complete	Marcos **fills out** a form to order a book.
get	to go after something	I'll **get** some milk at the store.
	to receive	I often **get** letters from my pen pal.
get ahead	to go beyond what is expected of you	She worked hard to **get ahead** in math class.
get along	to be on good terms with	Do you **get along** with your sister?
get out	to leave	Let's **get out** of the kitchen.
get over	to feel better	I hope you'll **get over** the flu soon.
get through	to finish	I can **get through** this book tonight.

Some Two-Word Verbs

Verb	Meaning	Example
give	to hand something to someone	We **give** presents to the new baby.
give out	to stop working	If she runs ten miles, her energy will **give out**.
give up	to quit	I'm going to **give up** eating candy.
go	to move from place to place	Did you **go** to the mall on Saturday?
go on	to continue	Why do the boys **go on** playing after the bell rings?
go out	to go someplace special	Let's **go out** to lunch on Saturday.
look	to see or watch	Don't **look** directly at the sun.
look forward	to be excited about something that will happen	My brothers **look forward** to summer vacation.
look over	to review	She always **looks over** her answers before she gives the teacher her test.
look up	to hunt for and find	We **look up** information on the Internet.
pick	to choose	I'd **pick** Lin for class president.
pick on	to bother or tease	My older brothers always **pick on** me.
pick up	to go faster	Business **picks up** in the summer.
	to gather or collect	**Pick up** your clothes!
run	to move quickly on foot	Juan will **run** in a marathon.
run into	to see someone you know unexpectedly	Did you **run into** Chris at the store?
run out	to suddenly have nothing left	The cafeteria always **runs out** of nachos.
stand	to be in a straight up-and-down position	I have to **stand** in line to buy tickets.
stand for	to represent	A heart **stands for** love.
stand out	to be easier to see	You'll really **stand out** with that orange cap.
turn	to change direction	We **turn** right at the next corner.
turn up	to appear	Clean your closet and your belt will **turn up**.
	to raise the volume	Please **turn up** the radio.
turn in	to go to bed	On school nights I **turn in** at 9:30.
	to give back	You didn't **turn in** the homework yesterday.
turn off	to make something stop	Please **turn off** the radio.

Adverbs

An adverb tells more about a verb, an adjective, or another adverb.

USE OF ADVERBS	EXAMPLES
An **adverb** can tell about a **verb**. It can come before or after the verb.	Our team **always wins** our basketball games. The whole team **plays well**.
An **adverb** can make an **adjective** or another **adverb** stronger.	Gina is **really good** at basketball. She plays **extremely well**.

TYPES OF ADVERBS	EXAMPLES
Adverbs answer one of the following questions: • How? • Where? • When? • How much? or How often?	Gina **carefully** aims the ball. She tosses the ball **high**, but it misses the basket. She will try again **later**. She **usually** scores.

ADVERBS THAT COMPARE	EXAMPLES
Some **adverbs** compare actions. Add **-er** to compare two actions. Add **-est** to compare three or more actions.	Gina runs **fast**. Gina runs **faster** than her guard. Gina runs **the fastest** of all the players.
If the **adverb** ends in **-ly**, use **more** or **less** to compare two actions. Use **the most** or **the least** to compare three or more actions.	Gina aims **more carefully** than Jen. Jen aims **less carefully** than Gina. Gina aims **the most carefully** of all the players on her team. Jen aims **the least carefully** of all.
Be careful not to use an adjective when you need an adverb. Never use an adverb after a **linking verb**.	Everyone plays ~~fair~~ fairly. My teacher is fairly.

Prepositions

A preposition comes at the beginning of a prepositional phrase.
Prepositional phrases add details to sentences.

USES OF PREPOSITIONS	EXAMPLES
Some **prepositions** show location.	The Chávez Community Center is **by my house**. The pool is **behind the building**.
Some **prepositions** show time.	The Youth Club's party will start **after lunch**.
Some **prepositions** show direction.	Go **through the building** and **around the fountain** to get to the pool. The snack bar is **down the hall**.
Some **prepositions** have multiple uses.	We'll make new friends **at the party**. Meet me **at my house**. Come **at noon**.

PREPOSITIONAL PHRASES	EXAMPLES
A **prepositional phrase** starts with a **preposition** and ends with a noun or a pronoun. It includes all the words in between. The noun or pronoun is the **object of the preposition**.	I made a new friend **at the party**. Next week I'm going to the movies **with her**.

Some Prepositions

Location		Time	Direction	Other Prepositions	
above	near	after	across	about	for
behind	next to	before	around	against	from
below	off	during	down	along	of
beside	on	till	into	among	to
between	out	until	out of	as	with
by	outside		through	at	without
in	over		toward	except	
inside	under		up		

Conjunctions and Interjections

A conjunction connects words or groups of words.
An interjection expresses strong feeling.

CONJUNCTIONS	EXAMPLES
A **conjunction** connects words, phrases, or clauses.	The zoos in San Diego **and** Atlanta have giant pandas. In China, giant pandas can be found in the wild **or** in panda reserves. Pandas will eat other animals, **but** mostly they eat bamboo. **Some Conjunctions** Conjunctions / Uses **and** — To connect two ideas that are alike **but** — To show a difference between two ideas **or** — To show a choice between two ideas
Some **conjunctions** introduce a **dependent clause** in a complex sentence. The conjunction connects the **dependent clause** to the main clause.	Pandas can't find enough bamboo to eat **because their habitat is being destroyed**. **If all the bamboo is wiped out**, the pandas will die. **Conjunctions in Dependent Clauses** after / because / since / till / where although / before / so that / until / while as / if / through / when

INTERJECTIONS	EXAMPLES
An **interjection** is a word or phrase that shows strong feeling. An exclamation mark follows an interjection that stands alone.	**Help!** **Ouch!** **Oops!** **Oh boy!** **Oh my!** **Wow!**
An interjection used in a sentence can be followed by a comma or an exclamation mark.	**Oh**, it's a baby panda! **Hooray!** The baby panda has survived!

Capital Letters

A reader can tell that a word is special in some way if it begins with a capital letter.

PROPER NOUNS	EXAMPLES

A common noun names any person, place, thing, or idea.
A proper noun names one particular person, place, thing, or idea.

All the important words in a **proper noun** start with a capital letter.

	Common Noun	Proper Noun
Person	captain	**C**aptain **M**eriwether **L**ewis
Place	land	**L**ouisiana **T**erritory
Thing	team	**C**orps of **D**iscovery
Idea	destiny	**M**anifest **D**estiny

Proper nouns include:

- names of people and their titles

Laura Roberts
Captain Meriwether Lewis

But: Do not capitalize a title if it is used without a name:

The captain's co-leader on the expedition was William Clark.

- abbreviations of titles

Mr. Ramos
Mrs. Ramos
Dr. Schuyler
Ms. Nguyen

Abbreviations of Titles

Capt. for the captain of a boat or in the armed forces

Pres. for the president of a country, a company, a club, or an organization

Sen. for a member of the U.S. Senate

Rep. for a member of the U.S. House of Representatives

- words like *Mom* and *Dad* when they are used as names

"**Mom**, can you tell me more about the expedition?" said Laura.

But: Do not capitalize names if they follow a word like my.

I ask my **mom** lots of questions.

- organizations

United Nations   Science Club   Wildlife Society   Lodi City Council

- names of languages, subject areas, and religions

Spanish   Mathematics   Buddhism
Vietnamese   Social Studies   Christianity

Capital Letters, continued

PROPER NOUNS, continued	EXAMPLES

- names of geographic places

Cities and States
Dallas, Texas
Miami, Florida
St. Louis, Missouri

Streets and Roads
King Boulevard
Main Avenue
First Street

Bodies of Water
Yellowstone River
Pacific Ocean
Great Salt Lake
Gulf of Mexico

Countries
Iran
Ecuador
Cambodia

Landforms
Rocky Mountains
Sahara Desert
Grand Canyon

Buildings, Ships, and Monuments
Empire State Building
Titanic
Statue of Liberty

Continents
Asia
South America
Africa

Public Spaces
Hemisfair Plaza
Central Park
Muir Camp

Planets and Heavenly Bodies
Earth
Jupiter
Milky Way

- abbreviations of geographic places

Words Used in Addresses

Avenue	Ave.	Highway	Hwy.	South	S.
Boulevard	Blvd.	Lane	Ln.	Square	Sq.
Court	Ct.	North	N.	Street	St.
Drive	Dr.	Place	Pl.	West	W.
East	E.	Road	Rd.		

Abbreviations for State Names in Mailing Addresses

Alabama	AL	Hawaii	HI	Massachusetts	MA	New Mexico	NM
Alaska	AK	Idaho	ID	Michigan	MI	New York	NY
Arizona	AZ	Illinois	IL	Minnesota	MN	North Carolina	NC
Arkansas	AR	Indiana	IN	Mississippi	MS	North Dakota	ND
California	CA	Iowa	IA	Missouri	MO	Ohio	OH
Colorado	CO	Kansas	KS	Montana	MT	Oklahoma	OK
Connecticut	CT	Kentucky	KY	Nebraska	NE	Oregon	OR
Delaware	DE	Louisiana	LA	Nevada	NV	Pennsylvania	PA
Florida	FL	Maine	ME	New Hampshire	NH	Rhode Island	RI
Georgia	GA	Maryland	MD	New Jersey	NJ	South Carolina	SC

South Dakota	SD
Tennessee	TN
Texas	TX
Utah	UT
Vermont	VT
Virginia	VA
Washington	WA
West Virginia	WV
Wisconsin	WI
Wyoming	WY

- months, days, special days and holidays

January	July	Sunday	New Year's Day
February	August	Monday	Mother's Day
March	September	Tuesday	Thanksgiving
April	October	Wednesday	Hanukkah
May	November	Thursday	Kwanzaa
June	December	Friday	
		Saturday	

PROPER ADJECTIVES	EXAMPLES
A **proper adjective** is formed from a **proper noun**. Capitalize proper adjectives.	Napoleon Bonaparte was from **Europe**. He was a **European** leader in the 1800s. Napoleon ruled the country of **France**. He was the **French** emperor.

IN LETTERS	EXAMPLES
Capitalize the first word used in the **greeting** or in the **closing** of a letter. Street, city, and state names in the address, as well as their abbreviations, are also capitalized.	Dear Kim, I wish you could explore the Academy of Natural Sciences with me. I've learned so much about the flora and fauna that Lewis and Clark found. The museum even has some of the original samples! I'll tell you about it when I get home. See you soon. Your friend, Jamal Kim Messina 10250 W. Fourth St. Las Vegas, NV 89015

IN TITLES AND QUOTATIONS	EXAMPLES
Capitalize the **first word** in a **direct quotation**.	Clark said, "**There** is great joy in camp." "**We** are in view of the ocean," he said "**It's** the Pacific Ocean," he added. "**We** are finally here."
All important words in a **title** begin with a capital letter. Short words like *a, an, the, in, at, of,* and *for* are not capitalized unless they are the first or last word in the title.	**book:** *The Longest Journey* **poem:** "Leaves of Grass" **magazine:** *Flora and Fauna of Arizona* **newspaper:** *The Denver Post* **song:** "The Star-Spangled Banner" **game:** Exploration! **TV series:** "Bonanza" **movie:** *The Lion King*

Punctuation Marks

Punctuation marks make words and sentences easier to understand.

PERIOD	EXAMPLES
Use a **period**:	
• at the end of a statement or a polite command	Georgia read the paper to her mom.
	Tell me if there are any interesting articles.
• after an abbreviation	There's a new restaurant on Stone St. near our house.
	It opens at 10 a.m. today.
	But: *Do not use a period in an acronym:*
	National Aeronautics and Space Administration **NASA**
	Do not use a period in the abbreviation of a state name written in a mailing address:
	Massachusetts **MA** Illinois **IL** Texas **TX** California **CA** Florida **FL** Virginia **VA**
• after an initial	The owner is J.J. Malone.
• to separate dollars and cents. The period is the decimal point.	The article says lunch today costs only $1.50.
• in an Internet address. The period is called a dot.	The restaurant has a Web site at www.jjmalone.org.

QUESTION MARK	EXAMPLES
Use a **question mark**:	
• at the end of a question	What kind of food do they serve**?**
• after a question that comes at the end of a statement	The food is good, isn't it**?**
	But: *Use a period after an indirect question. In an indirect question, you tell about a question you asked.*
	I asked how good the food could be for only $1.50.

EXCLAMATION MARK	EXAMPLES
Use an **exclamation mark**: • after an interjection • at the end of a sentence to show that you feel strongly about something	Wow**!** One-fifty is a really good price**!**

COMMA	EXAMPLES
Use a **comma**: • to separate three or more items in a series	Articles about the school, a big sale, and a new movie were also in the newspaper. The school will buy a new bus, 10 computers, and books for the library.
• when you write a number with four or more digits	There was $500,000 in the school budget.
• before the **conjunction** in a compound sentence	The school could buy books, **or** it could buy a sound system. All the teachers discussed it, **and** they decided to buy books.
• before a question at the end of a statement	We need science books, don't we?
• to set off the name of a person someone is talking to	Georgia, does the article say why the school is buying a new bus? Just a minute, Mom, let me look.
• between two or more adjectives that tell about the same noun	The old, rusty school bus is broken.
• after a long **introductory phrase**	**In the last few months,** the bus had to be fixed six times.
• after an **introductory clause**	**Because the bus is old,** it keeps breaking down.
• before someone's exact words	Mr. Ivanovich said, "It is time for a new bus!"
• after someone's exact words if the sentence continues	"I agree," said the principal.

Punctuation Marks, continued

COMMA, continued	EXAMPLES
Use a **comma** in these places in a letter: • between the city and the state • between the date and the year • after the greeting • after the closing	144 North Ave. Milpas, AK July 3, 2002 Dear Mr. Okada, I am really glad that we have computers at school, but ours are out-of-date. As principal, can you ask the school board to buy new ones next year? Sincerely, Patrick Green

QUOTATION MARKS	EXAMPLES
Use **quotation marks** to show • a speaker's exact words	"Listen to this!" Georgia said.
• the exact words quoted from a book or other printed material	The announcement in the paper was "The world-famous writer Josie Ramón will be at Milpas Library Friday night."
• the title of a song, poem, or short story	Her poem "Speaking" is famous.
• the title of a magazine article or newspaper article	It appeared in the magazine article "How to Talk to Your Teen."
• the title of a chapter from a book	On Friday night she'll be reading "Getting Along," a chapter from her new book.
• words used in a special way	We will be "all ears" at the reading.
Always put **periods** and **commas** inside quotation marks.	"She is such a great writer," Georgia said. " I'd love to meet her."

APOSTROPHE	EXAMPLES
Use an **apostrophe** when you write a **possessive noun**.	
• If there is one owner, add **'s** to the owner's name.	The **newspaper's** ads for yard sales are interesting, too.
	But: If the owner's name ends in s, *you can add* **'s** *or just the apostrophe. Either is correct.*
	Mrs. Ramos's chair is for sale.
	Mrs. Ramos' chair is for sale.
• If there is more than one owner, add **'** after the **s**.	The **Martins'** dog had puppies, and I want to buy one.
	But: If the plural noun that names the owners does not end in s, *add* **'s**.
	The **Children's** Choir is holding a yard sale.
Use an **apostrophe** to replace the letters left out in a **contraction**.	**Doesn't** the yard sale start today?
	I'd love to support the choir. **Let's** go to the sale!

Contractions with *not*

In contractions with a verb and **not**, the word **not** is usually shortened to **n't**.

Verb	Phrase	Contraction
are	you are n~~o~~t	you aren't
is	she is n~~o~~t	she isn't
was	he was n~~o~~t	he wasn't
were	they were n~~o~~t	they weren't
do	I do n~~o~~t	I don't
does	he does n~~o~~t	he doesn't
did	we did n~~o~~t	we didn't
have	I have n~~o~~t	I haven't
could	she could n~~o~~t	she couldn't
would	you would n~~o~~t	you wouldn't
should	we should n~~o~~t	we shouldn't
Exceptions		
can	you can~~no~~t	you can't
will	we wi~~ll~~ n~~o~~t	we won't
am	I ~~a~~m not	I'm not

Contractions with Verbs

In many contractions, the verb is shortened.

Verb	Phrase	Contraction
am	I ~~a~~m	I'm
are	you ~~a~~re	you're
	they ~~a~~re	they're
is	he ~~i~~s	he's
	it ~~i~~s	it's
	here ~~i~~s	here's
	that ~~i~~s	that's
	where ~~i~~s	where's
have	we h~~a~~ve	we've
	they h~~a~~ve	they've
will	I w~~ill~~	I'll
	they w~~ill~~	they'll
	she w~~ill~~	she'll
would	I w~~oul~~d	I'd
	he w~~oul~~d	he'd
	you w~~oul~~d	you'd

Spelling

Follow these rules and your spelling will get better and better.

HOW TO BE A BETTER SPELLER

Spelling Tips

1. To learn a new word:
   - Study the word and look up its meaning.
   - Say the word out loud. Listen as you repeat it again.
   - Picture how the word looks.
   - Spell the word out loud several times.
   - Write the word five or ten times for practice. Try to use the word often in a sentence until you are sure you know its spelling.
2. Learn the following spelling rules.
3. Use a dictionary to check your spelling.
4. Keep a notebook of words that are hard for you to spell.

Q + U	EXAMPLES
Always put a **u** after a **q**.	The **qu**ick but **qu**iet **qu**arterback asked **qu**antities of **qu**estions. **Exceptions:** Iraq Iraqi

IE, EI	EXAMPLES
Use **i** before **e** except after **c**.	The f**ie**rce rec**ei**ver was always ready to catch the ball. **Exceptions:** • **ei**ther, h**ei**ght, th**ei**r, w**ei**rd, s**ei**ze • w**ei**gh, n**ei**ghbor (and other words where **ei** has the long **a** sound)

PLURALS	EXAMPLES
To form the plural of a noun that ends in **x**, **ch**, **sh**, **s**, or **z**, add **-es**. For most other nouns, just add **-s**.	Their team was called the Fox**es**. Their players made great catch**es** in the end zone.

Y TO I	EXAMPLES
If a word ends in a consonant plus **y**, change the **y** to **i** before you add **-es**, **-ed**, **-er**, or **-est**.	The coach was the happ**iest** when his players tr**ied** their best.
For words that end in a **vowel** plus **y**, just add **-s** or **-ed**.	For five day**s** before the game, the team stay**ed** at practice an extra 30 minutes.
If you add **-ing** to a verb that ends in **-y**, do not change the **y** to **i**.	The players learned a lot from study**ing** videos of their games.

-ED, -ING, -ER, -EST	EXAMPLES
When a word ends in silent **e**, drop the **e** before you add **-ed**, **-ing**, **-er**, or **-est**.	The players notic**ed** what they did wrong. Lat**er**, they talked about their mistakes.
When a one-syllable word ends in one vowel and one consonant, double the final consonant before you add an ending.	Then they pla**nned** some new plays for the game. They got set for their **biggest** challenge.

PREFIXES AND SUFFIXES	EXAMPLES	
Add a **prefix** to the beginning of a root word. Do not change the spelling of the **root word**.	They **replayed** the video often. The team never got **discouraged**.	
When you add a consonant **suffix**, do not change the spelling of the **root word**.	We had a **lovely** day for the game. *Exception:* happy happiness	
For most **root words** that end in silent **e**, drop the **e** before adding a vowel **suffix**.	Our quarterback won the Most **Valuable** Player award for the game.	

Some Prefixes and Suffixes

Prefixes

anti-	in-	pre-
bi-	im-	re-
dis-	inter-	sub-
extra-	mis-	un-

Suffixes Beginning with a Consonant

-ful	-ly	-ness
-less	-ment	-tion

Suffixes Beginning with a Vowel

-able	-ent	-ish
-al	-er	-ive
-ant	-ible	-ous

Glossary of Literary Terms

Action/Reaction   Action/reaction tells how one event makes another event happen.

> See also **Characterization**

Advertisement   An advertisement is a notice of something for sale. It uses persuasive techniques.

> See also **Persuasion**

Alliteration   Alliteration is the repetition of beginning consonant sounds. An example from "Outside and In" is

> Sometimes people tell me,
> "You are graceful on the stage!"
> "Your voice is smooth and silky."

Article   An article is a short piece of nonfiction writing that often appears in newspapers and magazines.

> Examples: **"Many People, Many Intelligences," "When Disaster Strikes"**

Autobiography   An autobiography is a story that a person writes about his or her own life.

> Example: **"My Best Friend"**

Biography   A biography is the story of a person's life that another person writes.

Cause and Effect   A cause is an event that makes another event (the effect) happen.

Character   A character is a person or animal in a story. Characters can be real or imaginary.

> See also **Characterization; Character Traits**

Characterization   Characterization is the way a character is brought to life. It includes descriptions of how a character looks, acts, and thinks.

> See also **Character Traits; Motive; Point of View**

Character Sketch   A character sketch is a short description of a person.

> See also **Characterization; Character Traits**

Character Traits   Character traits tell what someone is like.

> See also **Character; Characterization**

Climax   The climax is the most important event in a story. In "A Mountain Rescue," the climax happens when Rudi lowers his clothes-rope into the crevasse.

> See also **Plot**

Conflict and Resolution   Conflict describes a character's problem. Resolution tells if the problem is solved.

> See also **Plot**

Description   A description tells about a person, place, or thing. Many descriptions use sensory words to tell how things look, sound, feel, smell, and taste. An example from "My Best Friend" is

> . . . we'd sit on the bottom step of Isabel's front porch with our bare feet on the ground. We'd draw pictures in the dirt while we talked and rub them out with our hands. Or we'd rake the cool, damp dirt on top of our feet and pack it down tight, then slide our feet out, leaving a little cave we called a frog house. And all the time, we'd be just talking.

Dialogue   Dialogue is what characters say to one another. Most writing shows dialogue in quotation marks. Plays do not.

Diary   A diary is a personal book written about the author's life as it happens. It describes events, thoughts, and feelings.

Essay   An essay is short piece of nonfiction writing that informs, entertains, or persuades.

Example: **"Common Ground"**

Exaggeration   Exaggeration is saying that something is larger or more important than it really is.

Fable   A fable is a short story that teaches a lesson about life. Many fables have animals as characters.

Examples: **"The Mouse and the Lion"** and **"The Monkey and the Camel,"** from **"The Qualities of Friendship"**

Fantasy   Fantasy is writing about imaginary characters and events. Fairy tales, science fiction, and fables are examples of fantasy.

See also **Science Fiction**

Fiction   Fiction is writing that an author makes up. Biographical, historical, and realistic fiction are based on real life. Other fiction comes from the author's imagination. Fiction includes novels and short stories.

Example: **"A Mountain Rescue"**

Figurative Language   Writers use figurative language to say something in an imaginative way. Imagery, metaphor, personification, and simile are examples of figurative language.

See also **Exaggeration; Imagery; Metaphor; Personification; Simile**

Folk Tale   A folk tale is a very old story that has been told and retold for many years. Most folks tales were told for many generations before people wrote them.

Example: **"Owl,"** from **"Unwinding the Magic Thread"**

Free Verse   Free verse is poetry that does not rhyme or have a regular rhythm. Free verse can sound like ordinary speech.

Examples: **"Discovery,"** **"Adobe,"** from **"Together, We Dream"**

See also **Poetry; Rhyme; Rhythm**

Genre   Genre is a type of literature. The four main genres are fiction, nonfiction, poetry, and drama.

Goal and Outcome   A goal is something that a character wants to do or have. The outcome tells if the character met the goal.

See also **Plot**

Historical Fiction   Historical fiction is a story based on real people or events. Writers add details that could have happened.

History   History is a record of events that happened in the past.

How-to Article   A how-to article gives step-by-step directions. It tells how to make or do something.

Imagery   Imagery is language that helps create pictures in readers' minds. It is sometimes called sensory language because it tells how things look, sound, taste, smell, and feel.

See also **Figurative Language**

Glossary of Literary Terms, continued

Interview   In an interview, one person asks questions of another person.

> Example: **"Could I Ask You A Question?"**

Journal   A journal is a personal record. It may include descriptions of events, stories, poems, sketches, reflections, essays, and other interesting information. It is like a diary.

Legend   A legend is a story about a person or event in the past. The characters can be real or imaginary. Legends often exaggerate things about a character or an event.

Letter   A letter is a message that one person gives to another. Friendly letters and business letters are two examples.

Memoir   A memoir is a story someone writes about a personal memory.

Metaphor   A metaphor compares two things by saying that they are the same thing. These are metaphors from "When I Taste Salt":

> She is a hero
> and a goddess
> and a mermaid

Meter   Meter is the pattern of stressed and unstressed syllables in a poem.

> See also **Rhythm**

Motive   A motive is the reason a character says, thinks, or does something. In "Owl," Owl runs away because he thinks his face is ugly.

> See also **Characterization**

Myth   A myth is a very old story that explains something about the world. Myths are usually about gods, goddesses, and other superhuman characters.

> Examples: **"Echo and Narcissus," "How the Ox Star Fell from Heaven"**

Narrative Poetry   Narrative poetry is poetry that tells a story. It has characters, a setting, and a plot. It can also have rhythm and rhyme.

> See also **Poetry**

Nonfiction   Nonfiction is writing that tells about real people, places, and events.

> Examples: **"Grandfather's Nose," "Many People, Many Intelligences," "My Best Friend"**

Onomatopoeia   Onomatopoeia is the use of words that imitate sounds. *Buzz*, the sound a bee makes; *hiss*, the sound a snake makes; and *gurgle*, the sound a stream makes are examples of onomatopoeia.

Pantomime   Pantomime is the use of gestures, body movements, and facial expressions to tell an idea. Words are not used in pantomime.

Personal Narrative   A personal narrative is nonfiction written from the first-person point of view.

> Example: **"Art Smart"**
>
> See also **Point of View**

Personification   Writers use personification when they give human characteristics to animals, things, or ideas. Examples are found in "The Mouse and The Lion" and in "The Monkey and The Camel."

Persuasion   Writers use persuasion when they want their readers to act or think a certain way. Persuasion is used in advertisements, editorials, sermons, and political speeches. For example, in "Evergreen, Everblue," Raffi uses the voices of nature to persuade the reader to help protect the planet.

Photo Essay   A photo-essay is nonfiction that includes photographs and captions. The photographs and words are both important sources of information.

Example: **"Teamwork"**

Play   A play is a story that is performed by actors. The story is told through the actors' words and actions.

Example: **"Earthquake at Dawn"**

Plot   The plot is the sequence of events that happen in a story, a play, or a narrative poem. Plot usually has four parts: problem or conflict, complication, climax, and resolution.

See also **Climax; Conflict and Resolution; Problem and Solution**

Poetry   Poetry is writing that tells ideas in few words. Poets choose words and phrases that are usually very imaginative. Many poems are written in sections called stanzas and use rhythm and rhyme.

Examples: **"We Could Be Friends," "Everybody Says"**

See also **Rhyme; Rhythm; Stanza**

Point of View   Point of view describes how a story is told. In the first-person point of view, the narrator is a character in the story and uses words such as *I, me*, and *we*. In the third-person point of view, the narrator is not in the story and uses words such as *he, she*, and *they*.

Example of first-person point of view: **"My Best Friend"**

Example of third-person point of view: **"A Mountain Rescue"**

Problem and Solution   A problem is something that a character has to deal with. A solution is how the character deals with the problem.

See also **Plot**

Realistic Fiction   Realistic fiction tells about imaginary characters who could be real and imaginary events that could happen.

Example: **"A Mountain Rescue"**

Repetition   Repetition is saying the same thing several times. For example, in the poem "Everybody Says," the phrase "everybody says" is repeated three times.

Report   A report is nonfiction writing that tells facts. Reports are different from essays because they do not include opinions.

Rhyme   Rhyme is the repetition of sounds at the ends of words. Rhyme adds to the rhythm and musical quality of poetry.

Examples: **"Just Me," "We Could Be Friends"**

Rhymed Verse   Rhymed verse is poetry that rhymes.

See also **Rhyme**

Glossary of Literary Terms, continued

Rhyme Scheme   Rhyme scheme is the pattern of rhyming words in a poem.

See also **Rhyme**

Rhythm   Rhythm is a musical quality created by the repetition of stressed and unstressed syllables.

Science Fiction   Science fiction is a fantasy story about real or imaginary science. It often takes place in the future.

Sensory Language   *See* **Imagery**

Setting   The setting is the place and the time a story happens. For example, the setting of "Earthquake at Dawn," is San Francisco, California, in the year 1906.

Short Story   A short story is short fiction that has a single problem and a simple plot.

Simile   A simile compares two things by using the words *like*, *as*, or *than*. An example from "Together We Dream" is

adobes. . .like some big chocolate bars

Stanza   A stanza is a group of lines in a poem. Stanzas are separated by spaces.

Examples in **"We Could Be Friends"**

Story   A story is fiction writing that has a setting, characters, and a plot.

Style   Style is a special way of writing. It includes choice of words, tone, sentence length, and use of imagery and dialogue.

See also **Word Choice**

Tall Tale   A tall tale is a funny story made up of exaggerated characters and events. Tall tales are not true.

Example: **"Pecos Bill,"** from **"The Art of the Tall Tale"**

See also **Exaggeration**

Theme   A theme is a main idea. It is the message a piece of writing has. For example, the theme of "The Monkey and the Camel" is that not everyone can do everything well.

Word Choice   Word choice is the kinds of words and language the writer uses to tell his or her ideas. Word choice is a part of an author's style.

See also **Style**

Glossary of Key Vocabulary

Many words have more than one meaning. The definitions in this glossary are for the words as they are introduced in the selections in this book.

Pronunciation Key

Symbols for Consonant Sounds

b	box		p	pan
ch	chick		r	ring
d	dog		s	bus
f	fish		sh	fish
g	girl		t	hat
h	hat		th	Earth
j	jar		th	father
k	cake		v	vase
ks	box		w	window
kw	queen		wh	whale
l	bell		y	yarn
m	mouse		z	zipper
n	pan		zh	treasure
ng	ring			

Symbols for Short Vowel Sounds

a	hat	
e	bell	
i	chick	
o	box	
u	bus	

Symbols for Long Vowel Sounds

ā	cake	
ē	key	
ī	bike	
ō	goat	
yū	mule	

Symbols for R-controlled Sounds

ar	barn	
air	chair	
ear	ear	
īr	fire	
or	corn	
ur	girl	

Symbols for Variant Vowel Sounds

ah	father	
aw	ball	
oi	boy	
ow	mouse	
oo	book	
ü	fruit	

Miscellaneous Symbols

shun	fraction	$\frac{1}{2}$
chun	question	?
zhun	division	$2\overline{)\frac{50}{100}}$

Parts of an Entry

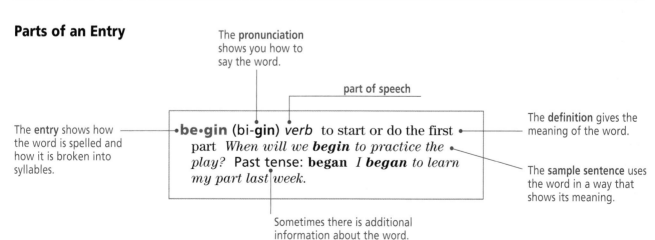

The **pronunciation** shows you how to say the word.

part of speech

The entry shows how the word is spelled and how it is broken into syllables.

•**be·gin** (bi-**gin**) *verb* to start or do the first part *When will we **begin** to practice the play?* Past tense: **began** *I **began** to learn my part last week.*

The **definition** gives the meaning of the word.

The **sample sentence** uses the word in a way that shows its meaning.

Sometimes there is additional information about the word.

A

absolute truth When something is completely true, it is the **absolute truth**. *Some people lied, but she told the absolute truth.*

ac·cept (ak-**sept**) *verb* When you **accept** something, you like it the way it is. *She learned to accept her friends' ideas.*

a·dapt (u-**dapt**) *verb* When you **adapt** to something new, you change to get used to it. *Juan learned to adapt to his new school.*

a·do·be (u-**dō**-bē) *noun* An **adobe** is a brick made of mud and straw that dries in the sun. *They put one adobe on top of another to build the house.*

adobes

a·dor·a·ble (u-**dor**-u-bul) *adjective* Something is **adorable** when it is pretty and delightful. *The new baby is adorable.*

ad·vise (ad-**vīz**) *verb* You **advise** someone when you tell what you think he or she should do. *Our parents advise us to stay away from strangers.*

aid (ād) *noun* Money, food, and supplies for people who need help is called **aid**. *The class sent aid to the flood victims.*

an·ces·tor (an-**ses**-tur) *noun* An **ancestor** is a family member who lived before you. *Marie likes to hear stories about her favorite ancestor, her great-aunt.*

an·swer (an-sur) *verb* You **answer** when you say or do something after you hear a question or a statement. *Please answer my question at once.*

at·ten·dant (u-**ten**-dunt) *noun* An **attendant** is someone who serves another person. *A flight attendant serves meals on planes.*

au·di·ence (aw-dē-uns) *noun* An **audience** is a group of people who watch and listen to a performance. *The audience clapped at the end of the show.*

B

bar (bar) *noun* A **bar** is a solid object that is longer than it is wide. *We used an iron bar to keep the door closed.*

be·liev·a·ble (bi-**lē**-vu-bul) *adjective* A **believable** event could really happen. *Her story seemed strange, but I thought it was believable.*

ben·e·fit (**ben**-u-fit) *verb* When you **benefit** from something, you are helped by it. *You will benefit from good food and exercise.*

best friend A **best friend** is the friend you like the most. *Kathy and her best friend do many things together.*

bless·ing (**bles**-ing) *noun* A **blessing** is something good that brings happiness. *After a long, dry summer, the rain was a blessing.*

blind (blīnd) *adjective* A **blind** person is someone who cannot see. *Blind people use other senses because they cannot see.*

brain power Your **brain power** helps you think, feel, learn, remember, and move. *People use their brain power to help them do many different things.*

brave (brāv) *adjective* A **brave** person does not show fear in a difficult situation. *The brave fireman saved the child from the burning building.*

C

care for People can **care for** each other by loving and helping each other. *My grandparents care for me in many ways.*

cause (kaws) *noun* A **cause** is something that makes something else happen. *The heavy rain was the cause of the flood.*

char·ac·ter (**kair**-ik-tur) *noun* Your **character** is what you are really like. *Kim has a shy, sweet character.*

climb (klīm) *verb* When you **climb**, you move yourself up with your hands and feet. *Bill tried to climb to the top of the tree.*

com·bi·na·tion (kom-bi-**nā**-shun) *noun* A **combination** is a mix or a blend. *Peanut butter and jelly make a good **combination** for a sandwich.*

com·mand (ku-**mand**) *noun* A **command** is an order; it tells what to do. *The trainer gave the **command** to stop.*

com·mon (**kom**-un) *adjective* **1.** If something is **common**, it may be ordinary or average. *Our dog is no special kind, he's just a **common** dog.* **2.** If something is **common**, it may be shared. *Our **common** interest in art brought us together.*

common ground Land shared by everyone is **common ground**. *The park is **common ground** that we all can use.*

com·mons (**kom**-uns) *noun* A **commons** is a piece of land that is shared by the whole town. *Our **commons** is used for many different events throughout the year.*

com·mu·ni·ty (ku-**myū**-ni-tē) *noun* A **community** is a group of people who live in the same place. *Everyone in the **community** helped to build a new playground.*

co·op·er·ate (kō-**op**-u-rāt) *verb* You **cooperate** when you work together. *If we **cooperate**, we will finish our work very quickly.*

co·op·er·a·tion (kō-op-u-**rā**-shun) *noun* Working together is **cooperation**. ***Cooperation** can help us do things we cannot do alone.*

count on When you **count on** someone, you need that person to help you. *We can **count on** Joan to take good care of our dog while we are away.*

crazy about When you are **crazy about** something, you really love it. *Pablo and I are **crazy about** funny movies.*

crop (krop) *noun* A **crop** is a field of plants that farmers grow. *Rice is an important **crop** that is grown in many countries.*

crop

crystal clean When something is **crystal clean**, it is clear and pure. *We took a long drink of the **crystal clean** water.*

cul·ture (**kul**-chur) *noun* People's **culture** includes their art, customs, beliefs, food, music, and clothing. *He wanted to learn about the **culture** of Japan.*

D

dam·age (**dam**-ij) *noun* Harm and destruction are kinds of **damage**. *Heavy rain caused **damage** to the bridge.*

dance (dans) **1.** *noun* A **dance** is a party where people move to music. *We had fun at the school **dance**.* **2.** *verb* When you **dance**, you move your body to music. *She likes to **dance** with a partner or all alone.*

de·cide (di-**sīd**) *verb* When you **decide**, you make up your mind about something. *We will **decide** what to do about the problem next week.*

ded·i·cate (**ded**-i-kāt) *verb* When you **dedicate** your work to someone, you make it for that person. *She will **dedicate** the book she wrote to her older sister.*

depend on You **depend on** things or people that you need. *The team members **depend on** the coach for training.*

dis·cov·er (dis-**kuv**-ur) *verb* When you **discover** something, you learn about it for the first time. *I **discover** new things about science every day.*

dis·re·spect·ful (dis-ri-**spekt**-ful) *adjective* You are **disrespectful** when you are rude and impolite. *It is **disrespectful** to laugh when someone makes a mistake.*

E

earth/Earth (urth) *noun* **1.** The ground or dirt is **earth**. *When she works in her garden, she likes the smell of fresh **earth**.* **2.** The planet we live on is called **Earth**. *The astronauts saw **Earth** from the moon.*

ech·o (**ek**-ō) *noun* You hear an **echo** when you hear the same sound repeated many times in a row. *You can hear the **echo** of your voice when you yell in a cave.*

ed·u·ca·tion (ej-u-**kā**-shun) *noun* You get an **education** when you learn. *We go to school to get an* **education**.

ef·fect (i-**fekt**) *noun* An **effect** is something that happens because of something that happened earlier. *The flood was the* **effect** *of the heavy rain.*

en·joy (en-**joi**) *verb* When you **enjoy** something, you like it. *I always* **enjoy** *parties with my friends.*

en·tire (en-**tīr**) *adjective* Something is **entire** when it is complete or whole. *Nana's* **entire** *family was with her on her 100th birthday.*

ep·i·dem·ic (ep-u-**dem**-ik) *noun* An **epidemic** is a sickness or disease that spreads quickly. *Everyone in town was sick during the flu* **epidemic**.

e·vac·u·ee (i-**vak**-yū-ē) *noun* A person who must move away from a disaster is called an **evacuee**. *One* **evacuee** *saved her belongings from the flood.*

eve·ry·bod·y (**ev**-rē-bod-ē) *pronoun* Everyone or every person is **everybody**. ***Everybody*** *in my class wanted to visit the museum.*

every chance we got When we did something **every chance we got**, we did it whenever we could. *We went to the beach* **every chance we got**.

ex·ag·ge·rat·ed (eg-**zaj**-u-rā-tid) *adjective* Something is **exaggerated** when it is bigger and wilder than the truth. *Jim's* **exaggerated** *story about a giant fish made us laugh.*

ex·press (ek-**spres**) *verb* You **express** when you show or tell something. *Her art was a way to* **express** *her feelings.*

ex·pres·sion (ek-**spresh**-un) *noun* Your **expression** is the way you make your face look. Smiling is an **expression** that shows happiness. *Her frown was an* **expression** *of sadness.*

F

fa·mil·iar (fu-**mil**-yur) *adjective* Things you know well are **familiar**. *She is* **familiar** *with the rules of the game because she plays it every day.*

family resemblance People in some families look like each other. They have a **family resemblance**. *He and his brother have a strong* **family resemblance**.

fea·ture (**fē**-chur) *noun* A **feature** is part of your face. *Her best* **feature** *is her smile.*

feel (fēl) *verb* When we **feel**, we can be happy, sad, scared, and so on. *I* **feel** *excited when our team wins a game.* Past tense: **felt** *We* **felt** *sorry for the team that lost the game.*

felt (felt) *verb* the past tense of **feel**

figure out When you **figure out** something, you learn how to do it. *He was able to* **figure out** *how to fix the bicycle.*

for·est (**for**-ist) *noun* A **forest** is a large area with many trees. *There are more than fifteen kinds of trees in our* **forest**.

forest

fossil fuel A **fossil fuel** is a source of energy found in the earth. Coal, oil, and natural gas are **fossil fuels**. *Gas is a* **fossil fuel** *that is used for cooking, heating, and running cars.*

full attention You give your **full attention** when you watch and listen carefully. *The students gave the teacher their* **full attention**.

G

gath·er (**gath**-ur) *verb* **1.** When people **gather**, they come together. *We will* **gather** *at the park for lunch.* **2.** When you **gather** something, you collect it. *The farmers will* **gather** *the crops in September.*

gene (jēn) *noun* A **gene** is the part of a cell that tells your body how to form and grow. *The baby has the* **gene** *for blue eyes.*

ge·net·ics (ju-**net**-iks) *noun* The science of **genetics** studies genes and how they are passed from parent to child. ***Genetics** studies why we are the way we are.*

ges·ture (**jes**-chur) *noun* A **gesture** is a movement you make with your hands and arms. *She raised her hand as a **gesture** that she wanted to speak.*

go out of my way When I choose to take a longer way, I **go out of my way**. *I **go out of my way** because I like to walk through the park.*

go over You **go over** to a place when you visit. *She will **go over** to her aunt's house tomorrow.*

goof around When friends **goof around**, they play together and have fun. *After they finish their homework, they can **goof around**.*

guide dog A **guide dog** is trained to help a person who cannot see. *The **guide dog** led the blind woman down the street.*

H

had our lives all planned out We knew what we wanted to do in the future; we **had our lives all planned out**.

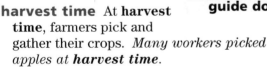
guide dog

harvest time At **harvest time**, farmers pick and gather their crops. *Many workers picked apples at **harvest time**.*

hold on When you **hold on** to something, you do not let go of it. *He tried to **hold on** to the ball, but he dropped it.*

hu·mor (**hyū**-mur) *noun* When something makes you laugh, it has **humor**. *He adds **humor** to his stories to make them funny.*

I

I (ī) *pronoun* If you are the person speaking or writing, you call yourself **I**. *I am the only one who knows what **I** am thinking.* Plural: **we** *We all know what **we** think about it.*

identical twins Two babies born at the same time are called **twins**. **Identical twins** have the same genetic information. *Sometimes we call the **identical twins** by the wrong names because they look exactly alike.*

i·den·ti·ty (ī-**den**-ti-tē) *noun* Your **identity** is who you are. *Carlos hid his **identity** by wearing a costume and mask.*

im·age (**im**-ij) *noun* If you are the **image** of someone, you look a lot like him or her. *Everyone said she was the **image** of her mother.*

im·prove (im-**prüv**) *verb* When you **improve**, you get better at something. *She tried to **improve** her grades by studying more.*

in·her·it (in-**hair**-it) *verb* When you **inherit** something, you get it from your parents or ancestors. *Mother hoped the new baby would **inherit** her green eyes.*

in·sist (in-**sist**) *verb* When you **insist** on something, you will not change your mind. *I **insist** that you take the last piece of cake.*

in·struc·tor (in-**struk**-tur) *noun* An **instructor** is a teacher. *The **instructor** helped the students understand the lesson.*

in·tel·li·gence (in-**tel**-i-juns) *noun* The ability to think, understand, learn, and express yourself is called **intelligence**. *His **intelligence** made school seem easy.*

in·tel·li·gent (in-**tel**-i-junt) *adjective* You are **intelligent** if you are smart. ***Intelligent** people often get good grades.*

in·ven·tive·ness (in-**ven**-tiv-nis) *noun* The ability to think up new things is called **inventiveness**. *His creative project showed his **inventiveness**.*

ir·re·spon·si·ble (ear-i-**spon**-su-bul) *adjective* People who are **irresponsible** do not do what they say they will do. *I am **irresponsible** when I forget to feed the dog.*

ir·ri·ta·ble (**ear**-i-tu-bul) *adjective* You are **irritable** when you get upset easily. *The hot weather made Tam tired and **irritable**.*

is·land (ī-lund) *noun* An **island** is land that has water on all sides. *She needed a boat to get to the island.*

island

J

jeal·ous (jel-us) *adjective* A **jealous** person wants what someone else has. *Scott was jealous of Sophia because she had a new bike.*

K

kind·ness (kīnd-nis) *noun* A **kindness** is something good that you do or say. *She showed her kindness by helping me carry the big box.*

L

la·bor (lā-bur) *verb* You **labor** when you work hard. *We will labor in the garden all summer.*

lay·er (lā-ur) *noun* A **layer** is one thickness of something. *We put a layer of frosting on the cake.*

la·zy (lā-zē) *adjective* A **lazy** person does not want to work or do anything. *I was lazy and didn't do my homework.*

lead·er (lē-dur) *noun* The **leader** of a group tells the others what to do. *The President is the leader of the United States.*

life (līf) *noun* **1.** Something that has **life** is alive. *He saved her life after the accident.* **2. Life** can also mean living things. *The ocean is full of sea life.*

log·ic (loj-ik) *noun* When something has **logic**, it makes sense. *We agreed with her because there was logic in what she said.*

look just like When you **look just like** a person, you look the same as the person. *Everyone says I look just like my sister.*

low·er (lō-ur) *verb* When you **lower** something, you move it downward. *If you lower the window, you will keep the cold air out.*

M

me (mē) *pronoun* *I* and **me** mean the person speaking or writing. *I want you to give me the answer.* Plural: **us** *Our parents gave us gifts.*

mem·ber (mem-bur) *noun* A **member** is someone who is part of a group. *Wilma is a member of the math team.*

mer·its (mair-itz) *noun* Someone's good points are called **merits**. *Kindness and honesty are some of her merits.*

miss (mis) *verb* When you **miss** something, you feel sad because it is not there. *I miss my sister when she goes away to school.*

my (mī) *adjective* **My** tells that something belongs to the speaker or writer. *I carry my books to school.*

my·self (mī-self) *pronoun* **Myself** is used with *I* or *me*, or to make a statement stronger. *I fixed my bike myself.*

N

na·tion (nā-shun) *noun* People who live in one country form a **nation**. *Our nation is the United States of America.*

natural resource A **resource** is something people use. A **natural resource** comes from the Earth. *Water is an important natural resource.*

O

op·ti·mis·tic (op-ti-mis-tik) *adjective* You are **optimistic** when you are cheerful and hopeful. *Joe was optimistic about passing the test because he studied hard.*

out·land·ish (owt-lan-dish) *adjective* Something is **outlandish** if it is very strange or odd. *He wore his most outlandish clothes to the costume party.*

P

part·ner (**part**-nur) *noun* A **partner** is a person or animal who works with you. *She chose Kim to be her **partner** in the game.*

peas·ant (**pez**-unt) *noun* A **peasant** is a very poor person who works on the land. *The **peasant** worked hard but made little money.*

per·son·al·i·ty (pur-su-**nal**-u-tē) *noun* Your **personality** is the way you act or what you are like. *Everyone likes Felipe because he has a friendly **personality**.*

pine (pīn) *verb* When you **pine** for something, you feel sad and sick because you want it. *When I'm away from home, I **pine** for my mom's good cooking.*

pi·o·neer (pī-u-**near**) *noun* The first person to go someplace new or do something new is a **pioneer**. *An astronaut is a **pioneer** in space.*

plan (plan) *verb* You **plan** when you think about how to do something before you do it. *We **plan** where to go before we leave.*

plan·et (**plan**-it) *noun* A **planet** is any one of the large objects in space that travel around the sun. *The **planet** we live on is called Earth.*

planet

plas·ter (**plas**-tur) *verb* When you **plaster** a wall, you cover it with material to protect it. *The room will look better after we **plaster** and paint the walls.*

plow (plow) *noun* A **plow** is a large tool that opens the earth for planting. *After the **plow** turns over the dirt, we can plant the seeds.*

por·trait (**por**-trit) *noun* A **portrait** is a picture of a person. *She painted a **portrait** of her father.*

pos·i·tive (**poz**-u-tiv) *adjective* You are **positive** when you are sure that things will work out well. *The baker was **positive** that his cake would be delicious.*

pres·ent (**prez**-unt) *adjective* **Present** means at this time. *We need a new classroom because our **present** one is too small.*

proud (prowd) *adjective* You feel **proud** when you are happy about something you did well. *I was **proud** of the good grades I got this year.*

pull (pool) *verb* When you **pull** something, you move it toward yourself. *We used a rope to **pull** the cart up the hill.*

R

rain forest A **rain forest** is an area covered by trees that gets at least 100 inches of rain each year. *Trees in a **rain forest** may grow as tall as 200 feet.*

re·al·i·ty (rē-al-u-tē) *noun* The way things really are is called **reality**. *She woke from her dream to face **reality**.*

re·cov·er·y (ri-**kuv**-ur-ē) *noun* When something gets back to normal after a problem, it is called **recovery**. *The town's **recovery** from the tornado took months.*

re·la·tion·ship (ri-**lā**-shun-ship) *noun* A **relationship** is how people connect with each other. Families and friends have **relationships**. *Joanna has a close **relationship** with her sister.*

rel·a·tive (**rel**-u-tiv) *noun* A **relative** is a person in your family. *Carlos met a new **relative** at the wedding.*

relief worker A **relief worker** is someone who helps people after a disaster. *A **relief worker** helped us after the fire.*

re·move (ri-**müv**) *verb* You **remove** something when you take it away. *Mom asked us to **remove** our toys from the living room.*

re·peat (ri-**pēt**) *verb* When you **repeat** something, you say it again. *He asked her to **repeat** the word because he didn't hear it clearly.*

re·quire (ri-**kwīr**) *verb* When you **require** something, you need it. *Beautiful gardens **require** a lot of work.*

rescue worker A **rescue worker** tries to save people in emergencies. *The rescue worker found the lost boy.*

re·spond (ri-**spond**) *verb* When you answer back, you **respond**. *When the teacher asks a question, we try to respond with the correct answer.*

restore power When you **restore power**, you get the electricity to work again. *We hope they will restore power soon so that our lights turn on.*

rise (rīz) *verb* When things begin to **rise**, they start to get up. *Farmers often rise before the sun is up.* Past tense: **rose** *We rose from our seats and clapped at the end of the play.*

rose (rōz) the past tense of **rise**

ru·ins (rü-unz) *noun* Fallen buildings, damaged roads, and bridges that cannot be fixed are called **ruins**. *After the earthquake, we looked through the ruins of our town.*

ruins

S

salt (sawlt) **1.** *noun* **Salt** is a natural product that adds flavor to food. *I added a little salt to my soup.* **2.** *verb* You can **salt** food to add flavor. *I salt my popcorn and add butter.*

sep·a·rate (sep-ur-it) *adjective* When something is **separate**, it is by itself. *The nurse put the sick child in a separate room.*

sew·er (sü-ur) *noun* A **sewer** is an underground tunnel that carries wastes from houses and buildings. *The sewer took the wastes to the ocean.*

shel·ter (shel-tur) *noun* People can stay in a **shelter** when they have no home. *The family lived in the shelter until their house was repaired.*

short·com·ings (short-kum-ingz) *noun* Someone's bad points are called **shortcomings**. *Laziness is one of Ted's shortcomings.*

show off When you **show off**, you show others how well you can do something. People **show off** to get attention. *She tried to show off by skating backwards.*

si·lence (sī-luns) *noun* When everything is quiet, there is **silence**. *Some students like to study in silence.*

sit·u·a·tion (sich-ü-ā-shun) *noun* A **situation** is something that happens. *When Alex lost his money, he was in a bad situation.*

skill (skil) *noun* A **skill** is the ability to do something well. *Learning a new skill takes a lot of practice.*

skirt (skurt) **1.** *noun* A **skirt** is a piece of women's clothing that hangs from the waist. *She wore a bright blue skirt.* **2.** *verb* When you **skirt** something, you go along its edge. *I will skirt the lake on my way home.*

solve problems When you **solve problems**, you find answers. *Teachers and parents can help us solve problems.*

source of The **source of** something is the place or thing it comes from. *The library is a good source of information.*

source of power A **source of power** is something energy comes from. *Running water is a source of power.*

stop to worry When you **stop to worry** about something, you take time to think about it. *He didn't stop to worry about being late for dinner.*

strange (strānj) *adjective* Something is **strange** when it is different from what people are used to. *Claire did not want to eat the strange food.*

stream (strēm) *noun* A **stream** is a small river of moving water. *The stream led us to a large river.*

strug·gle (strug-ul) *verb* When you **struggle**, you try hard to do something. *We had to struggle through the deep snow to get to school.*

sun·down (sun-down) *noun* Evening begins at **sundown**, when the sun goes down. *It gets dark very quickly after sundown.*

sun·up (sun-up) *noun* Morning begins at **sunup**, when the sun comes up. *The farmer starts his work at sunup.*

sup·plies (su-plīz) *noun* Materials that people need are called **supplies**. *The supplies we took to go camping included food, water, and raincoats.*

sup·port (su-port) *noun* Strength and encouragement are examples of **support**. *A good friend always gives you support.*

supposed to be The way things are **supposed to be** is how they should be. *He was supposed to be home before dark.*

sur·vi·vor (sur-vī-vur) *noun* Someone who is still alive after a disaster is called a **survivor**. *One survivor of the flood was a tiny baby.*

sus·tain (su-stān) *verb* When you **sustain** something, you keep it going. *We can sustain the forest by planting new trees.*

T

take care of When you **take care of** something, you give it your time and attention. *Juan has to take care of his sister when his mother goes to work.*

take good care When you **take good care** of someone, you give that person special attention. *Doctors take good care of people who are sick.*

tal·ent (tal-unt) *noun* When you have **talent** for something, you do it well. *She has musical talent and plays the guitar very well.*

talk and talk When people **talk and talk**, they talk for a long time. *Richard and I can talk and talk for hours.*

taste (tāst) 1. *noun* A **taste** of something is a small amount of it. *The cook took just a taste of his special dish.* **2.** *verb* You **taste** something when you put it in your mouth. *I wanted to taste all the different foods at the fair.*

team (tēm) *noun* A **team** is a group that works together. *Each player on the soccer team did her best.*

tend (tend) *verb* When you **tend** something, you take care of it. *I tend the horses every day after school.*

tent city A **tent** is a shelter made of cloth. A **tent city** is a large area with many tents. *After the hurricane, many people lived in a tent city until their houses were safe.*

tent city

ter·ri·fied (tair-u-fīd) *adjective* When you are **terrified**, you feel very scared. *She was terrified of being left alone in the dark.*

that was all there was to it When you were sure of how something would be, you could have said "**that was all there was to it**." *He would win the prize, and that was all there was to it.*

thick (thik) *adjective* When something is **thick**, it is big and solid. **Thick** is the opposite of thin. *The thick walls of our house kept us safe during the storm.*

threat·ened (thret-und) *adjective* If you are **threatened**, you are warned that something bad may happen. *The threatened man ran from the growling dog.*

tight·en (tīt-un) *verb* When you **tighten** the way you hold something, you grab it harder. *She had to tighten her hold on the bags so that they would not fall.*

took pity   If you **took pity** on someone, you felt sorry for that person. *We **took pity** on her and helped her find the money she lost.*

tra·di·tion (tru-**dish**-un) *noun*   A **tradition** is an action or a behavior that has been done for many years. *It is a **tradition** in my family to give gifts at the new year.*

train·ing (**trā**-ning) *noun*   When you get **training**, someone teaches you how to do something. *Tim had years of **training** before he could skate well.*

trait (trāt) *noun*   A **trait** is a person's way of looking or being. *Kindness is an excellent **trait**.*

trap (trap) *noun*   A **trap** is used to catch animals. *I caught a mouse in a **trap**.*

U

u·nique (yū-**nēk**) *adjective*   Something is **unique** if it is the only one of its kind. *You are **unique** because there is no one else just like you.*

u·nit·ed (yū-**nī**-tid) *adjective*   When people are **united**, they act together for common purposes. *They were **united** in working to stop pollution.*

up to me   When something is **up to me**, I am the one who should do something. *It's **up to me** to do my homework and get ready for school.*

us (us) *pronoun*   the plural of **me**

V

val·ley (**val**-ē) *noun*   A **valley** is the land between hills or mountains. *They walked through the **valley** and saw beautiful mountains on each side.*

valley

vil·lage (**vil**-ij) *noun*   A **village** is a small community. *Anna knows the name of every person who lives in her **village**.*

vil·lag·er (**vil**-i-jur) *noun*   A **villager** is a person who lives in a village. *The **villager** had a garden and kept chickens in his yard.*

W

wa·ter (**waw**-tur)   **1.** *noun*   Living things need **water**. *I was thirsty, so I drank some **water**.*   **2.** *verb*   You **water** plants to help them grow. *I **water** the garden every day.*

wave (wāv)   **1.** *noun*   In the ocean, water comes to the shore in a **wave**. *The **wave** crashed against the rocks.*   **2.** *verb*   You **wave** when you move your hand back and forth. *I **wave** to my friends when I see them.*

we (wē) *pronoun*   the plural of **I**

weath·ered (**weth**-urd) *adjective*   Something is **weathered** when it is changed by wind, sun, and rain. *The **weathered** house has peeling paint.*

weep (wēp) *verb*   When you **weep**, you cry. *She tried not to **weep** when she left her home.*   Past tense: **wept**   *He **wept** when his dog died.*

weight (wāt) *noun*   A **weight** is something heavy. *She used a stone as a **weight** to keep the papers from blowing away.*

wept (wept) *verb*   the past tense of **weep**

wood nymph   In Greek myths, a **wood nymph** is a spirit that lives in the forest and looks like a beautiful young woman. *The **wood nymph** ran behind a tree.*

wreck·age (**rek**-ij) *noun*   What is left after things are destroyed or ruined is **wreckage**. *After the storm, they walked through the **wreckage** of the town.*

Index of Skills

Language and Vocabulary

Index of Skills, continued

Reading and Learning Strategies, Critical Thinking, and Comprehension

Activate prior knowledge 14, 24, 36, 46, 55, 72, 82, 94, 104, 128, 137, 142, 156, 167, 172, 194, 208, 226, 242, 268, 280, 296, 308, 321

Analyze information 43, 217, 220, 237

Analyze story elements 104, 111, 135, 237, 238, 290, 307–308, 318–319

Ask questions 42, 94

Author's biases and point of view 208, 213, 216

Author's purpose 134, 149, 202–203, 216–217, 219–220, 299

Build background 14, 24, 36, 46, 55, 72, 82, 94, 104, 128, 137, 142, 156, 167, 172, 194, 208, 226–227, 242, 268, 280, 296, 308, 321

Cause and effect 46, 52, 164, 175, 198, 231, 237, 245, 247, 249, 283, 285, 287, 300–302, 304, 315

Character 237–238, 266, 290
 Feelings 111, 180
 Motive 51, 169, 232, 288, 308, 313, 315
 Point of view 29
 Traits 110, 238, 266, 273, 300, 302, 319

Clarify information 94, 268, 276

Classify 14, 19, 76, 216, 252

Comparisons 19, 24, 29, 52, 88, 99, 113, 137, 145, 164, 166, 211, 236, 239, 250, 273, 275–277, 282, 285, 287–290, 302–303, 311

Confirm word meaning 165, 268

Connect new information to known 194, 203

Details 16, 27–28, 39, 49, 75–76, 85, 87, 98, 107, 110, 111, 131, 133, 142, 145, 147, 149, 159, 161, 174, 176–177, 196, 198, 202, 231–232, 236, 245, 247, 249–250, 273, 282–283, 285, 287, 300, 315, 325

Draw conclusions 29, 147, 247, 250, 311, 324

Evaluate information 217, 220

Evaluate literature 52, 203, 217, 237–238

Facts and opinions 19, 28–29, 41–42, 52, 57, 77, 85, 88, 111, 133–134, 139, 149, 164, 177, 196, 203, 217, 250, 276, 288, 317–318, 324

Fantasy and reality 288, 290, 303–304

Formulate questions 30–31, 42, 151, 172

Generalizations 101, 275, 318

Generate ideas 9, 11–14, 19–24, 29–31, 33–36, 42–46, 52–55, 57–64, 67, 69–72, 77–82, 88–89, 91–94, 99–104, 111–120, 123, 125–128, 134–137, 139–142, 149–151, 153–156, 164–167, 169–172, 177–186, 189, 191–194, 203–208, 217–221, 223–226, 237–242, 250–260, 263, 265–268, 276–280, 288–291, 293–296, 303–308, 318–321, 324–332

Goal and outcome 104, 226, 308, 318

Graphic organizers 296
 Bar graphs 36, 342, 378
 Cause-and-effect charts and maps 52, 304, 340
 Character charts or maps 319
 Circle graph 14, 43, 342
 Classification charts 13–14, 19, 30, 54–55, 71, 77, 79, 81, 88, 93, 103, 137, 141, 204, 217, 221, 225, 237–238, 252, 267, 276, 307, 320, 325, 341
 Clusters 24, 35, 60, 65, 71, 94, 103, 121, 127, 207, 226, 242, 261, 280, 333, 340
 Comparison charts 29, 45, 151, 193, 250, 277, 279, 289–290, 341–342
 Concept maps *See* Clusters.
 Diagrams 175, 227, 246, 287, 299, 343–344
 Experience charts 115–116
 FATP charts 181, 256, 328
 Family tree 155
 Five Ws charts 59, 60
 Flow charts 127, 341, 363, 378
 Goal-and-outcome charts and maps 307, 318, 345
 Graphs 36, 342, 378
 K-W-L charts 194, 203, 341
 Line graphs 342
 Lists 43, 205
 Main idea charts and diagrams 149, 181, 182, 343
 Maps 26, 113, 136, 244, 246, 248, 253, 274, 286, 305, 379
 Mind maps 65, 121, 187, 261, 333
  See also Clusters.
 Organization charts 328, 341
 Outlines 255–256, 370–371

Pie graphs *See* Circle graph.
 Prediction charts 42
 Problem-and-solution charts and maps 111, 135, 205, 345
 Punnett Square 179
 Pyramid diagrams 242, 344, 366
 Rising-and-falling-action maps 347
 Semantic maps/charts *See* Clusters.
 Sequence chains 288, 311, 344
 Storyboards 99, 116, 134, 344
 Story maps 134, 295, 327–328, 344–347
 Story staircase maps 346
 T-charts 340, 378
 Tally chart 171
 Time lines 239, 296, 303, 343
 Tree diagrams 43, 149, 343
 Venn diagrams 20, 31, 344
 Vocabulary cards and charts 14, 36
 Word diagrams 242, 280, 343
 Word webs *See* Clusters.

Inference 39, 41–42, 51–52, 57, 85, 88, 97, 99, 107, 110, 133, 139, 161, 177, 196, 202–203, 213, 217, 231–232, 250, 275–276, 313, 324

Judgments 18, 52, 88, 134, 164, 177, 238, 276, 283, 303

Main idea and details 72, 77, 142, 149, 177

Monitor your reading 94, 156, 268

Opinions 19, 28–29, 41–42, 52, 57, 77, 85, 88, 111, 133–134, 139, 149, 164, 177, 196, 203, 217, 250, 276, 288, 317–318, 324

Outline 255–256, 370–371

Paraphrase 42, 57, 156, 164, 175, 268, 276, 324

Plan 20–21, 30–31, 43, 53–54, 60, 78–79, 89, 100–101, 112–113, 116, 135–136, 150–151, 165–166, 178–179, 182, 204–205, 218–221, 238–239, 251–253, 256, 277, 289–291, 304–305, 319–320, 325, 328, 340–344, 362–364, 366, 374–376, 378, 382–383

Predictions 18–19, 36, 42, 97–99, 107, 148, 208, 217, 271, 282, 313, 318

Preview 36, 172, 194, 208, 217, 268

Problem and solution 104,111, 205

Propaganda 220

Reading rate 280

Literary Concepts

Index of Skills, continued

Literary Concepts, continued

Problem and solution 104, 111, 326, 443

Proverb or saying 126

Quotations 61, 70, 92, 116, 122, 126, 140, 183, 192, 257

Rap 266

Realistic fiction 443

Repetition 167, 219, 443

Report 79, 305, 372, 443

Respond to literature 19–21, 29–31, 42–43, 52–54, 77–79, 88–89, 99–101, 111–113, 134–136, 139, 149–151, 164–166, 169, 177–179, 203–205, 217–221, 237–239, 250–253, 276–277, 288–291, 303–305, 318–320, 324–325

Rhyme 55, 167, 169, 443

Rhyme scheme 444

Rhythm 167, 169, 444

Rising action and falling action 347

Science article 36, 172

Science fiction 444

Self-portrait 46, 53

Sensory images 55, 325, 329, 444

Setting 148–149, 237, 290, 301, 326–328, 444

Simile 88, 394, 444

Song 140, 154, 208, 278

Stage direction 226

Story 104, 112, 126, 294, 303–304, 306, 310–311, 325–326, 444

Style 211, 219, 301, 303, 324, 444

Summary 115, 164, 177

Tall tale 296, 298–299, 304, 444

Theme 77, 211, 317, 444

Travel guide 320

Word choice 59, 61, 117, 217, 255, 393–394, 444

Writing

Audience 59–60, 116, 181–182, 256–257, 327–328, 392

Biography 136

Caption 207

Character sketch 238, 319

Character study 319

Collect ideas 59–60, 115–116, 181–182, 255–256, 328, 382

Conclusions 257, 289, 371–372, 398–399

Consistent point of view 398–399

Consistent verb tense 186, 260, 398–399

Critique 238

Dedication 165–166

Definitions 171

Description 19, 53, 58–64, 150, 178, 241, 267, 279, 305, 319–320, 325

Details 60–61, 115, 117–118, 149, 181–184, 250, 325, 328–329, 370–372, 383–384, 399–401

Draft 61, 117, 183, 218, 257, 289, 329, 384

Edit and proofread 64, 112, 120, 186, 218, 260, 332, 387

Effective paragraphs 115, 149, 181–182, 184, 238, 250–251, 289, 395–398

Effective sentences 63, 257–258, 267–277, 279, 289–290, 295, 304, 331, 394–395, 402–407

Elaboration 183–184, 400–401

E-mail 253

Essay 255–258, 260, 289

Evaluate your writing 60–62, 64–65, 116–118, 120–121, 182–184, 186–187, 256–258, 260–261, 328–330, 332–333, 389

Expository writing 21, 29, 31, 43, 52, 77, 79, 99, 101, 113–120, 136, 164, 166, 171, 204–205, 220–221, 239, 250–251, 253, 277, 288–291, 303, 305, 320, 366–372

Expressive writing 20, 100, 165–166, 169, 180–186, 203–204, 217–219, 237–238, 276, 320

Fact sheet 113

FATP chart 181–182, 256, 328, 382

Friendly letter 100, 219, 320

Graphic organizers 340–347

Haiku 218

Interview 30, 151

Introductions 257, 289, 371–372, 398–399

Labels 178, 305

Letter 100, 219, 320

Literary critique 203, 217, 238

Main idea paragraph 181–184, 186

Map 113, 136, 253, 305, 379

Narrative writing 111–112, 134, 149, 237, 277, 304, 326–332

News article/newscast 251

Opinions 203–204, 207, 217, 238, 255–258, 260, 276

Organization
In logical order 59–60, 115–116, 181–182, 397
In sequential order 99, 134, 288, 303, 327–328, 396
In spatial order 396
To make comparisons 29, 31, 113, 151, 166, 239, 250, 277, 279, 288–290, 341, 344, 396
To show causes and effects 52, 164, 205, 304, 340, 396
To show goals and outcomes 318, 345
To show problems and solutions 111, 135, 205, 255–256, 345
To show thesis and supporting arguments 255–256

Outlining 255–256, 370

Paragraphs 53, 77, 149, 164, 177, 181–184, 186, 204, 238, 241–242, 250–252, 280, 289, 395–397

Peer conferencing 62, 112, 118, 184, 218, 258, 289, 330, 385

Persuasive essay 399

Persuasive writing 221, 254–260, 397, 399

Photo essay 89

Play 237

Poem 20, 59–62, 64, 89, 169, 218, 219, 325

Portfolios 64–65, 120–121, 186–187, 260–261, 332–333, 389

Poster 21, 166, 253, 291

Prewrite 60, 112, 116, 150, 182, 256, 289, 325, 328, 382–383

Proofread 64, 120, 186, 260, 332, 387
See **Edit and proofread.**

Public service announcement 253

Listening, Speaking, Viewing, and Representing

Grammar, Mechanics, Usage, and Spelling

Technology and Media

Research Skills

Index of Titles and Authors

Acknowledgments continued

Children's Book Press (continued): "I Honor My Ancestors" by Stephen Von Mason, "I Honor My Father and Mother" by Enrique Chagoya, "I Honor My Grandmother" by Helen Zughaib from *Honoring Our Ancestors*. Pages 6–7 copyright © 1999 by Enrique Chagoya; pages 22–23 copyright © 1999 by Stephen Von Mason; pages 30–31 copyright © 1999 by Helen Zughaib. Overall book project copyright © 1999 by Harriet Rohmer. All reprinted with permission of the publisher, Children's Book Press, San Francisco, California.

Francisco X. Alarcón: "Collective Dream," "Adobes," and "Family Garden." Text copyright © 1999 by Francisco X. Alarcón. Used with permission of the Author. All rights reserved.

J. Paul Getty Museum: *Echo and Narcissus* by Antonia Barber. Copyright © 1998 by Antonia Barber. Reprinted with permission of the J. Paul Getty Museum.

Harcourt, Inc.: Excerpt from *A Guide Dog Puppy Grows Up* by Caroline Arnold. Text copyright © 1991 by Caroline Arnold, reprinted with permission of Harcourt, Inc.

HarperCollins Publishers: "A Boy and a Man" from *Banner in the Sky* by James Ramsey Ullman. Copyright © 1954 by James Ramsey Ullman. *Teamwork* by Ann Morris. Copyright © 1999 by Ann Morris. "My Best Friend" from *Childtimes* by Lessie Jones Little and Eloise Greenfield. Copyright © 1979 by Eloise Greenfield and Lessie Jones Little. All used by permission of HarperCollins Publishers.

Margaret Hillert: "Just Me" by Margaret Hillert. Used by permission of the author who controls all rights.

Homeland Publishing (CAPAC). A division of Troubadour Records Ltd.: "Evergreen, Everblue," "One Light, One Sun," "Big Beautiful Planet," and "Clean Rain" from *Evergreen, Everblue* by Raffi. "Evergreen, Everblue" words and music by Raffi, copyright © 1990; "One Light, One Sun" words and music by Raffi, copyright © 1985; "Big Beautiful Planet" words and music by Raffi, copyright © 1982; "Clean Rain" words and music by Raffi, copyright © 1990. All rights reserved. Used by permission.

Limousine Music Co. & The Last Music Co: "Family Tree" from *Family Tree* by Tom Chapin. Copyright © 1988 by John Forster & Tom Chapin. Limousine Music Co. & The Last Music Co. (ASCAP).

Myra Cohn Livingston: "We Could Be Friends" from *The Way Things Are and Other Poems* by Myra Cohn Livingston. Copyright © 1974 by Myra Cohn Livingston. Used by permission of Marian Reiner.

NASA/JPL/Caltech: "Mars Network." Courtesy of NASA/JPL/Caltech.

Dorothy Hinshaw Patent: Selected excerpts from *Grandfather's Nose* by Dorothy Hinshaw Patent. Text copyright © 1989 by Dorothy Hinshaw Patent.

Penguin Putnam: "Everybody Says" from *Here, There and Everywhere* by Dorothy Aldis. Copyright 1927, 1928, copyright renewed © 1955, 1956 by Dorothy Aldis. Used by permission of G.P. Putnam's Sons, a division of Penguin Putnam Inc.

Scholastic: Selected excerpts from *Common Ground* by Molly Bang. Published by The Blue Sky Press, an imprint of Scholastic Inc. Copyright © 1997 by Molly Bang. Reprinted by permission.

Mike Thaler: Question and answer from *Earth Mirth* by Mike Thaler. Used by permission of the author.

Burton Watson: "Peasant Song" from *Ancient China* by Edward H. Schafer. Used by permission of Burton Watson, translator.

Albert Whitman & Company: *How the Ox Star Fell from Heaven* retold and illustrated by Lily Toy Hong. Text and illustrations copyright © 1991 by Lily Toy Hong. Adaptation reprinted by permission of Albert Whitman & Company.

Diane Wolkstein: "Introduction" and "Owl" from *The Magic Orange Tree and Other Haitian Folktales* by Diane Wolkstein. Schocken, copyright © 1997 by Diane Wolkstein.

World Almanac Group: "Looking for Life Elsewhere in the Universe" from *World Almanac for Kids*. Reprinted with permission from *The World Almanac for Kids 1998*. Copyright © 1997 World Almanac Education Group. All rights reserved.

Photographs:

Michael Aki: pp172, 175 (Michael Aki family photos courtesy of Michael Aki.).

American Foundation for the Blind: p92 (photograph of Helen Keller courtesy of American Foundation for the Blind.).

Animal Animals/Earth Scenes: pp190–191, 220 (rain forest, Doug Wechsler).

AP/Wide World Photos: p75 (rowers, David J. Phillip) p227 (seismograph, Francesco Belini) p244 (Taiwan earthquake, Pat Roque) p248 (sandbaggers, Beth A. Keiser) p449 (guide dog, Christopher Barth).

Art Resource: p66 (Ringling Bros. Astounding Feat of Ernest Clark Circus Poster 1910, Scala/Art Resource, NY) p133 (Aesop by Domingo Velazquez, Scala/Art Resource, NY), pp152–153 (La Familia by Jose Clemente Orozco, Schalwijk/Art Resource, NY © SOMAAP 2000), p264 (Ad Marginem by Paul Klee, Giraudon/Art Resource, NY © 2000 Artist Rights Society [ARS], New York/VG Bild-Kunst, Bonn), p272 (Athena, Nimatallah/ Art Resource, NY) p273 (Peracles, Scala/Art Resource, NY), p284 (ruling class, Giraudon/ Art Resource, NY), p285 (emperor, Giraudon/ Art Resource, NY, scholars, Erich Lessing/Art Resource, NY, knights, Victoria & Albert Museum, London/Art Resource, NY).

Artville: p40 (coins).

The Bridgeman Art Library: p262, p333 (Ulysses and the Sirens, Musee du Bardo, Tuni, Tunisia).

Brigham Young University: pp226, 228, 237 (photograph of San Francisco City Hall 1906 courtesy of L. Tom Perry Special Collections, Harold B. Lee Library, Brigham Young University, Provo, Utah.).

Children's Book Press: p80("Making Tamales" and cooking pot reprinted with permission of the publisher, Children's Book Press, San Francisco, CA. Copyright © 1990 by Carmen Lomas Garza. All rights reserved.)

Comstock: pp72–73, 77 (rafters)

Contact Press: pp222–223 (earthquake damage, Alon Reininger).

Corbis: p16 (chessboard), p21 (George Washington Carver, Bettman/ CORBIS), p26 (Miami coast, Robert Landau), p27 (El Morro, Neil Rabinowitz, waterfall, Richard Bickel; coqui frog, Kevin Schafer), p32 (Caesar Chavez, Ted Streshinsky), p90 (granite), p91 (climbers, Warren Morgan), p102 (crevasse rescue, Joel W. Rogers; rescue inset, Lowell Georgia), p144 (storefront, Bettman/ CORBIS), p146 (Jelly Roll Morton), p212 (tulips), p7, p222, pp262–263 (rock texture), p231 (man watching fires, Bettman/CORBIS), p233 (San Francisco Earthquake, Bettman/ CORBIS), p262 (Parthenon) p272 (Acropolis, Doric Column, Bettman/CORBIS) p278 (emperor, Pierre Colombel) p448 (forest) p451 (planet) p 452 (ruins, John Dakers) p453 (tent city, Janez Skok).

Digital Stock: p6, p16, p209, p211, p215, p261 (Earth) p18 (beach) p210 (girl, boy, man and woman) p214 (tidal wave) p224 (roadway) p238, pp242–243, p250 (lightning) p265 (sunset) p447 (crop).

Doménico Fabrizi: pp321–323 (Olas en el Malecón).

Dorling Kindersley: p285 (peasant plowing statuette, courtesy of the British Museum)

DoubleClick Studios: p17 (soda can) p140 (autograph book) pp142–143, p149 (teacups).

Estefan Enterprises: p32 (photograph of Gloria Estefan, courtesy of Estefan Enterprises, Inc.

FPG International, LLC: p15 (hand w/key, VCG) pp32–33 (Albert Einstein) p70 (Amish women, David S. Strickler) p79 (ants carrying leaves).

George Contorakes: pp24–25, p29 (Téssely Estévez) p26 (Estévez family) p28 (Téssely at computer, Gilbert Socas).

Liz Garza Williams: pp10–11 (girl at mirror/ graduation girl) p15 (boy w/notebook) p16, p18 (boy's eye) p16 (boys reading) p17 (at science fair, dropping trash, refusing food) p18 (boy w/ribbon and boy recycling) p22 (bedroom, girl & interviewer) pp36–37, p42 (kids in theater) p38 (playwright, girl painting, actors talking) pp94, 95, 99 (boy & dog) p96 (trainer w/dog, trainer w/boy) p97 (trainer, boy & dog, boy & dog, boy & dog) p98 (boy & dog on obstacle course, elevator, boy & dog on stairs) pp137–139 (boy w/baseball and boy w/basketball) p143 (tablecloth) p145 (frog houses, feet in mud) p147, p180 (girl walking) pp167–168 (girl & portraits) p170 (ears) p287 (rice, millet, soy beans).

Rubin Guzman: p32, (Sandra Cisneros)

HarperCollins Publishers: pp143-144, 148 (Lessie Jones Little and Eloise Greenfield courtesy of Eloise Greenfield and HarperCollins Publishers.).

Henry Holt: p188 ("Seeing the World Through Pictures" reprinted with permission from the publisher, Henry Holt, Copyright © 1997 by Robert Silvers).

Robert Hsiang: pp32, 46, 47, p49 (Nancy Hom painting self portrait)

The Image Bank: p13 (boy with pig, Jay Silverman) p40 (women farmers, Ken Huang) p450 (island, Guido Alberto Rossi)

Index Stock: p446 (adobes, James Lemass)

Liaison Agency, Inc.: pp 68–69 (basketball team, Gamma Liaison, J.O. Barcelone Pool)

Major League Baseball Photos: p32 (Sammy Sosa, David Durochik)

MapArt: p15 (globe map) p244 (Taiwan map) p246 (Dominican Republic map)

Off the Wall: p124 (sunflower frame)

Patrick Tregenza: pp122–123 (boy's head); p294 (girl)

PGA Tour: p40 (Tiger Woods)

PhotoDisc: p10 (clouds) p22 (leopard, ferret, lizard, CMCD, giraffe, Jack Hollingsworth) p40 (measuring tape, C. Borland/PhotoLink) pp46–47, p52 (palette, C Squared Studios) pp55–56 (girl on mountain, Louise Oldroyd/Life File) p68 (basketball) p120 (newspaper) p146 (piano keys, Alan Pappe) p174 (scientist, Keith Brofsky) p192 (burning rainforest, Kim Steele) p210 (orchids, PhotoLink) p211 (sunset at lake, Jeremy Woodhouse) p212 (trees, pond, PhotoLink), p213 (buffalo drinking, Alan and Sandy Carey, pulp mill, PhotoLink, sewer, S. Meltzer/ PhotoLink) p214 (crops, C.Borland/PhotoLink, burned land, D. Normark/PhotoLink, log pile, Kent Knudson/ PhotoLink) p215 (planting tree, S. Wankel/PhotoLink, girl recycling) p220 (boy and girl, CMCD) p260 (record player) p238, 245, 247, 249 (droplet, PhotoLink) p332 (lightning on mountain, Bruce Heineman) p454 (valley)

PhotoEdit: p40 (cashier, Michael Newman), p63 (Tera, Tera and Ricky, Myrleen Ferguson), p119 (girl, David Young-Wolff), p224 (damage, cracked street, Jonathan Nourok), p227 (bridge, Mark Richards) p388 (family, Spencer Grant) p401 (boy holding basketball, Michael Newman)

Photo Researchers: pp124–125 (best friends, Richard T. Nowitz), p285 (peasant, Robert E. Murowchick, 1984)

Sea World: p22 ("Back from the Brink" poster © 1999 SeaWorld, Inc. All rights reserved.

Sarita Silverman: pp5, 122-123, 187 (family photos courtesy of Sarita Silverman.

Stockbyte: p67 (clown hat), p153 (family)

The Stock Market: p16 (scientist, Pete Saloutus) p19 (talking, LWA/Dunn Tardiff) p41(3 girls, John Henley) p151 (child & adult, Lance Nelson) p170 (DNA model, William Schick, molecular model, Jean Miele) p291 (modern China, David Ball)

Superstock: p44 (Vendredi I, Auguste Herbin © 2000 Artist Rights Society (ARS) New York/ ADAGP Paris) p90 (mountain climbers)

Stone : pp14–17, p19 (roadway, Stuart McClymont) p40 (carpenter, Don Smetzer) p73 (field workers in Vietnam, Oliver Benn) p74 (men carrying basket, Alan Le Garsmeur) pp172–173, p177 (double helix, Paul Morrell) p174 (family, Lawrence Migdale) p176 (different kids, Robert Mort) p215 (oil spill, Ben Osborne) p278 (planting rice, Yann Layma)

UN/DPI: p76 (United Nations)

University of Arizona: pp292-293 (Storyteller statue by Helen Sands, courtesy of the Arizona State Museum, University of Arizona.)

Woodfin Camp & Associates: p70 (barn raising, Paul Solomon) p73 (dancers, Ken Heyman) p74 (firefighters, Mike Yamashita; kids playing ball, spill clean-up, A. Ramey), pp 74, 288 (cows plowing, Ken Heyman), p75 (women quilting, cod fishermen, Eastcott/Momatuik, bee keeper, Timothey Eagan) p76 (family dinner, Ken Heyman) p238 (sandbaggers, Eastcott/ Momatuik).

Author and Illustrator Photos:

p32 (Nadja Halilbegovich, © J. Kevin Wolfe), p41 (Joanne Ryder); p47 (Margaret Hillert); p76 (Ann Morris); p87 (Francisco Alarcón, © Francisco Dominguez); p98 (Caroline Arnold, © Arthur Arnold); p110 (James Ramsey Ulman); p139 (Myra Cohn Livingston); p169 (Dorothy Aldis); p176 (Dorothy Hinshaw Patent); p202 (Molly Bang); p216 (Raffi, courtesy of Troubadour Press.); p237 (Kristina Gregory); p249 (Richie Chevat); p273 (Antonia Barber); p285 (Lily Toy Hong); p297, 298 (Chuck Larkin); pp309–310, p317 (Diane Wolkstein); p323 (Carmen Agra Deedy).

Illustrations:

Rick Allen: pp308–309, pp312–316, p318 (Unwinding the Magic Thread), **Michael Aki and Michael Bergen:** pp208–215, p217 (Protecting Our Planet), **Fian Arroyo:** pp296–297, pp300–303, p326 (Pecos Bill), **Molly Bang:** pp194–203, p254 (Common Ground), **Norm Bendell:** p206 (garden cartoon), **Chi Chung:** pp280–285 (How the Ox Star Fell From Heaven) p294 (King Solomon), **David Diaz:** p3, pp8–9, p65 (A Very Unique You) p304 (Tell an Original Story), **Rita Elsner:** pp229–230, pp234–235 (Earthquake at Dawn), **Chris Higgins:** pp116, 260 ("Show What You Did," "It's Cool" © Chris Higgins Proof Positive/ Farrowlyne Associates, Inc); **Sandra Holzman:** p228 (Earthquake at Dawn cover), **Kathleen Kinkopf:** pp82–88 (Together We Dream), **JoAnn E. Kitchel:** p126 ("Friendship"), **Bill Maughan:** pp104–109, 111 (A Mountain Rescue), **Paul Mirocha:** p227 (The Making of an Earthquake), p246 (Hurricane diagram), p272 (maps of Ancient Greece), p284 (maps of Ancient China), **David Moreno:** p266 ("Mount Olympus Rap"), **Barbara Johansen Newman:** p12 (girl), **John Patrick:** pp128–134 (The Qualities of Friendship), **Joel Spector:** pp268–273, p276 (Echo and Narcissus), **Carol Zaloom:** p154 (banyan tree)

The High Point Development Team

Hampton-Brown extends special thanks to the following individuals and companies who contributed so much to the creation of this series.

Editorial: Susan Blackaby, Janine Boylan, Bonnie Brook, Shirleyann Costigan, Mary Cutler, Phyllis Edwards, Ramiro Ferrey, Cris Phillips-Georg, Fredrick Ignacio, Barbara Linde, Dawn Liseth, Daphne Liu, Sherry Long, Jacalyn Mahler, Marlyn Mangus, S. Michele McFadden, Debbi Neel, Wilma Ramírez, Michael Ryall, Sarita Chávez Silverman, Sharon Ursino, Andreya Valabek, Alison Wells, Virginia Yeater, Lynn Yokoe, Brown Publishing Network, Ink, Inc., and Learning Design Associates, Inc.

Design and Production: Lisa Baehr, Marcia Bateman Walker, Andrea Carter, Darius Detwiler, Jeri Gibson, Lauren Grace, Debbie Saxton, Curtis Spitler, Alicia Sternberg, Jennifer Summers, Debbie Wright Swisher, Margaret Tisdale, Andrea Erin Thompson, Donna Turner, Alex von Dallwitz, JR Walker, Teri Wilson, Adpartner, Art Stopper, Bill Smith Studios, Chaos Factory & Associates, Ray Godfrey, Hooten Design, Proof Positive/ Farrowlyne Associates, and Rose Sheifer.

Permissions: Barbara Mathewson